Nathaniel Southgate Shaler

The Story of our Continent

A Reader in the Geography and Geology of North America

Nathaniel Southgate Shaler

The Story of our Continent
A Reader in the Geography and Geology of North America

ISBN/EAN: 9783337408954

Printed in Europe, USA, Canada, Australia, Japan

Cover: Foto ©ninafisch / pixelio.de

More available books at **www.hansebooks.com**

THE STORY OF OUR CONTINENT

A Reader in the Geography and Geology of North America

FOR THE USE OF SCHOOLS

BY

N. S. SHALER
Professor of Geology in Harvard College

PREFACE.

Those who read this book will at once perceive that both in the subject-matter and arrangement it departs widely from the ordinary text-books which give an account of North America. It should be understood that the end which the writer sought to attain is not that which may be secured by the ordinary school geographies. Such works undertake to afford the student a large body of detailed information concerning the existing state of the country, and with little or no reference to the steps by which the land came to its present estate. The aim of this work has been to present only those features which can be shown in their relation to the geological development of the continent.

The expectation of the author has been that this work will be used as a reader along with some geography which treats in a thorough way the facts of a political and economic nature, such as these text-books ordinarily present. Used in this manner, it will naturally lead the student to perceive how the present state of the country is due to the processes which have gone on in the remote past, and in this way to attain to some of the most enlarging conceptions which the geological history of the earth unfolds.

CONTENTS.

CHAPTER I.
GEOGRAPHY OF NORTH AMERICA 1

CHAPTER II.
THE GROWTH OF NORTH AMERICA 18

CHAPTER III.
THE PRESENT CONDITIONS OF NORTH AMERICA 76

CHAPTER IV.
THE ABORIGINAL PEOPLES OF NORTH AMERICA 153

CHAPTER V.
NATURAL PRODUCTS AND RESOURCES OF NORTH AMERICA . . 166

CHAPTER VI.
EFFECT OF THE FORM OF NORTH AMERICA ON THE HISTORY OF THE COLONISTS FROM EUROPE AND THEIR DESCENDANTS . . 233

CHAPTER VII.
THE COMMERCIAL CONDITION OF NORTH AMERICA . . . 246

THE STORY OF OUR CONTINENT.

CHAPTER I.

GEOGRAPHY OF NORTH AMERICA.

Method of study. Cause and effect of climate. Influence of geographic conditions on animals and plants; on the life of man. Character of the soil. Origin of its fertility. General influence of geologic and geographic conditions on mankind.

In beginning the study of the geography of North America, it is well for us to form a clear idea as to the object which we should have in view in this task. With a distinct aim before us, it is easily seen that labor may be spared in the effort. It is a large task to form even the most general idea of the history and conditions of a great area of the earth's surface. The amount of knowledge concerning any one of the continents is so vast that to secure a general view of its conditions we have to neglect the greater part of the details concerning its growth and structure. If our plan be clearly marked, we can more easily put the unnecessary learning aside.

The most of our school geographies seek to present to the student a picture of the existing conditions on the earth's surface, to show him the shape of the lands, the boundaries of states, the character of the important natural features, the conditions of commerce; in other words, to give him a picture of the earth, or a particular part of it, as it now is. In this little volume we are to consider something more than is commonly presented in such work, the intention being to show the student in a general way how the continent of North America has come by its shape, through what steps it has become a land, how the stages of its growth have affected its climate, and thus have influenced the character of living things which have found a place upon its lands, and finally in what manner the past history of the continent, by determining the store of mineral materials under the earth, the shape of its surface, the nature of its soil and climate, measures its fitness for the uses of man; in a word, how the history of its people has been influenced by geographic conditions, and thus depends on the laws which have controlled the development of a continental mass.

In the effort to see how the geography of any country has influenced the life of the animals and plants which have found a place upon it, it is well for the student to begin his task by noticing a number of familiar facts, so familiar, indeed, that they readily escape attention, which may serve to illustrate the effect of surrounding conditions on the sensitive living creatures. It is easy to see that all the living tenants of the lands and waters are readily and largely influenced by the conditions of the nature about them.

Any one who has made himself moderately familiar with the round of the seasons has observed the profound effect arising from changes of climate. In the regions north and south of the tropics each year brings periods of winter and of summer; with the change in the amount of heat the living beings pass from the sleep of the winter season to the activity of summer time. In the springtime, when the sun rises higher above the horizon and sends more heat to the earth, we perceive the effect of the alteration on the development of life. The seeds are stimulated to growth, and most of the animals which have reposed in hidden places come forth and enter on their busy lives. Every year thus affords a beautiful lesson on the effects of simple changes in the events of the outer world. As the sun ascends higher, it brings with it a tropical climate, which marches over the surface nearly to the poles; then as the sun returns south in its annual course, the conditions of polar cold sweep down towards the equator. The difference between the tropical belt of the world and the regions beyond it lies in the fact that within the tropics it is always warm with something like the warmth of summer in higher latitudes, while near the poles the temperature is tropical for only a short time. If the summer heat continued throughout the year in any high latitude, palms and other plants which cannot withstand the cold would develop over nearly all the earth's lands.

After we have in mind the effect produced by the alternate rising and sinking of the sun in high latitudes, it is well next to note the effects on the district about us caused by differences in the geographic character of the land. In any country where there is a range of heights of even a few feet, where there are streams and hills however small, we may with a little study see how the nature of the surface, by determining the character of the soil, and the amount of water it contains, affects the lives of the plants and animals. In a lake or arm of the sea we note that in the deeper water there are no plants such as we have upon the land; the vegetable life is limited to certain soft forms which are without leaves, or roots, or seeds of a distinct kind. These aquatic plants live altogether beneath the surface of the waters, or at times tolerate the air for a few hours at low tide. Close to the shore, where the water is shallow, we may, if the water be fresh, find certain higher plants, such as our lilies, and rushes, which have distinct leaves, roots, and seed, and can maintain themselves with their roots below the surface of the water, but with their upper parts within the air. Next the shore, if the ground happens to be marshy, — that is, neither wet nor dry, — bushes and a few kinds of trees may grow, forms which cannot inhabit the water, and are equally incapable of living on the high land. Passing yet further above the water to the lands of a medium degree of wetness, yet other forms of lowly plants or trees possess the land. On the arid hilltops we find another assemblage of plants unlike any of those which dwell on lower ground.

Although it is not easy to see that the animal life is limited in the same narrow way by geographic conditions as is the vegetable world, closer inquiry shows us that in fact most animals, because they depend for their subsistence on particular kinds of plants, are also profoundly affected by peculiarities of the soil. This is particularly the case with insects, a group which contains more kinds of creatures than all the rest of the animal kingdom put together. Most insects require particular parts of plants for their food. Even those forms which live on other insects have to maintain themselves where their prey is plentiful. The insects of the swamp differ in a clear way from those of the upland. Thus in the state of nature, in every country, the living beings are distributed with reference to the character of the soil, whence all land life springs. The character of this soil depends upon the geography of the country. The underlying rocks, the rivers, lakes, hills, and mountains, mainly determine the nature of that soil, whether it be wet or dry, of clay, sandy or stony. All these features are fixed by the geological history of the country: they can be accounted for only where we know its past history,—how it came to have its present form.

Not only is the higher life of a land shaped by its geographic conditions, but the life of man is influenced even more than that of any other animal by the circumstances which surround him. If he be a farmer, the character of the crops he cultivates will be determined partly by the nature of the soil, and yet more by the character of the climate,—the amount of heat which the sun sends to him, or the share of rainfall which comes to his fields. He rears those crops which are made possible by the heat, the rain, and the nature of the earth on which they fall. In the Southern states of this country cotton is the leading product of the fields. It is profitable to grow it there, for the reason that the plant requires a very long summer to mature its bolls, and during this summer there must be a considerable fall of rain, and all the while a rather high temperature. Moreover, cotton requires a sandy rather than a clayey soil, and the ancient history of that part of the continent, as we shall see hereafter, favored the construction of soils of this nature. The farmers of the Northwestern states find their profit in raising grain. That region is the granary of the continent,—indeed, we may say of

Europe as well, — for the reason that the short, rather dry summer affords a suitable climate for the development of such crops, and the soil is generally of a clayey nature, having this quality given it by the geological conditions of the rocks made in the time when the continent was forming. Geographic conditions, those now existing or those which have ceased to be, but have left their marks on the character of the soil, make it impossible for cotton to be profitably reared in the Northwest, or wheat in the Carolinas. Or, to take another instance, the state of Florida is unfit for the tillage either of grain or of cotton; the latter crop will grow there, but the soil is not of a nature to make it profitable. Florida is the field of fruit culture. Its semi-tropical climate favors the development of oranges, lemons, pineapples, and many forms of fruit and vegetables. The soil is generally so poor that these plants have to be grown with the aid of artificial manures, and so that portion of the country is by nature set aside for gardening. The character of the soil, combined with the character of the climate of a country, serves to fix the occupations of the people who win food from the earth. Now the soil, simple as it seems to be at first sight, has always a very wonderful history. So much depends upon this history that we must ask the reader to turn his attention for a moment to the nature and origin of this film of loose material on the surface of the earth in which the plants find root.

All soils consist in the main of fine bits of rock, the particles of clay and sand which have been worn from the compact, firm-set under-rocks of the earth, by the action of rain, frost, rivers, waves, and the roots of plants, as well as by the decay which the atmosphere brings to all rock material. If we take a pinch of soil and spread it out thinly upon a sheet of white paper and inspect it with a magnifying-glass, we find that the greater part of the material is commonly made up of tolerably coarse grains, large enough to be seen by the naked eye or by a simple microscope. Mixed with these hard bits there are very many fragments of decayed roots, leaves, and stems, which are in part so finely divided that they give the mass a dark color. Sinking through the soil, the rain-water constantly takes a little of the decayed rock into solution as salt dissolves in water. This dissolved rock material is taken up by the roots of plants, and affords the ashy matter of their bodies, — material without which they could not grow. On the proportion of lime, potash, phosphatic matter, soda, and various other materials which the decaying rock affords to the soil-water, depends the fertility of the soil; that is, its fitness to nourish crops, whether those of wild nature or of the tilled fields. If the bits which make the soil are largely composed of limestone, which generally contains not only lime, but some phosphatic matter, soda, potash, and the other materials required to make the bodies of plants, the soil will be fertile. If, however, it be in the main made up of quartzy bits of sand, the plants can obtain from the soil-water but little nutriment, and therefore the fields will be sterile, and the forests or the cultivated crops scanty.

The proportion of fertilizing materials contained in the soil depends upon the conditions which existed when the rocks from which the soil is derived were forming. Nearly all our rocks were formed on old sea-floors. If the geography of those old sea-floors, that is to say, the conditions of temperature and other circumstances, were such as to make a plentiful life of shellfish or corals on the bottom, then the rocks formed from the remains of these creatures will abound in materials fit for plant growth. When this rock matter is subjected to decay and accumulates in the soil, the plants will flourish upon it. Each wheat plant will appropriate the waste of these old creatures of the sea-floor, and convert the chemical materials which they contributed to the rock into good grain. Thus we readily see that the character of our soils depends upon geographic conditions in very remote time. A striking instance of this effect may be found in the case of the very fertile limestone lands which are found in the so-called blue-grass district of Kentucky and Tennessee. These soils are of extraordinary fertility and of such endurance to cultivation that they have been tilled in corn without manuring for one hundred years or more. They owe their fertility to the fact that the rock contains a large number of the remains of animals somewhat akin to the shrimps. These creatures had the habit of storing in their hard parts a great deal of lime phosphate, which is the most important ingredient in soils which are to feed grain. The rocks beneath the blue-grass district are thin sheets of limestone laid one above the other to the thickness of a thousand feet or more; here and there there are beds, generally only a few inches thick, mainly composed of the remains of these little creatures, which are exposed to the atmosphere. These beds decay to a fine powder which works down through the hillsides, mingles with the soil, and so gives it its great fertility for crops of grain and grass.

The growth of ancient animals which built their remains into rock was determined, as is the growth of creatures of to-day, by geographic conditions. Other circumstances of the earth's crust determined that in the course of time these old sea-bottoms should be elevated into dry land and exposed to the actions which make soil. Thus we see that each stage in the earth's history prepares the way for the later stages of its development. Our life of to-day depends upon the conditions of remote times.

Although it is through the soil and climate that geological conditions most intimately affect the life of man, there are very many ways in which the geography of the past and present influence his career. Let us, for example, note the influence of the sea on the occupations of men. Wherever men's dwelling-places are along the shore, they find a considerable share of their food in the animals of the sea. They are thus tempted to seafaring, to the construction of boats, and come to have the peculiar needs which such life imposes on man. Yet later in their development they find a profit in the trade which the fields of the sea lay wide open to those who dwell upon its borders. Thus, while inland people are limited to the district just about them for their field of action, the folk next to the shore have a vastly wider range of employment. The peculiarities of their life depend upon the way in which the lands have grown to their present shape.

The fitness of the shore for the uses of the mariner varies greatly. Where the coast is very sandy and there are no large rivers passing across the shore to the sea, there is apt to be a dearth of harbors. Only small boats which can be dragged through the surf to the dry land can be used, and so it comes about that the people along such coasts usually make but limited use of the ways of the ocean. On the other hand, in regions where harbors abound, as along the northern coast of the United States, both on its eastern and western faces, or in the region of Northern Europe, Scandinavia, Holland, and England, the people may become deep-sea sailors and range over the oceans to the furthest lands of the earth. These peculiarities of coast lines, whether they afford good harbors or no, depend upon the ancient history of the shores. As we shall see further on, the singular abundance of harbors about the North Atlantic, which have made the people of those lands the sailors of the world, is immediately due to the fact that in former stages of the earth's development this part of the coast was deeply carved by glaciers or streams of ice.

If now we turn our attention from the industries of men, which are related to the mere surface of the earth, to the work which depends on the underground features, we find a yet more striking instance of the effect brought about by the ancient history of our sphere. Next after the wealth which comes for man's use from the soil, we must place that which comes from the mines. In looking over a map of North America which shows the mineral fields of the country, we observe that, although more than half of its area has nothing of particular use to man to be won from below the soil, there are large districts where the under-earth is richly stored with a great variety of materials to be gained by mining. There are at present over fifty different substances of great use to man which are obtained in one way or another from the realm of the earth which lies below the soil covering. Iron, copper, lead, zinc, gold, and silver, and several other valuable metals; coal, petroleum, natural gas, materials which serve for light, warmth, and the sources of power; our building-stones; various substances which serve to fertilize the fields worn by crops; and a host of other less important supplies for our arts are derived from this nether realm.

Wherever these mineral substances abound, the profit from winning them is so considerable that often, to the neglect of agriculture, the population seeks subsistence from the deeper earth below the soil. Where these substances are won, as in most cases they are, by delving deep beneath the surface, the men who follow these pursuits become peculiar in their methods of life, their ways of thought and action. These peculiarities of the miner's life manifestly depend on the existence of particular substances in limited parts of the world. The presence of these substances in the crust of the earth depends upon the former history of the area in which they lie; in a word, upon its old geographic conditions. If the substance sought in the mine be coal, we know that it is present, because in a very ancient day that particular field was occupied by great swamps, in which peaty matter was deposited in the manner in which we may now see it accumulating in our ordinary bogs. After a thick layer of peat was formed, the land it occupied sank beneath the sea, and sand and clay were accumulated upon it, which, while concealing it and preserving it from complete decay, converted the mass to coal. By further change it has been re-elevated, so that it is accessible to man. Ancient climate and ancient geography, in other words, led to the production of the coal bed. So with all the other substances won by the miner; each owes its abundance in the particular field to conditions of the climate or of the other geological features which occurred in the past.

It is hard to give the reader a clear idea as to the intimate way in which the geography of the present day determines the life now existing on the earth's surface; yet it is important he should see something of these facts, even if the instances he can consider are but few in number. Perhaps the best illustrations of how closely the life of the earth depends upon surrounding circumstances are afforded by field and garden plants. A good example is found in the principal American grain, — the maize or Indian corn, which furnishes by far the most valuable grain crop of the continent. It is of the utmost importance to the farmer to have a crop of this corn; but in the northern parts of the tilled portion of North America, generally in the region north of the Great Lakes, the summer is too short for the plant to mature its seeds. They are killed by frost before they are fully developed. By carefully choosing each year the plants which mature earlier than their neighbors in the field, and using seed from these, varieties have been formed which hasten their growth, and so in a measure adapt themselves to the needs of the short northern summer. The maize of Alabama requires five months in its round from seed to seed; by selection particular varieties have been formed which will come to maturity in regions where it is but three months between the frost of spring and autumn. Further than this it seems impossible to go, and so there is a limit determined by the temperature beyond which the maize cannot be grown with profit.

The distribution of animals in the sea is even more closely determined by the temperature than that of the plants on the land. Thus in the warm waters south of Cape Cod there are many kinds of animals which cannot pass around this small cape into the colder waters of Massachusetts Bay. The most vigorous and active fish south of the Cape, the blue-fish, a creature there greatly developed, cannot maintain itself north of the Cape. Occasionally, in the last two centuries, it has in the warmer seasons worked around the promontory, and for a year or two gained a place in Massachusetts Bay. It has seemed likely that it would permanently win this new field, but each time it has been driven back by the cold of the water. The difference is also marked in the mollusca, or shell-fish; a number of species flourish just south of the Cape, which do not appear in the somewhat colder waters a few miles to the northward. The difference between the temperature of the waters north and south of Cape Cod is brought about by the influence of this small promontory, projecting only forty miles from the main shore, on the movement of the cold current which creeps down the coast of New England and Nova Scotia from the Arctic regions, and which is finally arrested in its movement by the hook of Cape Cod.

We need to comprehend these effects of differences of a geographic sort, and conceive them as applying, in a greater or less measure, to all living or extinct species of animals and plants, in order to understand how far the history of the earth in the past has served to affect the beings of to-day, particularly the highest of them, — man. Most animals and all plants are, as regards. heat, delicate thermometers. They are affected, too, by the winds, by the moisture of the air and soil, and by the qualities of the soil itself, the plants directly, and animals through plants; and so the world of life is swayed about by every accident which affects these circumstances. Every geographic change alters the height of the land or the shape of the sea, and thus affects the currents of the air bringing heat and moisture, the rivers which flow from the continents, or the marine currents which convey the waters of the sea hither and thither over its surface.

The most important lessons which naturalists have learned by the study of fossils contained in rocks concern the succession of life in various stages of the earth's history. At the present time there are somewhere about half a million different kinds of animals and plants on the surface of the earth. Each species resembles more or less closely other related species, so that we have to look carefully to see the difference between them, as, for instance, between the different kinds of sparrows or the several sorts of oaks. The greater number of groups are separated in character by wider differences, such as those which distinguish the beech from the oak; but the white oak does not produce anything but white oaks from its seed, and the sparrows each rear broods of their own kind. If we search the rocks which were formed on the earth's surface say half a million years ago, — a very recent time in the earth's history, — we find by the fossils they contain that there were also oaks and beeches and sparrows, and these were of species related to those now living, undoubtedly the forefathers of living forms, but they differed from them in most cases in a clear way: they differ as much from living oaks or beeches as the species of these plants now do from each other. Thus, stage by stage, we can go back into the remote past of the earth, each step separated, it may be, from the preceding by a million years, until we have found somewhere near a hundred different stages in the earth's history, each showing by its fossils that the life, though akin to that which went before and that which came after, had a particular character. Studying these facts, geologists have one and all come to the conclusion that all the life of to-day has come down to our time from ancestors of earlier days, and has indeed descended from the first beings which came into existence on the surface of this sphere.

A yet more important conclusion derived from the study of these plants and animals of the past and their relation to the living creatures of to-day is that, though many kinds of animals have perished at various periods in the past, leaving no descendants in our time, life as a whole, both that of animals and plants, has always steadily been going upward in its organization towards higher states of being. If we consider the earlier stages, — as, for instance, that known as the Cambrian, which is near the time when life came upon the earth, — we find in the fossils of the beds then laid down on the sea-floor no fishes, no insects; only animals as lowly in structure as our shell-fish, or worms, or certain kindred of our crustaceans. There were apparently no land plants, only imperfect sea-weeds, or perhaps mosses and lichens, on part of the continents which had arisen from the sea. There were no lizards, frogs, birds, or four-footed beasts of any kind. The lands were probably destitute of life, except for the lower kinds of plants and perhaps for a few worm-like animals, or, it may have been, the lowest grades of insects. In the latter chapters of the great stone book, the leaves of which are the strata or rock beds of the earth, we find stage by stage the higher animals and plants appearing. First among the plants come the ferns, and then palm-like creatures, and only in a relatively late day our flowering plants and those which bear fruit and large seeds make their appearance. The back-boned animals also show the same steadfast advance: first come the fishes; then, after a long time, the reptiles; then the birds, at first with long, lizard-like tails and teeth, then the higher song birds. Sucking animals are wanting until a late day; then they came with lowly forms related to the kangaroo. Later, higher kinds appear; and finally the history is rounded with the appearance of man.

All the while these wonderful changes which have led life upward in the scale of being have been going on, the continents have been growing, slowly rising from the sea-floor, gradually dividing the oceans into separate seas, shaping the paths of rivers, and generally determining the geographic influences which, as we have seen, have so much to do with the conditions of life. Every living species of plant and animal has been compelled to move hither and thither with the changes in the form of the land. The more active kinds, those which were better fitted to move here and there with the changes in the land and the consequent alteration of climate and other conditions, have lived because of their vigor, of their intelligence, their power of associating their own action with that of other creatures; and so in the changing geography of the earth the abler forms survive and leave their strong progeny to inhabit the world, while the weaker are destroyed through the process of change. Let us suppose that Cape Cod, which, as we have seen, is an important geographic feature affecting the climate of the sea-water on the coast of the United States, were swept away, as it might in a very easy way be removed by the waves. Then there would arise a contention between the creatures living to the north and south of it as to which should possess the portion of the coast formerly occupied by the Cape. The more vigorous would gain the ground, and in this way a slight effect towards peopling the earth with strong beings would be brought about. A vast number of such changes, some of far greater moment, have tested the qualities of animals and plants, their fitness to remain the masters of the earth. In these trials the lowly and weak have been destroyed, the higher and stronger have been preserved.

It is very hard to tell the story of life in the past within the limits of a few pages ; but further on we shall try to see in the history of North America, in a somewhat detailed way, how the advance of organic life has been promoted by the successive and ceaseless changes in the shape of the lands and the seas.

CHAPTER II.

THE GROWTH OF NORTH AMERICA.

Shape and grouping of the lands and seas. Effect of these features on the conditions of the earth. Method of interpreting the history of the land: process of growth of North America. Successive stages of the development in its geography and in its organic life. Brief history of the organic and inorganic changes in Cambrian, Silurian, Devonian, Carboniferous, Triassic, Jurassic, Cretaceous, and Tertiary times. The coming of man.

In this chapter we shall consider the manner in which the continent of North America has grown, and the effect of its growth on the part of the world in which it is situated. Looking upon a general map of the world, or, better, on a globe, which gives a clearer notion of the earth forms, we perceive that there are two great groups of land masses breaking the surface of the seas. These are the larger mass of the Old World continents, — Asia, Europe, Africa, and Australia, with their neighboring islands, — and the twin continents of the New World, — North and South America. The Old World continents are either close together, or connected with each other by archipelagoes. The New World continents, though tied into one mass by a long isthmus, are, except in the northwest corner of America, parted from the Old World by wide and deep seas. Three of the great continents are of distinctly triangular shape; Africa, North America, and South America are three-sided figures, rather acute triangles in general form, their points turned towards the south pole, their bases to the north. Asia has traces of the same form; and Australia, if we consider not only the part of the continent which is above the water, but also that which remains in the form of shallow seas, has also something like the form of Africa and the Americas.

The grouping of the continents and their place in the world of waters brings about one of the most beneficent arrangements in the system of the earth's machinery. By this arrangement the ocean currents are led from the tropics, where their waters are heated, towards the poles, where they give off the heat they acquired near the equator, thus warming the sea and the adjacent islands in a remarkable manner. For instance, the Gulf Stream, which, as it flows westward across the tropical part of the Atlantic as a broad current impelled by the trade winds, is turned to the northward by the northern part of South America and the southern portion of North America, and made to flow into the northern Atlantic. This current is very broad and deep; it carries many times as much water as all the rivers of the world; and this stream, warmed by the tropical suns, carries with its tide more heat into the Arctic circle than comes to the earth in that realm from the direct rays of the sun. If the continents did not form great walls across the seas, the equatorial current which the trade winds produce and send in a westerly direction would go straight around the earth, and none of its heat would be turned to high latitudes about either pole. In such a condition of the earth, Europe and the parts of North America north of the parallel of 45° would be uninhabitable by man, from the intensity of the cold.

This would also be the case with the southern parts of South America. At the same time, the heat of the tropics, not having the chance to escape, which is now afforded by the ocean streams which the continents divert towards either pole, would be far greater than at present, probably too great for the life of man. Thus, by their position in the seas, the continents in a very simple way operate to improve the climate of the earth, to make the realms both of land and sea better suited for the varied forms of living beings.

Next let us note the fact that the large surface of the continents affords a valuable site for the development of the highly organized creatures of the land. The sea has but lowly forms of life. With the exception of the whales and a few other suck-giving animals the creatures which dwell therein are, whether animals or plants, generally of a much lower organization than those which occupy the land. The studies of naturalists have made it plain that detached islands are by their conditions not favorable to the development of a high order of life. Even the greater of them, such as Madagascar, cannot include within their area any such great variety of conditions of soil and climate as even the smallest of the continents affords. If a considerable change of climate comes to such an island, the creatures upon it have but a small chance to move to and fro to realms which may better suit them. The chances of life in general are small in such an island district; and as the bettering of the life depends upon the opportunity to take advantage of varied conditions, such detached islands do not afford a favorable field for the development of organic forms. If the land areas of the earth had remained in the form of detached islands in which the continents began their growth, it seems certain that the air-breathing animals would never have attained anything like the high position which they have won on the ampler fields that now exist. It is because the development of the continents has so much importance in the history of life that we shall undertake in this chapter to trace the process by which the land of North America has grown to its present highly organized form.

Looking at the great united mass of the North American continent, it is hard to believe that it has grown to its present shape from the detached islands of the earlier geologic time. But the students of the past history of the earth are by their inquiries made sure that this apparently firm-set land has undergone a vast series of progressive changes connected with its increase, — changes which may not unfitly be compared to those that occur in the growth of any animal or plant. Before entering on our account of the development of North America it will be well for the reader to have in mind a general idea as to the way in which, from a study of the rocks, it is possible to ascertain how the solid land has acquired its present size and shape.

The easiest way to understand the methods of geologic study is by comparing them with those which are used in making out the history of men in countries where we have no historic records. Thus in Egypt, in Mesopotamia, and in other countries, the chronicles are either wanting or so imperfect that we cannot tell the varieties of people which have in succession occupied the land. The student of the ancient human races in those countries finds his way to the facts by studying the remains which the several folk in succession have left in the ground. Men often build their habitations for thousands of years on the same site. When a city is ruined by fire or earthquake, or devastated by an enemy, the place may remain for a little while uninhabited, but the reasons which led to the ancient settlement commonly led to the construction of a new town, and so to the depth of many feet in the same place the ruins of one age are piled on those of the next preceding. Now let us suppose that stray coins or other buried treasures of each age lie in the layers of debris formed during the several periods of occupation. By digging away the debris, one stratum after the other, it is thus often easy to determine the successions of the people even where coins are occasionally wanting; fragments of tools or of arms can be interpreted so as to show the student the successions of the races which have occupied the ground.

The work of the geologist in determining the successive ages of the world is in general principles precisely like that of the student who concerns himself with the ancient history of man. The likeness will be perhaps clearer to the reader if we suppose him to undertake an inquiry concerning the ancient inhabitants of North America. All over the Mississippi Valley, and in other parts of the country, he will find scattered the plentiful remains of the Indians who were recently expelled by the whites. Arrow-heads, stone hammers and hatchets, here and there bits of pottery, or ancient graves, show the recent possession of the country by savages. Now and then, below the level of the upper or soil stratum, we find remains of a slightly more cultivated tribe of aborigines, the Mound-builders, and those folk who made the great fortifications of the Mississippi Valley. It is easy to prove that these Mound-builders were earlier than the tribes known to the whites, by the fact that their remains lie generally below the level occupied by the fragments of worked stone and earthenware left by the later ordinary Indians who were known to our people. Now let us suppose that the observer has a mind to dig deeper, and to pass altogether through the soil coating. He will, at most points in the Mississippi Valley, — indeed, over much of the area of the continent, — come at once upon rocks which are full of fossils. The stone in which they are held is laid in successive layers, which were evidently deposited one after the other, each carrying, in general, numerous remains of animals or plants. He knows these remains to have once been living, by their general likeness to the creatures of to-day; but when he proceeds to compare them with the forms now dwelling on sea and land, he finds that they differ in a very striking way from those now in existence: probably not a single species will be of the same sort as those now dwelling on the earth. In a word, he has found written in the great stone book a chapter in the history of the earth which came long before the present stage in that history.

With his own labor, aided by the work of others, the student can then proceed to trace the distribution of these beds containing fossils. He is almost sure to learn that they exist not only where he has found them, but that they have a great extension over the continent. For instance, finding certain beds in the Ohio Valley, guiding himself always by observing that he has the same set of fossils in the beds, he will probably discover that, on journeying a few miles eastward, they become overlaid by strata containing another assemblage of fossils which were clearly formed at a later day. Yet further east, say in the state of New York or in Pennsylvania, he may come upon a place where the beds he originally found are upturned in mountains, or have had the higher-lying strata stripped off by the action of rivers or other forces; and so he finds himself once again on the same level in the rocks. Let us suppose that, from the character of the fossils, he has determined that the beds he is studying were formed on the sea-floor. This is generally easily ascertained, as, for instance, by the presence of abundant stony corals. We know that such corals never flourish save in the waters of the sea. Therefore the beds in which they are found were certainly old sea-floors; and so the student comes to the conclusion that wherever the given beds exist, that portion of the continent was, at the time when they were constructed, below the level of the sea. In his studies of the particular group of rocks it will often happen that, in going in a particular direction, he finds that sand begins to appear in the limestone beds, then pebbles, and finally he comes to a place where he can find marks of sea-shore action or other evidence of the beating of the waves, or even, in rarer cases, the imprint of raindrops on the muds left bare in the recession of the tide. He thus knows that there was an old shore line in this position, and that beyond it lay a portion of the continent which was above the level of the sea at the time when the strata he has been studying were laid down on the neighboring sea-floor.

After having determined the place of the sea and land in one stage of the earth's history marked by the beds he has been studying, he may take in succession the strata which are above or below those on which he began his inquiries, and so, after having examined a great many thousand feet in thickness of the beds, determine a great many different groups of fossils, each the ancestors of those in the following strata. The geologists, or rather many geologists working together for a hundred years or more, have succeeded in interpreting the history of the earth's past in substantially the same way as we determined the succession of peoples in Egypt or Mesopotamia.

In the way above described, geologists have sought to determine how the continent of North America has grown to its present form. So far this difficult task has brought us only a part of the truth we seek to know concerning the history of this continent. The story of a great land is not like the well-arranged history of a people: it is rather as if we had a volume describing the successive years of English history with the pages torn apart and buried in many different places; some of them so affected by decay as to be illegible, others utterly destroyed. To put this scattered work into a shape to tell a connected story would, as we readily see, require a great deal of skill and labor.

Nevertheless, this arduous work of tracing the history of North America has brought us to a few general conclusions concerning the history of this land. The most important of these we will now endeavor to set before the reader. Like the other continents, North America consists of a broad fold of the earth's crust, only a part of which rises above the level of the sea. As the Atlantic and Pacific oceans are in their central parts on the average more than fifteen thousand feet deep, this great continental ridge ascends to the height of nearly three miles before it comes above the level of the sea. In a very ancient time, when this uprising fold of the crust first began to break the surface of the waters, it did not appear as we now behold it, in the form of a great united land, but as archipelagoes, or groups of islands of varied size, the greater part of which appeared where now lie the northern parts of the continent.

So far as we have learned, the first of these lands, which were afterwards to grow together and form North America, came above the sea at the beginning of what is called Archæan time. We do not know just where these islands were; we can in fact only prove that they were above the sea by the fact that great quantities of stony waste worn away from them by rivers and waves were laid down on the bottom of the ancient ocean. We know nothing of the animals or plants which were on the land or in the sea in the Archæan age. We are, however, tolerably certain that living creatures abounded, for we find in the rocks then made a good deal of limestone, and coal-like matter known as graphite. It is generally believed that these beds of limestone were formed by shell-fish, corals, or other animals which build hard parts of lime, and dying, contribute the material to form limestones such as we may find in coral reefs or where beds of oysters abound. The beds of graphite were probably at one time coal which has been brought to its present unburnable state through the changes which geologic time brings about. There was probably an age when these limestones and altered coal-beds contained distinct fossils: the slow-going changes which take place in the earth's crust, such as those which make hard rocks out of the mud of the ocean floor, have altered every bit of these ancient rocks, so that the fossils have, like the coins in the goldsmith's melting-pot, utterly disappeared.

Those who have studied the matter most carefully are of the opinion that this earliest traceable beginning of the continent took place more than a hundred million years ago. It is impossible for any man to imagine such a duration of time; we can only write the figures on the page, but we can obtain no idea whatever as to their meaning. The most aged man who ever lived may have been able to remember something of the events which have happened in a hundred years. A single million years is ten thousand times as long. Some idea of this duration may be had by representing the time by a straight line such as is afforded by a long direct road. Calling the length of a long human life, say a century, the distance a man may easily step at one stride, which is about three feet, he would have to take ten thousand such steps, and would travel about six miles, before he had measured off a distance equivalent on our scale to one million years. He would go near six hundred miles before the distance would be proportionate to the time which has elapsed since the Archæan period.

At the close of the Archæan time, and in the beginning of the ages commonly known as the Cambrian, we have a clearer idea as to the conditions of land and sea and the life the latter bore in this part of the world. The emerged parts of North America at this time seem to have consisted of one or more large islands in the northeastern part of the continent arranged in a somewhat wedge-shaped form like a V, occupying the part of the continent where now lies Labrador and Canada as far south as near the St. Lawrence River, the region immediately north of Lake Superior, and east of Hudson's Sea. That great field of inland waters was probably then, as now, below the ocean level. With the elevation of this great island or archipelago above the sea, the northeastern part of the continent probably assumed something like its present shape. On the western and southern sides, however, the greater portion of its surface still lay below the level of the sea. Nevertheless, on the lines where now lie the Rocky Mountains of the west and the Appalachians of the east, lines of islands, some of them probably as large as Great Britain, indicated where these great mountain systems had already begun to grow and had elevated a portion of the rising continent above the level of the sea. Although the continent was as yet very incomplete in its outlines, the plan upon which it was to be built was at least in a general way determined.

Unlike the Archæan rocks, these Cambrian strata contain numerous fossils from which we can in a general way determine the character of the life which inhabited its seas. There are a great many different species of these forms, all of shapes entirely unlike those of the present day: there are among them many shell-fish, mostly belonging to the group of lamp-shells, or brachiopods, creatures which were more abundant in later ages, but are now rare. There were also many univalve shells allied to our sea-snails, many worms which inhabited shells, as well as shell-less forms which moved freely over the bottom. There were also jointed animals in the same class with our crabs, but very different from them, which received the name of trilobites. These creatures are particularly interesting for the reason that they probably were the first animals to possess eyes, and therefore the first to behold the light of those ancient days. The seas of that day contained no fishes; in fact, the whole group of back-boned animals was a much later creation.

From the beginning of the Cambrian to the close of the Lower Silurian time there are no notable additions to the life of the earth, so far as we can determine from the record of the rocks. About the beginning of the Upper Silurian, or shortly before, we have the first faint signs of land plants in traces of what appear to be ferns. It is probable that the earlier lands were occupied by a lowly vegetation consisting mainly, if not altogether, of mosses. In the last-named time we have the first remains of animals which dwelt upon the land. These come to us in the form of those curious insects which are known as scorpions, animals with bodies in general like those of the spiders with four pairs of legs for walking, and with a long, jointed, and hard abdomen terminating in a sting. The fact that this creature has a stinging apparatus shows pretty clearly that there were other and stronger animals alive at the same time on the lands.

At the close of the Silurian period there appear at once, both in this country and in Europe, plentiful remains of certain species which have a keen interest for us, owing to the fact that they belong to the series of back-boned animals, and are thus nearer kin to man than any of the creatures known in the earlier ages.[1] These first vertebrates are fishes, which occur in the

[1] Some remains found in Lower Silurian strata of the Rocky Mountains seem to indicate that the fishes were probably in existence during the lowest Silurian period.

rocks where we first find them in such frequent remains that we may be sure they fairly swarmed in those ancient seas. Although much unlike the fishes of the present day, we note certain kinships between these old-time forms and those which now inhabit the waters. Some of these are like certain living forms of shark; others akin to the sturgeons or to the gar-pikes of North America.

It is a peculiarity of an interesting kind that all these early fishes have jaws armed with strong teeth fit for attack and defence, while their bodies are often protected with amazingly strong and closely interlocked plates or scales of a bony nature. They remind us, indeed, of the clumsy warriors of mediæval times, when they were prepared for battle in their suits of armor.

Another interesting group of animals—a group which affords some of the most picturesque and beautiful creatures of the sea—begins to develop and rapidly take on an amazing variety of form in the Silurian periods. These creatures, which are akin to the more familiar star-fishes, had a body shaped somewhat like the blossom of a daisy with long arms where the petals of the flower stand, the mouth in the centre of the arms leading to a pear-shaped calyx or body, the whole supported on a long and slender stem made up of limestone disks arranged one on top of another like a pile of coins. The body and branched arms, as well as the stem, were composed of shapely hard bits which covered and protected the internal soft parts. Between the joined edges of each of these plates there was a thin living membrane which, by the circulation of the blood, brought ever-new supplies to the plates, so that they increased in size with the constant growth of the exquisitely organized body. Attached to the sea-bottom by strong root-like processes extending from the base of the stem, with the body held some feet above the slimy mud of the ocean bottom, and the many creeping animals which assail creatures prone upon its floor, with branched arms which could gather food from a wide space of water, these crinoids were singularly well fitted for life in the ocean depth.

Yet another very interesting group of animals which abounded in the Silurian time were the great kindred of the living pearly nautilus known by the name of orthoceratites, or straight-shelled animals. Those who are familiar with the features of the pearly nautilus can imagine the form of the orthoceratites by conceiving the shell of the nautilus unrolled from its coiled form and made into a very slender, tapering cone. Some of these straight-shelled forms were of gigantic dimensions. We not infrequently find them having a length of three or four feet, and a diameter at the larger end of five or six inches, and fragments have been discovered which must have belonged to shells having a length of nearly twenty feet. When young, these creatures dwelt in a shell which had but one chamber; as they grew in size and needed more protection, they built on a second wider and longer cell, withdrew their bodies from the old room, and sealed the space across, except for a single small opening. In the course of years they thus formed many successive partitions, and the most of their habitations — all, indeed, but the last chamber — were empty, but served a good purpose in buoying up the shell, which otherwise would, by its great weight, have anchored the animal to the bottom. In the empty places it is supposed that the animal secreted some gas, and that the shell was thus made so relatively light that it stood up in the water while the creature crawled along the bottom.

From the close of the Silurian through the Devonian, and down to the beginning of the time when the coal-measures were deposited, the growth of the continent was steadily advancing. The original islands were rising higher from the sea, and extending their shores so as to win more of the shallow bottom to dry land. The vast region of ocean, already in part walled in by the great Canadian or Laurentian islands and those of the Appalachians and Rocky Mountain system, though its floor was subjected to various irregular movements, gradually became more shallow. As it became shoaler its waters appear to have become more fit for life, until just before the coal-measures time the animals of the sea-bottom, particularly the crinoids, brachiopods, and ancient corals, flourished in a marvellously luxuriant way.

So abundant were they that the lime deposited from their skeletons formed beds of limestone which may have a thickness of one hundred feet or more. It is owing to the great thickness and purity of these limestones that the under-earth streams have been able to excavate in them the great caverns of Kentucky, Southern Indiana, and Southwestern Virginia.

During all these earlier ages of the continent, from the close of the Cambrian to the beginning of the coal-measures, the Mississippi Sea, as we may term the great field of waters now occupied by the valley of that river, was evidently the seat of a great ocean current which swept up from the southward. This was doubtless the same great tide of waters from the tropics, to which we give the name of the Gulf Stream, because it flows through the Gulf of Mexico, the diminished remnant of the ancient Mississippi Sea. In this olden day there was a wide path between the Laurentian land and the islands where now lie the Rocky Mountains of Canada, so that then as now this ocean stream had an open way to the Arctic Sea. We find evidence that such a current existed in various periods, from the presence, in the rocks formed at the several times, of coral reefs, which, as is well known, can only grow where a strong tide of very warm water flows against a shore. The first of these reefs to appear is found in Kentucky; the position of the corals indicates that the warm current came from the southward during the Lower Silurian time. The next succeeding system of reefs belongs to the Upper Silurian time. Yet later in the early stages of the Devonian, another great reef was built, — that which forms the falls of the Ohio at Louisville. Still later, in the sub-carboniferous, or cavern limestone, we find evidence that this ocean stream still swept to the northward through the Mississippi Sea.

Yet other proof that the ancient Gulf Stream flowed over what is now the central part of the continent is given us by a deposit which occurs in this valley, and is known as the Ohio or Devonian black shale. This formation consists of very thin layers largely made up of organic remains, derived from creatures which lived in the water above the bottom of the warm seas, which occupy the central part of such great circling currents as the Gulf Stream. At present the Gulf Stream has between the northward-flowing current of the American shore and the southward-flowing water of the European shore, a great oceanic area which has near its surface a great deal of sea-weed which grows as it floats in the water. This plentiful vegetation nourishes a great quantity of animal forms, whose remains are contributed to the sea-floor. It seems probable that this Ohio shale was accumulated on the ocean floor beneath an ancient sargasso, or sea-weed sea. When it was formed, the old Gulf Stream probably flowed between the present site of the Mississippi River and the old islands which were formed by the growing Rocky Mountains.

When the Carboniferous period began, a great extent of sea-floors, which with the uprising of the continent through the earlier ages were gradually coming nearer to the surface of the water, finally arose above the sea, so that the several ancient islands and archipelagoes, which had in a way prefigured the form of the continent, were at length united in one great land. From this time, indeed, we may fairly date the beginning of the continental history of this country. It seems likely that this continent of the coal-measures was at least in some of the ages of that enduring time almost, if not quite, as extensive as it is at the present day. Its general shape, also, was probably much the same then as now. On the northeastern shore it probably extended somewhat farther into the Atlantic than at present; and on the south what is now the Gulf of Mexico probably covered the area now occupied by the whole of Florida, Mississippi, and Louisiana, as well as a part of Virginia, the Carolinas, Georgia, Alabama, and Texas. It is also probable that the Pacific then occupied a considerable portion of the country east of the Rocky Mountains, from Mexico to the high north. It is possible, indeed, that nearly all the Rocky Mountain country was at this time below the level of the sea, and thus the continent, as a whole, lay somewhat to the eastward of its present position.

Before we pass to our brief study of the coal-measure time, we must note certain interesting changes in the marine life of the seas about the continent, which took place just before the coal-beds began to be formed on the newly emerged land. Of the many alterations, we can notice but few. The first of these to be remarked is the rapid disappearance of the great group of trilobites, which had been for so long a most picturesque and important group of animals in those early seas. Gradually, after the close of the Silurian time, these creatures diminish in variety, and the remaining forms decrease in size, until finally, in the sub-carboniferous limestones, they are represented by small species which speedily disappear, and so ends the history of all the kind.

The crinoids, successors of the forms which we have already noted as existing in the earlier ages, attain a singular perfection of growth and number of species as well as of individuals in the seas which deposited the carboniferous limestones. The most remarkable as well as the most numerous crinoids of that day were more perfect structures than those of earlier times, in that they had arranged a system by which the excrements of the body were conveyed to a distance from the mouth. In the earlier forms, the mouth and the further extremity of the alimentary canal were very near together and at the same height above the sea-bottom. In these peculiar carboniferous crinoids a tall, conical, chimney-like shaft was built up to the height of some inches from the mouth, and through this the waste of digestion was poured forth into the sea at a point where it would not readily harm the breathing or feeding of the creature.

Owing, perhaps, to the advantage which this sewage system gave these crinoids, they multiplied exceedingly, and attained such numbers that they stood, very often, as thick as the wheat stems in an ordinary field. Between their close-set columns a great variety of other living forms flourished and contributed their limy matter to the growing stratum. New crinoids sprung up in every available interspace, and swiftly took the place of those which perished. The result is that the limestones of this time are much more massive than those of most other ages in which the beds were commonly formed of molluscan shells, the shell-fish being destroyed by the violent stirring of the mud on the bottom by earthquake shocks or sudden changes in the marine currents. A large part of the great caverns of this country, all those of noteworthy size, in Indiana, Kentucky, and Tennessee, as well as those of many foreign countries, are excavated in beds of this age. The great thickness of the strata of these sub-carboniferous limestones is owing to the habit of growth of the crinoids, and the majestic avenues of the caverns are thus in a measure due to the peculiar habit of growth of these ancient "sea-lilies."

With the close of the sub-carboniferous period all these peculiar proboscis-bearing crinoids just described disappear. Most of the other simpler forms also pass away. A few of the principal groups only have remained; some of them surviving in slightly changed shapes to the present day. The cause of this rapid destruction of creatures, which appear to have been successful for a long time and over a large part of the earth's surface, is probably to be found in the rapid increase in the variety of fishes which occupied the ocean at that time.

The fishes in the sub-carboniferous seas were clearly in great variety and remarkably provided with effective jaws. To a great extent they had abandoned the system of plate and scale armor so common in the earlier ages, replacing these instruments of mere defence with those which serve for attack. They had stronger and more serviceable teeth, and their bodies seem to have been shaped for swifter movement through the waters. Among these fishes were some forms which had the teeth placed like paving-stones over the inside of the mouth, covering the parts where the tongue and roof of the mouth lie. These animals appear to have fed on the crinoids, the bodies of which they could readily crush in their powerful jaws.

Yet another momentous change in the character of animal life consists in the appearance, in these carboniferous rocks, of certain animals belonging to the backboned group, which probably were developed from fishes, but were much higher in the scale of being. These are the earliest members of the class to which the frogs and toads, the newts, water-dogs, and salamanders belong. As is commonly known, these amphibians are born as tadpoles; they have swimming-tails like the common fishes, but no legs; gills, but no lungs; thus they are fitted for swimming, but not for walking, and for breathing the air which is dissolved in the water. They do not, as is the case with land animals, even in their youngest state, take the air into their lungs. After a time of growth in the tadpole stage, these amphibians almost always drop their tails and gills, and in their place develop limbs and lungs, and are thus fitted to dwell on the dry land.

The gigantic salamanders of the Carboniferous period

attained a greater size than any of their kindred species now living. They appear to have lived in fresh water, and were probably nearly as large as the alligators now found in Florida. It is probable that they were the largest land animals of the vertebrate series which at this time dwelt upon the earth. There may have been no others of this group.

Many other important changes in the character of the life took place in the early stages of the Carboniferous period, but we cannot pause to consider them. Another feature of the age demands attention, — the extensive coal-deposits which were then formed, — deposits not only of interest as showing the condition of the continent of that time, but also because of their effect upon the history of its civilized peoples. This effect seems destined to be greater in the future than it has been in the past.

THE COAL-MAKING TIME IN NORTH AMERICA.

Although coal-beds, or at least layers of a coaly nature, had been formed in an imperfect manner in the earlier geologic ages and have been formed in considerable abundance at various times since the Carboniferous period, that period really deserves the name of the coal-bearing age; for more deposits of carbon were probably buried in the rocks in that period of the earth's history than in all the other ages put together. Moreover, the coal formed in this middle age of the continent's history, owing to its pure quality and its wide distribution over the surface of the land and the ease with which it is won by the miner, is extremely valuable as a source of heat, light, and mechanical power. The formation and preservation of this valuable material were due to the peculiar conditions upon which the continents entered at the beginning of the Carboniferous time. These conditions we must now consider.

We have already remarked that just before the coal-making age the slow upward growth of the continental mass brought a wide area of seas into the state of shallows, and that the last stage of the elevation converted a great area previously covered by the oceans into dry land. At first this land was low; much of it which has since been upheaved into mountains, was then in a condition of broad plains extending eastwardly and westwardly from the narrow Blue Ridge or original mountainous Appalachian archipelago. The surface of this land recently lifted from the sea was probably equal in area to at least one-third of the existing continent. In form, this land probably resembled that now existing in the great sandy district of Eastern North and South Carolina, or the plains which ascend from the Mississippi westward towards the foot of the Rocky Mountains. It is probable that the surface was not anything like as high above the sea as the above-mentioned districts of plain and prairie.

For a long time after the elevation of these lowlands from their condition of sea-bottom they did not become what we can properly term dry land. The climate of this period was evidently made very moist by a considerable and very constant rainfall. This favored the formation of extensive swamps, which appear to have covered all the low-lying fields of the continent with a dense mass of water-loving vegetation akin to the ferns and rushes of the present day.

While these conditions of climate prevailed, the surface of the land was extremely unstable; again and again, to the number of scores of successive movements, it was alternately lowered a little below the level of the sea or slightly lifted above its plane. We do not know whether these alterations were due to actual uprisings and downsinkings of the solid part of the continent, or to swayings in the height of the sea itself. It is quite possible that both sea and land varied slightly, though frequently, in their height; and so neither held a fixed place for any great geologic time. It is to the action of these two conditions, the extreme humidity of the climate and the instability of the land with reference to the sea, that we owe the formation and preservation of the coal-measures. The way in which these results are brought about afford one of the most interesting features in the geologic record. It is well worth the attention which we shall now have to give to it.

In endeavoring to account for any peculiar conditions in the ancient stages of our world, it is best first to search for facts which, in the present condition of the earth, are most like those we seek to explain in the past. Let us therefore look closely at the characteristic aspects of a coal-bed, and see what features it presents which need explanation, and then seek in the work of the world in our own day the means of accounting for them. In a coal-bed we perceive that we have at the base some rocks of ordinary character, such as sandstone or layers of thinly bedded clay; next above these a layer which the miners term a dirt-bed, and which closely resembles the soil. Then comes a layer of coal, which often attains a thickness of from six to twelve feet, but is rarely of greater depth. Above this coal come again other layers of sandstone, conglomerates, or clays. After a succession of these last-named layers we are likely to find dirt-beds overlaid by coals and covered in turn with sandstones or shales, and so in succession, until there are twenty or more such series of deposits lying one above the other.

Looking more closely at the relations of the coal to the under-clay or dirt-bed, we readily perceive that this deposit found beneath the coal was a true soil; for we find it to contain abundant roots of plants allied to the tree ferns, the reeds, rushes, and other plants now living. The stems of these we can often trace upwards for a considerable distance into the coal-bed itself. A close examination of the coaly matter by the naked eye, and with the microscope, shows us that the whole of the material is commonly made up of bits of plants partly decayed and pressed close together, along with a little mud of the fine-grained character which settles in stagnant pools. It is evident, in a word, that coal-deposits were made from the remains of vegetable matter which grew in swamps, and fell into the water when the plants perished. All doubt on this point is removed by the fact that in certain coals we frequently find the remains of fishes associated with those of various fresh-water plants.

We find that a close likeness exists between these beds of coal formed in the ancient time and the peat-bogs which are now accumulating so plentifully in all regions where the climate is moist and tolerably cool, but not so cold as to prevent the growth of an abundant vegetation, and where the surface is not too steep to prevent the growth of bogs. All the level low-lying lands of Great Britain, Ireland, the northern shores of Germany, and the Scandinavian peninsula were originally covered by such bogs, though these accumulations have been to a great extent cleared away to convert the land into tilled fields. At the present time the climate of North America is prevailingly too dry to permit the freest growth of peat-bogs. But in the northeastern portion of its area, and as far south as Florida, and in high latitudes west to the Red River of the North, we find a vast number of these swamps. Within the limit of the continent they are best seen in Labrador and Newfoundland. The bogs of Ireland and Scotland, however, furnish the best means of comparing existing bogs with those of the coal-measures time. Wherever in these countries a natural or artificial pool of fresh water is found, the spores of certain mosses take root along its margin, and in the moist air they soon form a thick coating of sponge-like interlacing stems. This sheet of vegetation rapidly extends off over the surface of the water, at first floating on the surface; but as it thickens, gradually sinking until the mass rests upon the bottom. The upper part of the moss sheet alone is living; the lower portion is dead. This lower part does not completely decay, as it would if freely exposed to the open air, but is converted into a blackened mass of soft woody matter which gradually adheres together, making a uniform deposit of a very dark color known as peat, and which we may regard as the first stage of coal.

In moist air, such as is found in Scotland and Ireland, the moss not only extends out over the water of the pool on the margins of which it began to grow, but also climbs up the neighboring slopes, provided they be not too steep, and extends as a mantle over the surface of the country. In these elevated situations the moss is able to grow by virtue of a large amount of

LAKE DRUMMOND, DISMAL SWAMP, VIRGINIA.

water which it holds in exactly the manner in which water is retained in a sponge. Although, as on the surface of the lake, the lower part of the moss dies, it is kept from perfect decay by the water with which it is surrounded, so that there also it becomes converted into peat.

Peat is in fact very like coal in most regards, except its compactness, and we may fairly assume that all coal-beds were originally in the condition of our bogs. What is now firm material could originally be cut by a spade as our peats can be. Peat, when dried in the sun, affords the poor fuel, which serves the country people in Northern Europe, and it is sometimes still used in this country. The material was brought into its firmer shape in the following way: after the deposit in the swamp had been formed in the manner above described, though through the agency of other plants than the living mosses, a change in the height of the sea carried the morass to some depth below the level of the water, where in time it became buried beneath layers of clay, sand, or, more rarely, limestone. These deposits brought a certain weight upon the soft peat, which tended to drive its particles more closely together, and to squeeze out the water. Certain chemical processes generated gases in the mass, which tended still further to expel the water and to bring the vegetable matter nearer to the state of ordinary bituminous coal, that which burns with a free flame.

With the many uprisings and downsinkings of the land which took place in this singular period of the earth's history coal-beds, all, indeed, save those latest formed, were sure speedily to become deeply buried, and thus, by the conditions which deep burial brought about, to be changed to firm coal. In certain cases, indeed, the alteration of the original peat has gone so far that the material is converted into anthracite coal; that is, coal in which all the material which by heat can be readily converted into gas has been driven off. In certain rare cases, indeed, it has been changed into the unburnable form of carbon known as graphite, or plumbago, a substance which is used in making lead-pencils and vessels which are destined to receive the highest heat which furnaces can apply.

When the coal-measures were formed, the climate of North America, as well as of those portions of the Old World which face the region of the North Atlantic, was much moister and had a more equable temperature than in the present time, or perhaps than in any other period of the earth's history. We know this by the fact that the delicate vegetation which occupied those ancient swamps was able to flourish up to and within the Arctic circle, and that plants of the same nature also formed peat-bogs as far south as Central Alabama. Some geologists are of the opinion that the peculiar climate of the Carboniferous period was brought about by the same conditions that produced the glacial period which has just passed away. They think that when the coal-beds were formed there were alternating times when in rapid successions, — that is to say, quickly returning, in a geologic sense, — the surface of the land was occupied by a vast glacial sheet and by far-extending morasses; when the glaciers spread out from the mountainous elevation, bearing into the shallow seas great quantities of waste worn from the rocks, the sandstones and pebble beds which so often lie between the coal-deposits were formed. When these ice-sheets disappeared, and the continents, disburdened of their weight, rose above the sea, its surface was repossessed by the swamp-making vegetation, and so by alternation of these conditions frequently repeated the beds of the coal-bearing age were accumulated.

It is not yet certain that this was the true condition of climate in this age of the earth's history, but the facts are better explained in this than in any other way. Moreover, as we shall see when we come to consider the history of the continent during the Glacial period, which is the last great event in the earth's history, the character of the deposits much resembles those made during the Carboniferous time.

When the coal-measures were first formed, they extended over a great part of the continent, from which they have since been swept away by the action of the sea, the rivers, and of glacial ice. Thus the coal-beds of Indiana, Illinois, and Western Kentucky, which are now separated from those of Ohio, Tennessee, and Eastern Kentucky, by a wide space occupied by Silurian and Devonian rocks were once united by continuous coal-fields. It is probable, that the area of carboniferous rocks was originally more than twice as extensive as it now is.

The carboniferous beds are overlaid by those of the Permian age, which were formed during a time when the climate was becoming dryer, and the swamps from which the coal-beds were formed ceased to be developed, though most of the plants and animals continued to live. In a word, the Permian period marks a great and gradual change in the atmospheric state of this part of the world, a stable land and a dry air taking the place of the previous oscillating land and humid climate.

In the Carboniferous age there appear to have been no considerable mountains built. The movements of the land were probably limited to the frequent uprisings and downsinkings of the broad flat lands, which so strikingly marked this continent during the period when the coal-measures were deposited. In the period immediately following the last or Permian stage of the Carboniferous, commonly known as the Trias, we have evidence of much mountain-building. A good deal of the flat land whereon the coal-measures were laid down was wrinkled into great mountainous folds. All the great chain of the Alleghanies lying to the west of the old Blue Ridge, and extending from near Albany, N.Y., to Alabama, was about this time thrown into mountain folds, the higher summits of which rose six or eight thousand feet above the sea. These foldings took place also in the region to the east of the Blue Ridge, and led to the formation of mountains in Eastern New England and in the region about the Gulf of St. Lawrence. It is likely that at the same time a great deal of mountain-building was done in the Rocky Mountain region; the only extended portion of the continent, indeed, which is not affected by the wrinkling movement of the strata was the district of the Mississippi Valley and that which lies to the north of it in British America.

In a small part of the continent, viz. that which lies in Eastern Virginia and Middle North Carolina, the conditions for the formation of coal persisted during this Triassic time, and in this portion of the continent several coal-beds were formed. Elsewhere the deposits consisted of heavy conglomerate composed of large pebbles and bowlders, coarse sandstones, and layers of sandy shale, all evidently derived mainly from the waste of the recently made mountainous land.

The changes in the condition of sea and land consequent on the alterations of the form of the continent which took place shortly after the close of the Carboniferous period were very great. Nearly all the earlier groups of genera and species were destroyed or driven away from this part of the world. The alteration was, as is generally the case, greater in the air-breathing forms than in those which inhabited the water. To the changed lands there came by migration from some other region a host of air-breathing animals of great size, somewhat akin to our frogs and salamanders, but differing from them very much in form and size. These amphibians are best known to us by the very numerous footprints which they have left upon the sandstones of the Connecticut Valley in Massachusetts, prints which they formed on the old sea-shore, and which have been preserved by being buried by sand which was blown or washed upon them. When the quarrymen lift the slabs of stone from their place in the beds, they often find them thickly covered with footprints which these extinct creatures impressed upon them. Often the impressions are as numerous as those made by a flock of sea-fowls on the soft margin of the existing coasts.

At first these footprints were supposed to have been made by birds; on close study, however, it is easy to see that the creatures were clearly not bird-like. Although most of the tracks were evidently made by animals which usually walked on two feet, we find here and there the impressions of two smaller sets of toes which they occasionally rested upon the ground. Moreover, we occasionally find impressions of a tail where it dragged upon the surface of the mud. Naturalists have therefore concluded that these creatures were, in most cases at least, really quadrupeds, and from the study of their skeletons they have determined that they were most likely animals which were born from the egg in the tadpole state, and afterwards in the manner of frogs and their kindred developed lungs and limbs, becoming thus fitted for life upon the dry land. In size, these strange animals, of which we know little, save from their footprints, varied from that of a robin to that of creatures much larger than an ostrich. Some of the impressions made by the feet have a length of fifteen inches, and from the depth to which they penetrated the wet sand it seems likely that the animal weighed several hundred pounds. Besides the creatures which made the footprints of the Connecticut Valley, and which were probably more nearly akin to the frogs than to any other living animals, the Triassic period is remarkable for the great number of true reptiles more or less nearly related to the crocodiles and lizards, and which differ from the amphibians, in being born with limbs and lungs, as well as in less important particulars. These higher creatures were very plenty and of very varied form. So far as we yet know, these were the first species in North America belonging to the group of back-boned animals which breathed the air directly by means of lungs from the time when they came forth from the egg.

By far the most interesting addition to the life of the continent which was made during this period, consists of a species which belonged in that group of suck-giving animals which bear their young for a while after birth in a pouch. This little creature was related to the opossums which still live in North America, as well as to the numerous kindred of the kangaroo which dwell in Australia. It was not larger than a small domestic cat, and probably fed on insects such as beetles.

The plants of the Trias differ less from those of the Carboniferous age than do the animals. Ferns continue to abound as before, but it is evident that the narrow-leaved trees akin to the cypresses and pines were becoming more abundant.

It does not seem likely that the new forms of living beings which so plentifully appear in the Triassic deposits of North America originated within the limits of the continent; it is more probable that they migrated to this land from other regions over some bridge from other countries. Whence they came we do not know.

Next after the Triassic period come the strata of the Jurassic age. It is doubtful if deposits of this age exist in any part of North America east of the Mississippi River except along the borders of the Arctic Ocean. In the Cordilleras, however, these beds occupy a large area. From them alone we may judge as to the character of the American life. It seems likely, indeed, that the eastern half of the continent was, during the Jurassic period, much higher above the sea than it is at the present time, and that the strata which were then laid down are now hidden beneath the ocean along the Atlantic coast.

The plants of the Jurassic time are but scantily known in North America. It seems likely, however, that they differed in no important way from those of the Triassic period. It is otherwise with the animals, however; for many groups of them show great changes and advances in structure. These are most conspicuous and important in the groups of mollusca and in the reptiles. Though all the life shows signs of progress, the gain is most conspicuous in the above-named classes.

In the mollusca we find that the cephalopods, a group which began in the earlier ages of the earth's history, and which long continued in the form of chambered shells, takes on in North America, in the Jurassic period, an important variation of form. This change, which began in Europe in the Triassic period, consisted in the growth of the animal outside of its shell in such a manner that the hard parts, which had hitherto served to encase and protect the creature in the manner of the snail's covering, became an internal skeleton supporting the soft parts of the body which were now defended from assault by the vigilance and strength of the animal. While its ancestors, the nautilus and the orthoceratite, were slow-moving creatures with little power of attacking other forms, these Jurassic cephalopods were among the most active inhabitants of the sea. On their strong arm-like processes about the head they had hooks for capturing their prey; their mouths were provided with powerful beaks; they swam with fins and by squirting the water through a tube from the space about their gills. They had an organ which secreted an ink-like substance which when thrown out clouded the water so that their pursuers could not observe the direction of their flight.

These creatures closely resemble the living squid and cuttle-fishes, to which in time they gave birth. The squids, however, are much more perfect and vigorous forms. They are, indeed, among the most masterful creatures of the waters at the present day.

The greatest changes in the living beings of the Jurassic period occurred in the group of reptiles. These were far more varied and of higher forms than their kindred of the Triassic age. Among them we find a number of gigantic species, one of which, the Atlantosaurus, was nearly a hundred feet in length. It must have been nearly as large as the greater whales. Others, known as Pterodactyls, were provided with wings much like those of bats, and were as well fitted for flight as any of our birds. Some of these were of great size, measuring twenty feet or more between the tips of the extended wings.

It is doubtless in this time in North America, as in Europe, that the birds began to develop from the reptiles; some of the fossils which have been found in the Cordilleran region appear to indicate this beautiful change which gave us the most charming of all the lower animals.

The mammals, or suck-giving creatures, which, as we have seen, appeared in the Triassic time, become more abundant in the Jurassic period. There are a number of different kinds, but, so far as we can judge from their teeth, they were still limited for diet to insects, and were all of the pouch-bearing group. It was only in a later day that these creatures of the mammalian series acquired the habits of eating vegetables or of preying on the larger animals.

The great section of the earth's history known as the Mesozoic, or middle-life, time was closed by a period known as the Cretaceous. Like the most of the other names for the geological formations, this term was first applied to the rocks succeeding the Jurassic by European students, particularly those of England. In the latter country the most important deposits of this age are those of fine, soft limestone, or chalk, such as is used on blackboards. Therefore the rocks of this age received the name of Cretaceous, which comes from the Latin word meaning chalk. It is supposed that the chalk was deposited in what was then a tolerably deep sea, the waters of which swarmed with small creatures of the lowest animal organization known as foraminifera. A somewhat similar deposit is now making on the deep-sea floor of the North Atlantic. There are no chalk-beds known in North America, the deposits of Cretaceous age consisting mainly of sandstones and clays, containing only a moderate amount of lime. These deposits occupy an extensive area in North America, extending from Southern Massachusetts through New Jersey as a narrow broken fringe, occupying a large field in the states which lie just north of the Gulf of Mexico, and a great part of the Cordilleran region and the Pacific border.

The beds of Cretaceous age in North America are very thick, being in some parts of the Rocky Mountains seven or eight thousand feet in depth. We thus see that a large part of the continent, probably nearly one-fourth of its whole surface, was below the level of the sea, and that in places it remained long submerged. It seems likely that during this time North America was much smaller than it is at present, or had been at any time after the close of the Carboniferous period.

The greatest change which took place in the living beings of North America in this age is exhibited in the plants which appear in the uppermost Cretaceous; for in addition to the great groups of lowlier forms developed in the earlier ages, we now find in the uppermost beds of this age trees related to the ordinary broad-leaved forms of our forests, such as oaks and maples, as well as many of our plants which bear edible fruit. The palms, also, are first known in this age; in fact, for the first time in the history of the continent its surface was occupied by woods which would have looked familiar to men of the temperate regions.

One of the most remarkable additions to the animal life of North America appears to have consisted in the introduction of feathered animals, creatures which, though distinctly bird-like, differed from ordinary birds in that they had very long jaw-bones armed with pointed teeth. Some of these birds were of very great size: one of them, a water-bird not unlike a loon, was, when standing, five or six feet in height. Although the most of these Cretaceous birds have teeth, we can see that these parts are in process of disappearing. In certain forms they have ceased to grow in the front part of the jaw; in yet other kinds they have entirely disappeared, and in their place we have the ordinary beaks; and with this latter change all conspicuous marks of the relation of the feathered creatures to the reptiles are lost.

Perhaps the most important change in the life of this as well as of the other continents consists in the nearly universal destruction of the great reptiles which, from the beginning of the Triassic period down to the close of the Cretaceous, occupied the sea and land. There had been hundreds, if not thousands, of species of these reptilian forms during the Mesozoic time. From their great abundance, this portion of the earth's history has been well termed the age of reptiles. Before the end of the Cretaceous we note that these great beasts of strange aspect are diminishing in the number of their kinds, and at the close of that period they nearly all disappear.

Another group, the cephalopods, the kindred of the pearly nautilus and the squid, also loses some of its ancient and interesting representatives in this time. The chambered shells, which began in the Silurian period, and finally gave birth to the beautiful series of the ammonites, almost vanish from the seas at this time. The end of the Cretaceous sees the last of the ammonites; and only one important chambered form, the nautilus, remained.

The cause of these great changes, and many others which cannot here be detailed, which took place near the close of the Cretaceous period, has not yet been determined. It does not appear to be due to any great alteration of climate such as might have destroyed the animals and plants, but rather to the spontaneous death of these creatures as their places were taken by other and more advanced forms. They appear to have died as human beings die of old age, the species disappearing from the earth in the same manner as the individual being.

During the Cretaceous period, as well as during the most of the earlier ages, the continent of North America appears to have been divided by a long arm of the Gulf of Mexico extending from the tropics to the Arctic sea, so that on the west was the great though narrow island of the Rocky Mountains, and on the east the more extensive land composed of the Appalachian and Laurentian islands and the districts of the Ohio and upper Missouri valleys. All the lowlands from Massachusetts to the Rio Grande, including the whole of Florida, Mississippi, and Louisiana, were beneath the sea-level, as was also the greater part of Texas and Alabama.

The climate of North America during this stage of its development was probably in the main warm and equable. This is shown by the abundance of great reptiles in regions which are now subjected to very cold winters. The greater part of these beasts were probably, like their living kindred, cold-blooded, and therefore unable to maintain themselves on the surface of the earth in freezing weather. We easily see that they could not, in the manner of our living snakes and lizards, have found refuge from the cold by creeping into holes in the earth. It would have required a Mammoth Cave to have afforded refuge for the larger species, and all the caverns would not have served as sufficient housing for them.

That the climate of this time was moist is indicated by the occasional occurrence of coal-beds, at least in the western part of the continent. The plants in general evidently grew in a luxuriant manner, and many of the greater reptiles doubtless fed upon them. In the swamps of this time many of the reptiles, especially the great turtles, probably dwelt. One species of the latter group, the remains of which have been found in Kansas, was of enormous size, the distance from tip to tip of fore-limbs exceeding fifteen feet.

Following the Cretaceous period comes the last great division of the earth's history, that known as the Tertiary. There appears to have been no great development of mountains in this time of change, but the continent underwent a general uplift which brought it nearly to the present form. It is probable that the great strait connecting the Gulf of Mexico with the Arctic Ocean was closed at this time, so that the Arctic regions and the adjacent northern portions of the continent became colder than they had hitherto been. Most of the lowland districts of the Atlantic and Gulf border, and of the belt of country along the Pacific coast which had been below the sea during the Cretaceous period, still remained in the possession of the ocean; but the water which covered them probably was shallower than before.

The greatest change which occurred in the beginning of the Tertiary period consisted in the introduction of many forms of animals and plants of higher organization than any which had lived before. Most noteworthy of these new groups of animals are the higher of the placental mammals. As we have seen before, there were in the long ages of the reptilian time a number of species of marsupials living on this continent. These were suck-giving animals which were born in a very immature state, and had for a long time to remain continuously attached to the nipple of the mother, where they were protected by the curious pouch. The result of this arrangement was, and it remains a characteristic of the living pouched mammals as well, that all the species are of rather small size, few of them weighing over a hundred pounds. Moreover, they seem incapable of making any of the variations of form which enable the higher mammals to live under great variety of conditions. None of the pouch-bearers live in the water, as our whales, or are even amphibious, as are the seals, the otters, and a host of other familiar animals. None of them have hoofs or horns like those of our bulls or horses; none of them can fly as the bats; none burrow under ground in the manner of the moles; none of them can stand a strenuous winter, as do many of the well-known beasts of this continent. As a whole, the pouch-bearers are small, feeble, weak-witted creatures; and we are not surprised that for ages they made no head against the reptiles of the Jurassic and Cretaceous times.

The higher non-pouched mammals begin their life within the mother in a different way from the marsupials. In the kindred of the opossum and kangaroo, the young, when it escapes from the egg, forms no attachment to the mother's body. In the higher mammals a union between the unborn creature and the mother is created by means of a structure called the placenta, which comes away when the infant is born. Through this placenta the mother's blood nourishes the young creature in such a manner that it is generally born, not in the immature state which it has in the marsupials, but so far developed that it can quickly care for itself. It often can follow the mother about in the manner of calves and colts, and does not have to be carried by the parent, as is the case with the pouched animals.

Owing probably to the more rapid and perfect development of the true mammals in the earlier part of their independent life, they attain to much greater vigor than their lower kindred; their forms vary to suit almost every condition which the earth affords; they are swift runners, strong flyers, alert swimmers, effective delvers in the earth; they afford great beasts of prey, such as the lions and tigers, and quick-footed forms like the antelopes, which are able to escape any pursuers. Their brains are larger and their intellects more able than all the lower mammalia which have no placenta. Step by step we find the measure of intelligence increasing, the animals ever helping themselves more and more by instinct and reason, until in man we have the great dominating intelligence of the world, a creature who depends vastly more on his mental powers than upon all the physical gifts which have been afforded him. The earliest of the higher mammals appear to have been creatures of much more simple structure than those of the present day. Like their predecessors, also, probably their ancestors, the reptiles, they had five toes on each foot, and were fitted for walking over the earth or for tree-climbing. By gradual changes from this rather simple creature, probably more nearly akin to the sloth than to any other living form, the placental mammals varied along many different lines of change. One group of these five-fingered creatures, that which finally gave us the horse and its kindred, which now has but one toe or finger to each foot, appears to have undergone its development in North America, principally in the region about the head-waters of the Missouri, in the district known as the Bad Lands.

From the numerous and beautifully preserved fossils which have been gathered in that district, all the important steps of this change from a five-toed to a single-toed animal have been traced. In the early Tertiaries we have the Orohippus, where the fore-limbs had four toes, and the hinder, three. In the next stage, in the Miocene, the fourth toe ceases to have any hoof, and does not project beyond the skin; the central hoof, or that on the middle toe of both front and hind legs, becoming much larger than the others. In the third step the side toes fade away, until they lose the semblance of hoofs, the remaining toe growing yet larger than before; and finally, in modern times, there is but one evident hoof, the others being reduced to the slender splint-bones of the horse, which serve no purpose whatever save to show us how the creature has changed from the conditions of his ancestors. The single hoof of the horse is a great advantage to the creature, as it provides him with a stronger limb by which he is enabled to escape pursuit. Moreover, as all know, this solid bony hoof is a powerful instrument of defence. A few years ago, in an American Zoölogical Garden, a lioness escaping from her cage pounced upon a donkey and was killed by the blows of the animal's feet.

We may note, also, in this horse series, the admirable development which takes place in the teeth, step by step, with the advance in the structure of the feet. The earliest of the horse kindred had low, flat teeth, with short roots of a shape calculated to wear out and become useless to the animal in a short time. Gradually the teeth become longer from the grinding surface to the end of the roots: the part exposed beyond the gums extended so far that they would endure the rough work of grinding hard and sandy grasses for a much greater period than any of the earlier forms.

Though the horse appears to have been developed on the continent of North America, it is a curious fact that none of these creatures existed on this continent or in the neighboring land of South America when man came to occupy this part of the world. From North America, they appear to have migrated over some temporary isthmus which for a time connected the Old World with the New. This complete disappearance of an important group of animals from the region where they were developed seems to indicate that some destructive accident befell them. It is not necessary, however, to suppose that the cause of the destruction of the horse on this continent is to be found in any change of climate or in the subsidence of the land beneath the sea. It may have been due to the ravages of some insect which killed these creatures as a certain fly destroys all the horses in a portion of Southern Africa.

The most notable change in the animal life of the Tertiary period, both on this and other continents, consists in the great increase in the number of insects. These creatures had evidently existed from very early times, some of their remains being found as early as the Devonian period, and specimens of a scorpion have been discovered in Silurian strata; but in the Tertiary time these animals rapidly became more numerous and varied in their kind. The increase is particularly noticeable in those forms of insect life which seek honey or pollen from the blossoms of flowering plants, as do the bees and butterflies. The bees and their kindred the common ants are the most intellectual of insects; except perhaps the white ants, they are the only members of this group which have learned how to associate their labor in well-organized communities which build permanent habitations for their societies.

The plants of the Tertiary time on this and other continents steadily increase in the number of their flowering forms. As compared with the earlier forests and fields, the plants of this age are conspicuous for their blossoms, fruits, and nuts. The fact is, that in the Tertiary time the vegetables have varied in order to secure the help of insects, birds, and mammals in the fertilization of their flowers and the diffusion of their seeds. The bright colors, sweet odors, and nourishing fruits which they have developed in these latter geological ages served to secure these ends. The insects resorting to them for honey or pollen serve to cross-fertilize the seed. The fruits, because they are palatable or nutritious, are eaten by many animals, and the strong seeds, not being digested in the stomach of the animal, are scattered far and wide over the field. Yet other plants have their seed provided with hooklets which may catch in the hair of animals as they pass by the plant, and thus be carried to great distances, giving the species a chance to win its way over the land.

In these and many other ways the animal and plant life in the Tertiary ages became more closely knit together than they had been in the earlier times. Much of the rapid variation and advance in the structure of both these great realms of life came about through this advance in the accommodation of animals and plants to each other. The plants changed their form to secure the assistance of certain animals, and to protect themselves from the assaults of others, and the animals varied so as to obtain ever greater advantages from the vegetables on which they mainly fed. In this way, contending against and helping each other, and ever varying to accomplish these ends, these two great armies of living beings have undergone vast changes, and have secured great advances in structure since the beginning of the Tertiary time.

The student should understand that the precise way in which these variations are brought about is still a matter of debate. By far the greater number of naturalists are of the opinion that the change from one species to another in the progressive alteration of animals and plants in the course of the earth's history is due to the fact that the descendants of any individual are very numerous, — often to be counted by thousands, — and of this multitude only one or two can commonly come to maturity, the others perishing from lack of food or being devoured by their enemies. Those which survive are enabled to do so because they vary from the others in some advantageous way, as, for instance, by having more vigorous seeds, being swifter in flight and chase, or with keener intelligence. These advantages the fortunate parent is apt to hand on to its descendants, and so in a given country a somewhat peculiar variety is formed which has an advantage over its kindred in the struggle for existence. The individuals which have this advantage breeding together, make the beneficial peculiarity yet more marked than it was before, and so from generation to generation the change becomes intensified. This, in very brief statement, is the Darwinian theory, and it seems likely that it explains many of the changes which, in the course of the ages, living forms have undergone. Whatever be the final determination as to the value of Mr. Darwin's view, there can be no doubt as to the steadfast progress of organic life through the geologic ages, each species in turn perishing, in most cases, after it had given birth through some process of change to a form better fitted for the conditions of existence in the region in which its ancestors lived.

Although the bodily forms of animals gained immensely in effectiveness during the Tertiary age, the greatest advance in this higher life is found in the addition to the intellectual power of its species. The brains grow larger in all the mammalia as we go from the earlier to the later stages of this time; the intelligence increases with the development of the machinery which serves its needs; the creatures develop habits of life which are controlled by instincts or reason; beavers build their dams; squirrels, birds, and mice, their nests;

the larger animals in the fields institute the method of life by herds, where the individuals protect and defend each other; in a word, in this later age mind comes to play a part unknown in the earlier times and lower states of being.

One of the effects arising from the increase in the measure of intelligence in these later stages in the earth's history is found in the greater sympathy which exists in the more highly organized beings. If we could have observed the earth during the reptilian period, we should doubtless have found that there were no animal sounds in the woods or fields save, perhaps, the chirping of creatures like the crickets and grasshoppers or the piping of some creatures allied to our frogs and toads. The song of birds, the hum of bees, the lowings and bellowings and chatterings of our mammalian species, were probably wanting. All these sounds, like the speech of man, indicate that the higher animals are becoming more conscious of and dependent on their kindred. Thus all the more advanced life exhibits the progressive gain in sympathy between individuals which is the basis of human relations.

By no means all the changes which took place in the animal life of North America and other great lands during the Tertiary period led to the elevation of that life. Many forms, in order to secure the means of subsistence or protection from their enemies, underwent changes which led to their degradation. The most conspicuous instance of such downgoing is exhibited by the serpents. The ancestors of these forms were originally four-limbed animals like the lizards; but in order to secure the peculiar advantages which the snake's form affords for constricting the prey and seizing it at a stroke, the form became altered so as to give the body great length and flexibility; the limbs were lost, and in their place motion was effected by movable scales and the waving flectures of the body. So, too, the whales have been formed by progressive degradation from four-limbed animals which dwelt upon the land. In fact, all changes of species probably serve to fit the creature to accomplish particular deeds. Sometimes it is advantageous for an animal or plant to inhabit a peculiar station or to do certain acts which require a less highly organized body than was possessed by its ancestors. It remains, however, a great and most important truth that these changes generally lead to more perfect states of being. Not only is it true, but a yet greater truth remains to be stated concerning the development of animals. This is, that the speed with which the advance takes place is in ever-increasing measure. Thus during the Tertiary age, which includes the time in which we now dwell, animal life has made greater advances in all that regards the development of intelligence than were accomplished in all the long ages of the earlier times. It is certain that the Tertiary periods do not include one-tenth, and they possibly do not amount to one-fiftieth, of the duration which we must assign to the preceding ages, and yet they have carried forward the process of growth in the most important features of animal life to an extent vastly greater than had been secured before. We thus see that this continent, as indeed are all the fields of the earth, is still fresh and vigorous, better suited than ever before to give nurture to its living tenants.

Near the close of the Tertiary period, or rather, we should say, in a recent geologic time, though it may have been a hundred thousand years ago, the continent of North America experienced a wonderful change in its physical conditions. At this time it had a form which probably did not vary much from that which it at present exhibits. It is probable that if we could compare a map of the continent made at the time we are considering with one which shows its present geography, we should perceive only slight differences in the outlines of the shore and in the shape of the interior regions. At this time, however, there came upon the land in its northern part a vast coating of ice which occupied nearly all the present land-surface of British America, a large part of Alaska, and about one-third of the area of the United States. This glacial envelope was not peculiar to North America; for it formed at the same time over nearly all the British Islands, Scandinavia, Switzerland, and perhaps Siberia. Similar great ice-fields were probably simultaneously developed in the southern part of South America and in New Zealand.

Just before this great glacial change came upon North America there was a warm climate, one which permitted the development of plants which cannot withstand vigorous winters, as far north as the middle portion of Greenland, a region now so cold that only a few plants of the hardiest sort can maintain a scanty growth. When the ice-fields began to extend from the regions about the poles southward, and from the colder mountain tops to the plains, all the animals and plants which had occupied the northern realm were forced to change their abodes to more southern lands or to perish from the earth. It is probable that many thousand years were occupied in this migration; for the ice must have won its way slowly to the possession of the great field it came to occupy, so that time was allowed for the species gradually to extend south of the field from which they had been dispossessed. In this great exodus of animals and plants a good many kinds perished, and of those which survived a great number underwent changes in their shapes. It is a surprising fact, however, that as a whole organic beings do not seem to have been very greatly disturbed by the change in the climate and the geography of the continent which the last glacial period brought about.

While the ice lay upon the northern portion of the continent, the surface of that area appears to have been borne down by the weight of the ice to a considerable depth below its present level. At the same time in the southern part of the continent, the region not occupied by the glacier, or, in general, that section south of the Ohio, the Potomac, and the Missouri rivers, appears to have been subjected to a considerable elevation. The upward movement of the land seems to have been enough to have extended the shores of the Southern states farther towards the equator than they are at present placed. The northeastern portion of the continent appears to have been more deeply depressed than the other portions of its surface, probably for the reason that the ice was deeper there than elsewhere. It seems likely that in this district the surface was lowered more than a thousand feet, perhaps several times that amount, below its present position.

After a period of unknown duration, which can probably be reckoned as thousands of years in length, this ice-sheet disappeared. As it was when thickest more than a mile in depth, it doubtless required a long time to depart. As it disappeared, the northern part of the continent rose again above the sea-level, while the southern **portion** of the land from New York southwardly along the Atlantic and along the Gulf of Mexico sank down beneath the sea. While this southern section had been elevated, the rivers had carved deep and wide valleys. When the land sank, the sea overflowed much of the valley lands near the shore, forming great bays such as the Delaware, Chesapeake, Albemarle, Pamlico, and Mobile bays. All these bays have been somewhat filled in by mud washed down by the rivers since the shore came to its present level. The greatest of them, as, for instance, that in which now lies the Mississippi in the part of its course between the junction of the Ohio with the great river and Southern Louisiana, has been filled with mud and sand brought from the highlands of the great central valley.

While the glacial sheet was upon the northern part of the continent, it moved slowly from the interior part of its field towards its margins in the sea and on the land. Its first effect was to sweep away all the soil which had previously covered the country. It then attacked the harder rocks, cutting them away in the following manner: fragments of stone imprisoned in the hard ice and projecting from its bottom acted as gouges as they were dragged over the bed-rock in the forward movement of the glacier; at the same time streams of fluid water flowing over the bottom on which the ice rested washed a great deal of fine debris from the inner parts of the glaciated district towards the edge of the field.

For a long time the front of the ice stretched across the continent from the Atlantic seaboard to near the foot of the Rocky Mountains in Dakota. The front remained in this position for the reason that the southward movement of the ice was just sufficient to supply the waste which took place in the mild climate to which it attained. As the glacier was constantly carrying forward quantities of stone which dropped out when the ice melted, and as the under-ice streams deposited their coarser sediment where they escaped from the ice-arches at the front of the glacier, the result was that a considerable accumulation of gravel, sand, and bowlders was made along this line. In many places this moraine, as it is called, has the height of several hundred feet, and extends in the form of a long ridge parallel to the margin of the glacier. More commonly, however, the front of the ice did not remain in exactly the same position for any great time, and so there are several lesser ridges parallel to each other, and it may be a few miles apart, forming a belt of morainal deposits. The greatest of these belts extends from Eastern Massachusetts, where it is well exhibited on the promontory of Cape Cod and the neighboring islands on the south, westward through Long Island, New York, thence across the mainland of New Jersey, through parts of Pennsylvania and New York, Central and Southern Ohio, and thence in a northwestward direction through Dakota. When the ice lay over the northern and eastern parts of the continent in the form of a vast sheet, it doubtless presented an unbroken upper surface over which the observer could have journeyed from the Potomac to Greenland, or from the valley of the Saskatchewan to Newfoundland, without observing any trace of the hills and valleys which were beneath him. We know from a recent examination of the central part of Greenland that such a continental glacier smooths over hill and dale as a winter's snowstorm hides the irregularities of a ploughed field or the hills where Indian corn has been grown.

When the continental glacier was deepest and ex-

GLACIAL BOULDERS, MOUNT DESERT, MAINE.

tended farthest to the south, there were many smaller glaciers in the mountains of the Cordilleras and probably also in those of Virginia which were not connected with the main ice-sheet. In the Cordilleras some of these detached glaciers were of great size, as for instance that of the upper Arkansas, which occupied the part of the valley in which Leadville now stands, with an ice-sheet of great depth and thickness. These lesser detached glaciers also formed morainal walls, which were often of great size. The accumulation of these deposits shows that in the case of these valley glaciers, as in that of the greater ice-sheet, the ice remained for a considerable time with its front in nearly one position.

As the great ice-sheet ceased to be well fed by winters' snows, its margin retreated to the northward. Here and there we find in small moraines evidence that for a little while the ice frequently paused in its falling back. It probably, from time to time, after having retreated a good ways, readvanced to near its original front. But after a time it utterly disappeared from all the region east of the Cordilleras, and remains there only in the form of very limited glaciers which, like those of Switzerland and Norway, occupy high-lying valleys in the mountains.

When the continental glacier was thick, the part of its mass within a few hundred feet of the ground contained a good deal of mud, sand, and stones which had been riven from the underlying rocks. When the glacier disappeared, this stony matter fell down upon the surface of the earth, forming a coating of stony and clayey material, commonly known as till. In some places this deposit was a hundred feet or more in thickness. Here and there, sometimes over large fields, this till was washed away by the melting waters of the glacier, the waste being accumulated in beds of clay, sand, and pebbles. The most of the brick clays of this country have been derived in this way by the sorting of the glacial waste.

All the soils in the glacial districts are mainly formed of this glacial detritus, which by the growth of plants upon it has gradually been commingled with vegetable matter, and so made fit for the husbandman's use. These soils are very variable in quality. In those regions where a great amount of pure siliceous sand has been deposited the soil may be too sterile to give any profitable crops, but where the material remains in the form of till, the farmer generally finds a strong soil, which, if properly cared for, is very enduring to the tax which agriculture puts upon the earth. In most parts of the country the soils which are upon the till contain a great number of pebbles, which are in part composed of feldspars and mica. They also often contain small quantities of apatite or crystallized lime phosphate. These minerals as they decay furnish potash, soda, lime, and phosphorus to the soil, and these are the materials which are most necessary for its refreshment. Thus we see that the bowlders which are in the way of the plough and give a sterile aspect to a large part of the glaciated districts are really to be considered as magazines, in which plant food is stored away in a manner which permits it to be slowly yielded to the soil.

At the close of the glacial period, when the rain waters began to move once more to the sea in a fluid form, the surface of the area over which the ice had lain had a very imperfect drainage. The valleys of many of the small streams excavated before the last glacial epoch were entirely destroyed, owing to the fact that the ice had worn away the rocks in which they lay. The basins of all the considerable rivers remained, but in a much altered form. When the streams of fluid water carved them, they made their surfaces slope everywhere continuously downward towards the sea; but when the ice overrode them, it changed these inclined planes to slopes of a pitted and irregular character. Fluid water coursing to the sea, except in the pot-holes about a waterfall, never excavates a pit; but a glacier can cut out deep excavations in soft rocks which may have a depth hundreds of feet, and be walled all round with rocks which were of harder character and therefore wore a less amount. The result is that when the ice went away, the free water accumulated in these basins, forming lakes of all sizes from tiny pools to very extensive basins. Moreover, the heaps of debris which were left by the ice blocked a great many channels with sand or clay, so damming in yet other lakes.

The result of these embarrassments of the streams was the formation of innumerable lakes in the northern half of the continent. There are certainly tens of thousands of these basins still occupied by water, but when the ice went away they were many times as numerous. The greater part of these basins have been filled in with peat or by the sand and mud washed in by the streams which enter them, while yet others have been drained away through the cutting down of the barriers through which the outflowing streams have passed. These lakes are still gradually disappearing, but they will long remain as the most beautiful of the many topographical features which give charm to the scenery of the glaciated district, and which are derived from the singular actions which the ice effected on the surface over which it flowed.

There were some interesting changes in the character of the organic life in North America, which appear to have occurred just after the disappearance of the ice. So far as we have learned, no great alterations in the plants or the lower animals occurred either in the onset or the disappearance of the continental glacier. But among the higher mammals many important alterations were effected. Probably before and during the glacial period, and certainly in the closing stages of that time, a number of great herbivorous animals occupied this continent which have since disappeared from the earth. Among them we reckon two great species of elephants, the mammoth and the mastodon, which appear for a considerable time to have existed in large numbers on this continent. It is probable that the American mammoth was of the same species with those of Siberia, which, as we know from the remains preserved in the mud at the mouths of the great rivers of Northern Asia, were hairy elephants, as well protected against the Arctic cold as are the polar bears. The mammoth was as large as the greatest living elephants, perhaps larger, and though closely akin to them, must have presented a very different appearance. The great tusks were curiously curved in the form of a sickle, with the points turned back towards the shoulders of the animal. Owing to the long hair, which on the back of the neck appears to have had the form of a shaggy mane, these creatures must have had a truly formidable aspect.

The mastodon was a much smaller creature, being rather less in size than our largest living elephants. Like the mammoth, it appears to have dwelt mostly in and about the swamps and streams, and it is in the mud of such situations that we commonly find their remains preserved. Along with these creatures there dwelt in the fields from which the glacial ice had recently passed away even as far south as Kentucky a large variety of musk ox, the descendants of which, much reduced in size, now occupy certain limited fields within the Arctic circle. The caribou or American reindeer, or a closely related kinsman of the species, ranged southward into Kentucky, where its bones are found in the Big Bone Lick. There was also a species of bison, taller and slenderer limbed than the living form of North America, which disappeared from its surface as the ice-sheet went away. A gigantic beaver, several times as large as the existing form, is also to be counted among these recently vanished animals. A curious variety of dog appears to have existed at about this time, as is shown by certain bones found in the caverns of East Tennessee.

This great change in the character of the higher life, while the lower species were not much altered, shows us how swift are the changes which are taking place in the more advanced kinds of animals. The higher the grade of a creature's development, the more sensitive it becomes to the conditions of climate and the other circumstances which affect its existence. Any conditions which affect the distribution of its food are apt to lead to its destruction or force it to extended migrations.

The last great change in the organic life of North America consisted in the appearance of our own species on this continent. It is not known at just what time man first won his way to the surface of this land. In the opinion of certain observers, bits of shaped stone having the appearance of rude implements which occur in the beds of gravel near Trenton, N.J., are to be regarded as evidence that men were here during the time when the ice-sheet was most extended. Well-shaped tools and a fragment of a human skull have been found in California, in ancient river beds which were filled with the lavas from volcanoes so ancient that their craters have been destroyed, and the country about the old valleys so far worn down that the place where the old rivers lay is now upon the hilltops. We do not know just how long ago this Californian man lived, but it seems likely that he inhabited that part of the continent at least as far back as the beginning of the glacial time. Similar evidences of the antiquity of man have been found in Europe, where it now seems certain that savages hunted the hairy mammoth beside the extended glaciers of the ice-epoch.

Although the glacial period was only in the geological yesterday, we know as yet but little concerning the details of its history. It will probably be a long time before we shall be sufficiently well informed as to what took place during this singular period, to form any judgment as to the cause of the great revolution in climate, or its precise effects upon the living beings which inhabited the earth.

The present day is really a part of the glacial age; remnants of the ice-sheet which recently desolated half the continent still remain in the valleys of the Cordilleras of British America and Alaska, and cover the greater part of Greenland. We have already noted the fact that, just before the last glacial period, a tolerably warm climate prevailed in North America up to near the pole. It seems likely that, in time to come, these conditions of warmth will revisit the portions of the land which are now sterilized with excessive cold. The change, however, will doubtless require a vast time for its accomplishment.

All the evidence which the geologist has gathered concerning the continent of North America serves to show that this land — as are, indeed, all the lands of the world — is in its youth. It is still growing up from the sea at such a rate that the ceaseless beating of the waves and the washing of the rains does not serve to diminish its area. On the contrary, its area is probably greater at the present time than it ever has been before.

CHAPTER III.

THE PRESENT GEOGRAPHIC CONDITION OF NORTH AMERICA.

The present condition of the continent. Comparison with other continents. Its mountains, islands, rivers, and other geographic features. Forests of North America. Prairies. Climate. Distribution of rainfall. Indian summer. Storms. Scenery of North America. Waterfalls. Cañons. Caverns. Dead seas. The continental shelf. Coral reefs.

WE have already traced, at least in outline, the history of the continent of North America. We have seen how, slowly but steadily, this great elevation has arisen from the ocean, and how it has maintained itself against the ceaseless assaults of the waves of the sea and the currents of the rivers. It has ever been wearing away, but always growing upward; portions of its surface have swayed downward beneath the ocean, while parts of the shallows near the coast have at the same time risen above the water. Again and again this elevation has changed its shape; but from the beginning the continent has always endured, and has constantly become better fitted to be the dwelling-place of the higher plants and animals which find their habitations on the land. These changes have gradually converted what was originally a group of islands into a wide field of land suited to be a home for great peoples. It is now our task to consider the existing form, climate, soil, and other features of the continent, and their influence on their living tenants.

As will be seen from the map, North America has a distinctly triangular shape, the only considerable departure from this form being due to the indentation of the Gulf of Mexico, the last remnant of the original central ocean of the continent, and to the peninsulas and islands which border it on the east. This great triangle is considerably longer than it is wide; its narrow side or base lies against the Arctic Ocean; its length is 3750 miles; and the long sides have an extent of about 5000 miles. On the east lies the Atlantic, and on the west the Pacific Ocean. Thus, North America and the twin continent of South America are so placed that they part the vast ocean into two great basins. The same parting is effected by the Old World group of lands, but the division which this latter group of continents effects is less definite and complete. The American barrier extends nearer to both poles than that of the Old World.

If we compare the continent of North America with the united land masses of Asia and Europe, we are struck with the fact that, while the shores of this land mass are generally straight and with few neighboring island masses, the lands of the Old World are, except in the case of Africa, singularly fringed with peninsulas and islands. Bearing in mind the story of the growth of North America as it is set forth in the preceding chapter, it is easy to see the reason for this difference.

In North America there are few of those mountain systems which form the centres of growth in the land, there being in all in this continent about half a dozen of such systems of elevations, while in the great mass of the Old World which constitutes Europe-Asia there are about four times as many of these mountain groups, each forming a distinctly separated region of elevation. When, as is frequently the case, the lowlands between these elevations have not been lifted above the line of the sea, the uplifted region appears as an island, at least until, by the process of growth, it so far rises above the ocean as to be united with the mainland. The consolidated form of North America is thus due to the fact that its mountain systems are few in number, and they have generally grown for a sufficiently long time to uplift the regions about them into dry land.

There is only one mountain system connected with North America which is so new and so imperfectly elevated that it gives rise to a considerable group of islands. This system is indicated in the long archipelago which bounds the Caribbean Sea on the east and north, generally known as the Antilles. This curious elevation rises from deep sea on either side, and has at the highest parts a height above the floor on which it rests of ten or fifteen thousand feet. It appears to have begun to grow in relatively modern geologic times, and to be still in process of upheaval. In its present state it closely resembles the ranges of the Appalachian and the Cordilleran mountains in the earlier stages of their history, when they formed narrow, strip-like archipelagoes composed of the emerged mountain tops. In time the system of the Antilles will probably, by continuous growth, lead to the emergence not only of the mountains themselves, but of broad fields of what are now sea-bottoms, thus repeating the process of growth which has gone on in the older regions of elevation of the continent.

It is evident that North America is composed of

several mountainous fields which, by their long-continued growth, have lifted not only their ridges, but much of the sea-bottom above the plane of the ocean waters. It is less evident, but still to the geologist plain, that in the northern and eastern part of the continent the mountains almost or entirely ceased to grow at a distant period in the earth's history, and at the present time the powers which construct these elevations appear to be active only in the region about the southern and western portions of the continent. As a whole, the mountain-building work of Eastern North America was done in an earlier day, and has not been continued to as late a time as in Europe and Asia. One of the results of this diversity in history is that the mountains of America have been more worn down than those of the Old World. They have been longer exposed to the action of the rock-destroying agents of the atmosphere, and consequently have lost a good deal of their original height.

The northeastern part of North America consists of a remarkable group of islands separated from each other by shallow and generally narrow arms of the sea; the largest of these islands is Greenland which covers an area of about seven hundred and fifty thousand square miles, or fifteen times as large as New York state. The form of Greenland is rudely triangular; in its shape it resembles the regular continents, but this resemblance is probably accidental. The surface of this extensive district is of a mountainous nature, at least in those parts of it which are open to view; but only a small portion of the land in the southern extremity and a narrow and interrupted strip of the eastern and western shores are visible: the remainder of the surface is covered by a deep coating of snow and ice which probably rises in the central parts of the island to the height of from five to eight thousand feet above the sea. This icy covering is the remnant of the glacial sheet which, in recent geologic times, covered the northern half of this continent. If it could be removed, the apparently connected land underneath it would probably prove to consist of a series of islands separated by shallow straits like those which lie nearer to the northern mainland of the continent. These land areas, slightly detached from the continent, which are such a peculiar feature of the northern part of North America, are not islands of the same decided nature as those which compose the Malayan Archipelago or those of the Antilles; they are probably parts of the continent wherein the valleys, formed during the time when the land was somewhat higher than it is at present, have been depressed below the level of the sea. The Malayan islands, those of Japan, the Antilles, and the most of the other large insulated lands, are, in fact, the summits of mountainous districts or the crests of volcanic peaks which have not been united with the adjacent continents, and not merely portions of the continent separated by river or ice-worn valleys from the neighboring continents.

Except Greenland, none of the islands about the northern part of North America have a decided mountainous character; they are only moderately elevated, their irregularities having the general nature of hills; that is, they owe their shape to the action of water or ice in carving out hollows in generally horizontal strata. If this archipelago of Arctic America were not unfit for life on account of its extreme cold, it would be a very suitable region for the use of man. The surface is diversified; the rocks have much mineral wealth, and are of a nature to form a fertile soil; the numerous inlets of the sea would afford good advantages for shipping. Sometime before the last glacial period this part of the world had a temperature much higher than it has at present; and judging by the fossil plants which have been preserved, the winter climate was probably not colder than that which is now found in Southern England or the lower parts of the Mississippi Valley; but there were no men at that time to enjoy the benefits of these favorable conditions. It is not impossible that in future geologic ages the climate of this region may once again become of a temperate character, making it fit for the life of man.

The mainland of North America contains in its northeastern part a singular enclosed sea which bears the inappropriate name of Hudson's Bay. It is not a bay, but rather a basin like the Black Sea or the Gulf of Mexico. On the east it is separated from the North Atlantic, except for a narrow strait by the peninsula of Labrador, a mountainous land, the elevations of which are very ancient, and have been worn down to their roots by the action of rivers, glacial ice, and sea-waves. On the north it is bordered by the peninsulas of the continent, and on the west by the irregular plain-land district of the central part of the continent. Hudson's Bay or Sea, as we should call it, is many times as large as Lake Superior, and is the most conspicuous and peculiar feature in the northern part of this continent. The conditions of its formation are not yet well known, but it seems likely that it is a part of a great valley of the continent which may never have risen above the level of the ocean; or if ever so elevated, it has been, like many other of the northern valleys of this level, again lowered below the plane of the sea. It is probable that Hudson's Sea may be, like the Gulf of Mexico, a remaining fragment of the ocean which in the early history of the continent divided the eastern mountains of North America from those on the western border of that land area. It may have been deepened and widened by the grinding action of the ice during the glacial periods, as the Great Lakes have been, but it cannot be considered as altogether due to the erosive work of ice acting during those stages in the earth's history.

Continuing our sketch of the irregularities of the coast-line of the continent of North America, we notice the group of islands at the mouth of the St. Lawrence. These islands include Newfoundland, the greatest of the islands which lie near the northern shores of North America, unless, indeed, Greenland should be a single island mass, and not an archipelago united by a sheet of ice. Along with Newfoundland we have the neighboring considerable islands of Anticosti and Cape Breton and the peninsula of Nova Scotia, which is almost separated from the mainland by the deep indentation of the Bay of Fundy. These several masses of land are parted from the continent by very shallow, though in some cases wide, arms of the sea. These straits seem to be old valleys which were excavated when this part of the continent was higher than it is at present, and have subsequently been lowered below the level of the sea. They have also been deepened and widened by the action of the glacial streams which have flowed through them since they were originally formed. All these islands except Anticosti and Prince Edward Island are composed of ancient rocks which have been much folded into mountain ridges and subsequently greatly worn down by the action of rain and sea-waves. These last-named islands have in the main escaped the influence of the mountain-building process. They are probably the remnants of high table-lands bordering old valleys which have been in part buried beneath the sea.

South of Nova Scotia there are for a good distance to the south no important islands near the shore of North America. Along the northern coast of New England is found a fringe of small isles such as border the hard rock shores of all districts which have been subjected to glacial action and constitute the so-called fjord or inlet and island zone of such regions. These small islands owe their separation from the mainland to the lowering of old valleys beneath the sea and to the cutting action of the glacial sheet, which has worn away the rock in a very irregular manner. We can form an idea of the way in which glacial wearing formed these numerous islets by taking two pieces of smooth wood, one of clear timber, and the other thickly beset with knots, then rubbing each of them for a time with sandpaper, taking pains to apply the friction equally to every part of the surface: we soon observe that the knotty timber, because of its varied hardness, wears irregularly, each knot remaining as an elevation while the softer parts wear away. On the other hand, the clear wood wears down in a uniform manner. A like difference is observable where the glacial sheet wears upon different kinds of rock: if the rock be of horizontally stratified beds, it generally is of uniform hardness like the clear wood; if, however, the rock be crystalline, as it is along the most of the northern parts of this continent, then it is certain to be of very diverse degrees of hardness, and so it wears down in an irregular manner under the action of the glacial scouring. In this way the surface of crystallized rocks, such as granite and gneiss, always becomes very irregularly shaped when worn by ice-streams, and the plane of the sea forms many inlets and islands along the shore which is formed of such materials.

South of Boston Bay we have in Cape Cod, Martha's Vineyard, Nantucket, Block Island, and Long Island, N.Y., a number of detached masses of land which owe their origin to another effect of glacial action. They are in the main fragments of the great frontal moraine, or heap of bowlders, clay, and sand which have been scraped from the bed-rocks of the region over which the ice moved and carried forward to the front of the ice-sheet. The sea has swept away a large part of these materials, which, not being firmly bound together, fall an easy prey to the waves; but the remnants preserved in these islands form a curious feature in the geography of the Atlantic coast.

South of New York the shore is generally bordered by a fringe of sea-beach islands which form a barrier enclosing a strip of shallow waters which sometimes expand into considerable basins, such as Albemarle and Pamlico sounds. So continuous is this strip of land, that it is possible to travel in a canoe through the water they enclose almost all the way from the mouth of the Hudson River to Cape Florida. The conditions which lead to the formation of these beaches, and consequently to the enclosure of the lagoons, are very easily understood. When the bottom of the sea shelves gently to the seaward, the waves of great storms cannot attain the shore, but are compelled to break in water twenty or thirty feet deep, it may be some miles out from the coast-line. The tumult of waves stirs up the sand and drives it forward to the point where they break; and as in breaking they cease to move forward, this sand is cast into a heap which soon rises above the level of the sea. Subsequent storms form more sand upon the new island, the wind sweeps the sand of the shore into hillocks or even considerable hills called dunes, and so in time a considerable strip-like island may be formed parallel to the shore.

Along no other coast are these sand-beaches so continuous as on the southern shore of the United States. They extend from New York, with few interruptions, to the mouth of the Rio Grande, which separates the United States from Mexico. They enclose an almost continuous strip of shallow water navigable for light boats. Along the coast of Florida, from Cape Canaveral to the Tortugas, for a distance of about two hundred miles, there is another peculiar class of coast islands, — the coral reefs. These reefs are constructed in part by the solid portions of certain stone-making corals, and in part by the remains of other forms of marine animals and plants which secure a favorable place for their life through the protection which the masses of coral afford.

Finding a lodgement on the sea-bottom at a depth of less than about one hundred feet, these corals, where there is a strong current of warm, clear sea-water sweeping by them, swiftly grow upward until they reach the surface of the ocean. Where the Gulf Stream sends its tide of warm water against the shores of Southern Florida, the most favorable conditions for the growth of coral-making animals is secured: bathed in very warm water, with suitable food brought to the mouths of each of the tiny animals, they grow and multiply with amazing rapidity, and in a very brief time form barriers which seem at first sight exactly like the lagoon islands of more northern shores. But on closer view we see that these reefs are altogether composed of fragments derived from the decay of the coral and of the other animals which dwell amid its branches. The waves beat the coral to pieces and cast the fragments on the top of the reef, the winds blow the fine lime sand into low hills on the top of the reef, and so in time a place is made for the palms and mangroves and other plants which clothe these islands.

The southern part of Florida, perhaps about a third of the peninsula, is composed of coral reefs which have grown in succession to the southward against the Gulf Stream, gradually restricting the exit place of the water until it is confined to a comparatively narrow channel. On the eastern side of the stream the coral reefs of the Bahamas have likewise pressed outward and westward, still further confining the path of the great current. We thus see that the colonies of coral animals, though the individual creatures are tiny, can do a great geologic and geographic work. It is probable that this hampering of the movement of the Gulf Stream has affected in some measure the temperature of Northern Europe, to which its warm waters carry heat and with it the possibilities of life.

On the continental side of the sand and coral island barrier of the Atlantic coast and the Gulf of Mexico we find numerous extensive sounds or bays which deserve attention. Those of the Delaware, Chesapeake, Albemarle, and Pamlico are the most conspicuous on the Atlantic coast; that of Mobile is the largest on the northern shore of the Mexican Gulf. There are many other of these bays of smaller size than those mentioned. These enlargements of the sea are explained in the following manner: In recent geologic time the southern coast of the United States has been at a higher level than at present. In this time of elevation the rivers cut wide valleys as they swung their channels to and fro in the endless movements which characterize all streams whose beds are not limited by hard rock. After these valleys had been cut, the land was lowered and the ocean admitted to them. At present these sounds or bays are being filled up by the sand and mud which is constantly pouring downward towards the sea. Thus the Mississippi River recently discharged near Cairo, at the junction of the upper river and the Ohio, into a long, broad bay, which extended south to the Gulf; but it has filled the whole of its basin with silt, and has extended the deposit beyond the mouth of the depressed valley. In time all these sounds will be filled by the land waste, and the shore be brought to a straighter form.

On the Pacific coast there are fewer irregularities to be considered, and of these we know less than of the features of the Atlantic coast. In Alaska we find a singular group of islands which extend in a long crescent from the American shore to near that of Asia. In general character, these islands resemble the Antilles, but they are of much less importance. They appear to be the emerged peaks of a growing mountain range, a branch from the great system of the Cordilleras. They are, so far as we have learned, composed mainly of volcanic deposits. The whole of this series of elevations is separated from the mainlands of Asia and America by deep water. They are therefore not to be considered as a definite part of either continent, but are most likely connected with North America, as a fringe of its great mountain system.

South of Behring Strait, and thence to the mouth of the Columbia River in Oregon, the shore abounds in islands, which probably owe their separated nature to the same conditions that have produced the islands along the shore, from Massachusetts Bay to Greenland; namely, to the erosive action of old glacial streams, and the submergence beneath the sea of old valleys. From Oregon to the southern limit of the United States the shore is almost destitute of islands, and has few sounds or bays. The most important of these rare indentations, that of San Francisco, is probably due to the lowering of the land, which had previously been shaped into a set of valleys below the level of the sea. That such bays are rare on the Pacific coast is probably to be explained by the infrequency of rivers on that portion of the seaboard of the continent and the consequent lack of valleys, which, when depressed beneath the sea, might afford harbors.

Lower California forms the largest and most interesting peninsula of North America. It has a length of 800 miles, and a width of 140 miles, in size being exceeded by few such tongues of land. Unlike Florida, which appears to have owed its formation, in large part, to the action of the Gulf Stream, in promoting the rapid growth of marine animals, which secrete limestone in their skeletons, the Californian peninsula is a mountainous district, and contains very elevated land. It is a spur, or rather a continuation of the mountain range, which extends along the coast of California. The base on which this southern part of the range rests, has not shared in the elevation, which has lifted the northern part so high that it is united to the mainland. This peninsula of Lower California is the eastern barrier of the great gulf of that name, which is the largest indentation on the western coast of the American continents, and on the east is only surpassed by the Caribbean Sea and the Gulf of Mexico.

South of the United States we come into the isthmus portion of the continent, the narrowing lands which connect the northern with the southern continent of the New World. There are no large islands in this district, and only one peninsula which demands notice. This is the singular promontory of Yucatan, which in form departs widely, as does the neighboring peninsula of Florida, from the prevailing shape of the other great capes of the continent. All the other promontories of considerable size, such as those of Greenland, Nova Scotia, or even California, trend with the shores against which they lie; but those of Yucatan and Florida are set at an angle to the neighboring coast line. We have seen that the Floridian peninsula may be mainly accounted for by the supposition that a good part of its mass is formed of animal remains. It is thus a great monument of organic life built against the shore. The peninsula of Yucatan is not to be thus explained; its origin is yet to be accounted for, though it is probably in part composed of coral reefs.

Having considered its coast line, we now turn our attention to the interior portion of the continent of North America. The preceding chapters have made it plain that the growth of this land-mass, as indeed of all the lands which deserve the name of continents, has been brought about by the development of mountain systems: the continents are created by the uplifting of the surface either in the form of sharp ridges or of the broad table-lands which grow upwards as the ridges arise. We will therefore first review the greater among the mountain systems of this continent, then take into consideration the rivers which have their positions determined in good part by the mountains which bound and shape their valleys, and lastly consider the lakes and plain-lands. There are three very distinct groups of mountains in North America, besides several relatively unimportant systems of elevation which have had little to do with the shape or history of the continent. The three great mountain groups are, in the order of their importance, the Cordilleras, the Appalachian, and the Laurentian systems. We will consider them in the order in which they are named, which is also their succession in importance measured by their size or the part they now play and have played in determining the climate and other conditions of life in this land.

The Cordilleran mountain system is the northern half of the longest district of elevations on the earth. It extends from the northern part of North America to the southernmost extremity of South America, everywhere forming the west coast portion of the twin continents. Only in the Isthmus of Darien do we find a distinct break in this line of elevation; there for about a hundred miles the ridges sink down to near the level of the sea. A little to the north of the Isthmus of Darien the range rises to a height of some thousands of feet above the ocean, and we find on its flanks the distinct table-land elevations which almost invariably are formed along with the crumpling of the rocks which construct a true mountain range. As we go north the ridges become more developed, they occupy a wider field, the table-land as well as the peaks are higher, and the result is the wider land of Mexico, a region of elevated plains which upholds several mountain chains. Thence northwards to the northwestern extremity of the continent the mountain ranges of this system are numerous and their table-lands, at least on their eastern side, distinct. The field they occupy is on the average a thousand miles in width. Numerous peaks rise to about fifteen thousand feet in altitude, or, say, three miles above the sea-level, and the pedestal or table-land district on which they rest rises to the height of about a mile above the ocean shore.

Approaching the Cordilleras from the east, everywhere, except in the region of Central America and Mexico, we find that we begin to climb up a wide plateau by slow degrees, from a point some hundreds of miles from the mountain ridges: then we come suddenly to a true mountain range. Beyond it lies a district of table-lands where the rocks, though uplifted, are not much, if at all, crumpled. Further west there is another crumpled district, then another irregular strip of table-land, and this succession continues until we reach the Pacific Ocean. On the western side of the mountains the table-land is not so evident as on the eastern or continental border of the system. It seems possible that it has been carved away by the long-continued action of the sea. We shall find the same arrangement in the case of the Appalachian Mountains; the table-land on the interior side of the mountain belt is much plainer than on the side which faces the sea.

Besides the principal ridges of the Cordilleras which extend in a general north and south direction, leaning a little to the west, there are many less important ranges of mountains which lie crosswise of the main system, having a general east and west direction. The result is a tangle of elevations which have to be considered in a map to show the true nature of the system. So considered, it is clear that the forces or strains which folded these mountains, acted in the main in an east and west direction. Let these pages of paper represent the rocks of that part of the earth's crust occupied by the Cordilleras, the right hand side the east, the left side the west, as on a map: press them together from the sides and we can fold them into ridges. This pressure, and the consequent corrugations of the paper, represent in a rude, diagrammatic way the force and effects of the pressure which created the main chains of the Cordilleras. Press the sheets less strongly in the plane from top to bottom of the book, and we find that there is a tendency to form folds which run across the page. This experiment is imperfect in its results, because the sheets of paper are thin, small, and very flexible; but we may with some thought conceive how thick beds of rock, occupying a field a thousand miles across, might fold in two different ways under the influence of pressure acting in two diverse lines.

It must not be supposed that the Cordilleras or any other mountains owe their shape to the work of the uplifting forces alone. While their height above the sea is due to these constructive powers arising from the shrinking of the earth, their actual shapes are greatly affected by the various wearing actions which their exposure to the air brings about. Frost, streams of ice, above all, the endless wearing of torrents and rivers ever shifting their beds and always wearing the rocks away, have together taken from this mountain district far more of the total amount of elevated land than now remains there. The mountain peaks and ridges are now fragments of the arched rocks of which they were formed. This is the history of all the elevations of this planet. Their shape is determined by the opposing forces which on the one hand lift them upward and on the other work to bring them down to the level of the sea.

The wearing action of rain-water or of glaciers in the Cordilleran mountain district is now slight, for the reason that this part of the earth is at present subjected to singular conditions of drought. In former geological periods the rainfall was far greater than at present, and the mountain torrents and rivers which they fed were proportionately greater and more efficient in covering the land. At this comparatively recent time great lakes fed by large rivers existed where there are now arid plains or shrunken sheets of salt water such as the Salt Lake of Utah.

The Appalachian system of North America lies near the eastern shore of the continent, as the Cordilleran borders the western coast. The eastern system presents many points of likeness and of contrast with the more extreme western mountains. The Appalachian system is smaller in every way than the western Cordilleras. Its length is half as great, it is less than half as wide, and both the ridges and table-lands much less than half as high as those features in the western system. Except in the section from Virginia northward, the ranges of this system do not touch the coast, while those of the Pacific slope everywhere border the sea. There are no distinct cross ranges in the Appalachians such as we find in the Cordilleras. The mountains run in a general northeastward and southwestward path, varying little from that trend. They do not make as continuous a barrier between the sea and the interior of the continent as do the elevations of the Rocky Mountain district.

The Appalachian mountain system extends from Newfoundland, where it is obscurely united to the Laurentian system, which is yet to be described, to Northern Alabama, where the ranges sink downward and pass beneath the level of rocks which were formed since these mountains were elevated, disappearing as lesser ridges may under a thick coating of snow. This system is composed of numerous successive ridges lying parallel to each other, with intervening valleys which are, like the ridges, much narrower and lower than the like features in the Cordilleras. There are many subordinate parts of this great assemblage of mountains, each with its own peculiar character and history. The core or centre of the system is the Smoky Mountains, Blue Ridge, and the connected mountains which bear other names. This ridge is obscurely exhibited in Northern Georgia and Alabama; it rises in height in Western South Carolina, and attains its maximum height in North Carolina, where it exhibits the highest and most bulky mountains found in the eastern part of the continent. From North Carolina northward this Blue Ridge set of mountains diminishes in height and width; in Virginia it gradually descends, until at the Potomac it is a narrow range of elevations rising to less than two thousand feet above the sea. In Maryland and Pennsylvania it sinks down and is barely traceable in obscure, slight elevations.

On the eastern side of the Hudson, at its mouth,

this system of the ancient Appalachians rises again above the level of the sea in the range of elevations known as the Berkshire Hills in Massachusetts and Connecticut, and as the Green Mountains of Vermont. These pass obscurely into the White Mountains, and are yet more obscurely continued to the eastward and northward in the ancient mountains of Northern Maine, Nova Scotia, and perhaps some of the elevations of Newfoundland. This old axis of the Appalachians was partly in existence in the very ancient stages of the earth's history, known as the Cambrian time, and in part grew up during the immediately succeeding periods: it is thus all old land. Its age is indicated by the profound erosion by rain and glaciers which it has received, and also by the fact that we find fragments of its rocks in all the later-formed strata which have been built on the sea-floors near the foot of these mountains.

On the west of the Blue Ridge division of the Appalachians we have the numerous and sharper ridges of the Alleghany division of these mountains: these elevations were formed after the coal-measures were laid down, and they show their relative newness by the comparatively small amount of wearing to which they have been exposed. They appear to any observant eye as if fresh from the factory, while the Blue Ridge hills have a battered and worn-out look. In good part the preservation of these ridges of the Alleghany division is due to the fact that they lie on the continental side of the Blue Ridge, and have thus been protected by those elevations from the action of the sea, which has in the long history of the continent cut back the eastern face of this last-named barrier to the distance of some scores of miles from the present shore.

The Alleghany chain of mountains may be traced from Northern Alabama to the Catskills in New York. They vary greatly in character; generally they have the form of distinct foldings, somewhat like plaited or frilled cloth, but in Eastern Tennessee long fractures or faults often change their shape. In this district, for some reason, the rocks did not evenly crumple as in more northern parts of the same field, but rent apart, and were shoved about under the action of the pressure which forced them up into folds.

East of the Blue Ridge and its northern continuation lies a belt of mountains which were formed in part, at the same time as the Alleghany division of the Appalachians, and in part at a later day. These various mountains have been worn down to their roots, so that they no longer appear on the maps as mountain ranges, and are not recognized as such by the eye of the ordinary traveller. The geologist sees, however, that the beds of rock have been folded into great dislocations, and that these ridges have been cut away by the waves of the neighboring sea. At various times since these mountains began to grow the sea has stood at a higher level than at present, and so has beaten against the upturned folds of the old strata for a very great time, and thus has worn away their summits, leaving only their foundations to tell of the once great elevations which were here. These easternmost Appalachians are most distinct in North Carolina and Virginia. Traces of them are found northward in the region between New York, and Eastport, Me., and faintly in Nova Scotia as well. Some of these elevations appear to have developed in geologically recent times: thus on the island of Martha's Vineyard rocks of tertiary age are crumpled into mountainous forms, the movement having taken place in the last stages of the earth's history.

The pedestal or table-land of the Appalachians is much less conspicuous than that of the Cordilleras, and as in that system it is most conspicuous on the interior continental side of the ranges. In Central Tennessee and Eastern Kentucky it rises to about fourteen hundred feet above the sea, locally to yet greater elevations. With varying height it follows the line of the mountain folds to the northeastward to the region of the Catskills in New York, where it attains its greatest elevation of about four thousand feet above the sea. North of this point it falls away; for the mountains to which it immediately belongs, the Alleghanies, die out near the Mohawk River. In the Catskills this table-land is so high, that, being cut up into sharp peaks by the action of rivers, the mass appears to be a noble chain, but looking closely we perceive that the strata are horizontal, and the peaked character is due to the excavations of the valleys; in a word, that the Catskills are really very great hills, their strata not having the folded character we find in true mountains. The table-land or pedestal of the Appalachians on the eastern side has to a great extent been worn away by the sea; still the mountains of this system rest generally upon a broad elevation which rises to the height of several hundred feet above the level of the ocean.

The Appalachian mountain system is greatly intersected by large rivers, presenting in this as in other features a marked contrast to the Cordilleran system. These rivers at several points almost completely divide the mountain belt. Thus the French Broad, a tributary of the Tennessee, starts in the eastern part of the Blue Ridge district, and continued in the main stream traverses the Western or Alleghanian section, and falls into the Mississippi. The James River heads against the westernmost distinct ridge of these mountains and flows to the Atlantic. The waters of the Susquehanna traverse all the important ridges of Pennsylvania, and flow into Chesapeake Bay. The Mohawk turns around the northern end of the Alleghany ranges and falls into the Hudson, which flows in the valley between these ranges and the northern continuation of the Blue Ridge range. Thus the Appalachian system lacks the geographic solidity of the system of the Cordilleras, which is not so completely intersected by rivers, but remains a vast wall between the central and eastern, and the western parts of the continent.

We have already noticed several points of contrast between the structure and aspect of the Appalachian mountains and the Cordilleran elevations. We must now note the fact that, while volcanoes recently in active operation — some still in a state of half activity — are abundant in the western district, no trace of such volcanic peaks is found in the eastern mountain system. It is tolerably clear that no volcanic outbreaks have taken place in the eastern part of the continental mainland for many geologic ages: the last accidents of this nature occurred in the time of the Trias — not long after the coal-measures were formed — at the time when the red sandstones of the Connecticut Valley and of New Jersey, and also the coal of the basin near Richmond, Va., were forming. In all this vast period since the Triassic time the region east of the Mississippi seems to have been exempt from the disturbances which volcanoes bring to a country.

The third mountain system of North America is that of the Laurentians, an imperfectly explored mountain country lying north of the St. Lawrence and the Great Lakes. Comparatively little is known of this vast field of old mountain ridges: the district it occupies is inhospitable to man, and has been but seldom visited by geologists. Indeed, its superficial geography is as yet but imperfectly determined. From the insufficient explorations we can make out only the merest outlines of the history of this interesting district. The form of this Laurentian upland is rudely that of the letter V, the eastern side being the peninsula of Labrador, and the western extending in the trend of the western side of Hudson's Sea, which occupies in part the space between the two belts of low mountains. Wherever examined these mountains appear as low, worn-down hills of very ancient rocks, — rocks which are, indeed, of the oldest period known to geologists.

This northern district was, in a certain sense, the primitive nucleus or germ of North America: from its mass has come a very large part of the sands and mud which have gone to form the stratified rocks of the eastern part of the continent, worn away by the rains and ice of unimaginably long periods; it is therefore to be expected that these mountains would appear as mere wrecks of the original elevations. In fact, they nowhere now attain a height above three thousand feet. The destruction of the elevations in the Laurentian district is so complete that we cannot make out the original trend of the several ranges; as in an ancient city where the devastation wrought by time leaves nothing but a confused ruin which we only know to have been the dwelling-place of men by the nature of the materials, so this old mountain field can only be shown to have been at one period like the newer systems of the Cordilleras and the Appalachians, by the waste of its former structures. The shape of the Laurentian mountain field is very peculiar; indeed, unexampled among such systems of elevations. All other systems form nearly straight lines or gentle curves, while this has, as before noted, the form of a letter V. It seems likely that there are two or more distinct sets of elevations in this district which may have been formed at different, though very ancient times. As a whole these mountains must be regarded as the remnant of a system which once had a great part in the geography and climatal history of the continent, but which long since ceased to have any decided influence on its conditions. Unlike the Cordilleras or the Appalachians, it does not at present in any decided way affect the existing conditions of the land.

The subordinate mountain systems of North America, those groups of elevations which cannot be distinctly connected with the three great fields before mentioned, are interesting but mostly of small importance, except so far as they show the wide range of the forces which bring about the wrinkling of the earth's crust. In Greenland, and in various parts of the Arctic district of the northeastern portion of the continent, there are elevations of a mountainous nature which have not been much studied by geologists. Within the United States we have several mountain-built districts which cannot be referred to any of the systems above mentioned. Of these the most notable are the Adirondacks of New York, the Black Hills of Dakota, and the Ozarks of Missouri and Arkansas.

The Adirondacks appear to be more closely related

to the Laurentian system than to any other field of mountains; but they are not distinctly connected with that system, for they are parted from it by the deep and wide valley of the St. Lawrence, as they are also separated in an equally distinct manner from the Appalachians. The Adirondacks form a nearly circular field of mountains, having an area of about six thousand square miles. In this field there are some scores of peaks from two thousand to five thousand feet high. No very distinct order of arrangement is observable in these elevations, for they, like the Laurentians, are very old mountains, worn down by the action of the elements to mere relics of their former mass. It is a peculiar feature of this group of elevations, that it is everywhere surrounded by lowlands which rise at most to a few hundred feet above the sea.

The Black Hills of Dakota are an outlying mountain district, separated from the Rocky Mountains by a region of a plain-like character having a width of about two hundred miles. The general structure of the ridges shows them to be closely related to the Cordilleran system. The mountains rise to the height of over 7250 feet, and occupy a field of about eight thousand square miles. The Ozark district of Missouri, the Indian Territory, and Arkansas is the most detached group of elevations in the continent. They lie about midway between the Cordilleras and the Appalachians, their only neighbors being a number of similarly detached elevations in the Indian Territory and in Northwestern Texas. The elevations of this system occupy an area of about ten thousand square miles, and rise to the height of about two thousand feet above the sea. This little mountain system, like the Adirondacks, seems to have been formed in the early geological ages in a time when the greater systems in the east and west had not begun the most important development which they afterwards underwent. Although a conspicuous feature in the lowland where they lie, the Ozarks have not in any considerable way affected the physical history of the continent. At several points in other portions of the great central plain-land of the Mississippi Valley the rocks show the existence of the strains which built them into folds, but the elevations they have produced are of even less consequence than the scattered systems we have just described.

The great valleys of the continent have their position determined in the main by the distribution of the principal mountain systems.

Our study of these elevations has prepared the way for our account of the greater troughs of the land, and the rivers which occupy them. At the outset we should notice that valleys are naturally divided into two groups, — the greater, which occupy broad fields between the separate systems of mountains, and the lesser, which owe the existence of their troughs entirely to the cutting action of the stream itself. In the first group, to which the most of the longest rivers of the world belong, their valleys are shaped by the distribution of mountain systems; in the second, the stream generally lies in good part within a single mountain system and determines the form of its valley by its own carving power.

Beginning our account with the northern valleys and rivers of the continent, we find that into the Arctic Ocean there falls but one river of considerable size, the Mackenzie, the least of the three great rivers of North America. The valley of this river appears to be formed

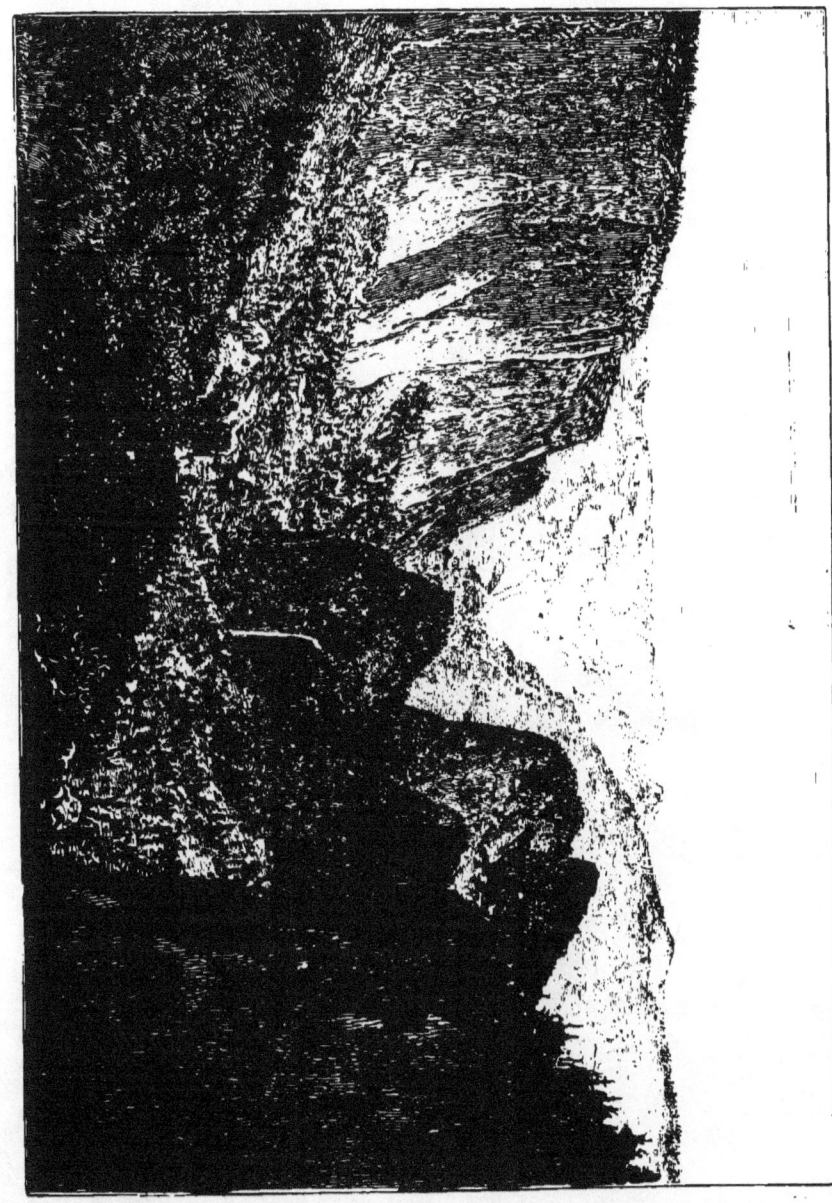
YOSEMITE VALLEY, CALIFORNIA.

by the barriers of mountain systems, that of the Cordilleras on the west and the obscure and as yet unexplored ridges which continue the western line of the Laurentian Mountains towards the Arctic Circle. Owing to the forbidding cold of this region, the valley of the Mackenzie is almost unknown except along the greater water-courses which are traversed by the agents of fur companies. From the little which is as yet ascertained about it, this valley appears to be essentially like that of the Mississippi, except for the lowness of the mountains on its eastern border. There are the same broad plains on either side of the stream as we find in the greater southern river. The stream of the Mackenzie carries much less water than the Mississippi, and differs from it in certain ways determined by the extremely cold climate of the country through which it flows. Like the rivers of Siberia, this stream often freezes to the bottom in the winter. Its sources being much farther south than the main channel, a great tide of water is poured into it before the ice has melted away from the channel. The result is that this ice acts as an obstruction to the floods, and causes the northern portions of its bed to wander about in a very irregular manner.

Like the St. Lawrence, the Mackenzie receives the waters of many great lakes. Next after that stream it is the most extensively fed from lakes, of any river on the continent. Although the total area of lakes draining into this stream is only about half that which goes to the St. Lawrence, they serve to give it the steady flow which characterizes the larger stream. This great extent of lake basins in the northern part of North America is a peculiar feature of the continent, and is mainly to be explained by the peculiar actions which took place during the glacial period.

South of the central head-waters of the Mackenzie we find the valley of the Churchill River, a stream of the third order of size, which flows to the eastward and falls into Hudson's Sea. It is but obscurely separated from the greater river of the north, and also from the valley of the Nelson on the south : it also draws away the water from a number of large lakes.

On its path to the eastward the Nelson River passes across the line of the western Laurentian district of elevations, which here has hardly any value as a barrier, for it is crossed by several streams. This stream, like the Mackenzie, gathers the greater part of its waters in the district of the Cordilleras, through the branches of its principal tributary, the Saskatchewan : it also receives the tribute of the Red River of the North, which heads against the upper branches of the Mississippi. These, its two principal confluents, unite in Lake Winnipeg, a noble area of fresh water as large as Lake Ontario. It also receives the waters of many other large lakes.

The valley of the Nelson is so slightly separated from those of the Mississippi and the St. Lawrence that it is possible in the spring-time to pass in a canoe from the waters of the more northern river to those of the neighboring southern streams with but little if any carriage of the boat at difficult places. The reason for this lies in the fact that there are no mountain barriers between the head-waters of these rivers ; they all rise in the relatively flat central trough of the continent formed between the eastern and western mountains.

East of the Nelson there are numerous small streams

which flow from the west, south, and east, into the great basin of Hudson's Sea. They are not well known. They all, however, are small, and do not command our attention.

The basin of the St. Lawrence is the second in importance among the river valleys of this continent. In certain regards it is akin to the other northern rivers we have been describing. Like them, it draws away the water from a great number of lakes; indeed, it is, except perhaps the Nile, the greatest of all the lake-fed rivers of the world in the volume of water it discharges: it drains a greater area of fresh-water basins than any other stream. The river systems of the northern and eastern part of the continent are noteworthy for the vast extent of their natural storage reservoirs, and among them the St. Lawrence has the foremost place. The conditions of the St. Lawrence Valley are peculiar. On the north it is bounded by the Laurentian uplands, but on the south from the outlet of Lake Superior to the rapids of the St. Lawrence there is no such high wall as we are accustomed to find on each side of a great river valley. At the southern end of Lake Michigan there is only a few feet of height separating the waters of that great lake from the tributaries of the Mississippi, which head up against the southern border of this inland sea: in Ohio and New York the edge of the barrier rises only to two or three hundred feet above the neighboring lakes of Ontario and Erie.

The absence of a distinct southern wall to the basin of the St. Lawrence, gives to that valley a character unknown in that of the other rivers of North America, and apparently unexampled in the other great stream basins of the world. The St. Lawrence is also peculiar in the fact that its waters do not descend, as in the case of most rivers, by a gentle declivity from the source of the stream to its mouth, but find their way to the sea by several great steps in falls or rapids, with long, nearly level intervals between them. The uppermost of these steps or benches is occupied by Lake Superior, from which the Laurentian waters descend to their next lower platform by the Sault Ste. Marie, or rapids which lead to the lower level of the other great lakes, Huron, Michigan, and Erie. The second descent is made where these waters pass over the rapids in the great fall of Niagara. By yet another step in the rapids between Lake Ontario and Montreal, the waters of the main St. Lawrence attain the level of the sea; but they course for the further distance of several hundred miles in a tidal estuary which gradually widens until it debouches into the Gulf of St. Lawrence. Taken altogether, the St. Lawrence is, for the volume of water which it passes to the sea, the least distinctly river-like of all the great streams in the world. It mostly consists of great lakes and a long arm of the sea: even where, as at the Straits of Detroit, near Niagara Falls, and between Lake Ontario and Quebec, it seems river-like, the well-trained eye perceives that it has not the character of an ordinary stream, for the reason that it has hardly a trace of sediment in its waters. It is characteristic of nearly all other great streams that they have to struggle on their way to the sea with a vast amount of alluvial matter brought to the valleys from the beds of torrents by which they are fed. All such materials in the basin of the St. Lawrence, except the small amount contributed by the affluents which join it below Lake Ontario, are deposited on the floors of the Great Lakes.

Owing to these peculiarities, the St. Lawrence has no alluvial plain; its clean waters have very little cutting power on the rocks; and it has no delta, or deposit of sediment, at its mouth, — a feature which is almost invariably found at the mouths of great rivers when they enter the sea.

South of the St. Lawrence and north of the Gulf of Mexico there are a number of lesser rivers, only a few of which deserve mention in this general account of North America. The first of these to be noticed is the Hudson. The main channel of this stream, extending from near Lake George to its mouth, occupies a broad valley which has only been in small part excavated by the river itself. It consists mainly of a trough between the Catskill Hills, or remnant of the Alleghanian tableland, on the west and the Berkshire Hills on the east. At the close of the last glacial period this valley was occupied by an arm of the sea which extended up through the depression in which lie Lakes George and Champlain, and thence to the strait of the St. Lawrence, then much wider than it is at present. The recent elevation of this valley has not entirely deprived the Hudson of its character of a marine inlet, for in the lower half of its course it is still rather to be classed as an arm of the sea than as a river.

East of the Hudson we have in the Connecticut one of the noblest of the New England group of rivers, which deserves mention on account of certain peculiar features. Like the Hudson it occupies a trough between two districts which owe their elevation to mountain-building forces. On the west lie the Berkshire Mountains and their northward continuation, the Green Mountains of Vermont, and on the east a broadly elevated district which is likewise to be reckoned as mountainous. At the close of the glacial period the valley of the Connecticut, like that of the Hudson, as well as all the other parts of the continent lying to the northeastward, was depressed to the depth of some hundred feet below the sea-level, and in this time it formed a great inlet extending from the present shore-line to the northern part of Massachusetts, or perhaps into Vermont. During this time the floor of the great fiord became deeply covered with the debris washed in from the neighboring higher ground, the wreckage of the rocks produced during the glacial time. When the valley was re-elevated, the broad, flat deposit of mud and sand was carved by the stream into beautiful terraces which are perhaps the best examples of such structures which are to be found in this country.

It is characteristic of all the other rivers in the New England district, in which we may include New Brunswick as well, that the rivers commonly discharge into arms of the sea and have more or less distinct remains of terraces, at least in the parts of their valleys which are some distance back from the shore. It is also characteristic of these streams that they carry tolerably uniform volumes of clear water. This feature is due to the fact that they drain from districts thickly covered by a coating of glacial drift composed of sand and gravel, which to a great extent stores the rain-water in the wet seasons and delivers it to the channels in times of drought. Where these streams flow from the north southwardly they generally have steep descents, falling usually at the rate of a foot or more in a mile. Where, however, their waters move, as is the case in certain rare instances, from the south towards the north, they have very sluggish streams which sometimes, as in the case of the Concord River, wind their way deviously through marshes to the sea. The cause of this difference in the slope of the streams is found in a change which has taken place in the position of the continent in its northeastern part, occurring since the glacial ice passed away from its surface. This part of the land has been bodily tilted up to the northward and eastward, so that all the old shore-lines which mark the ancient sea-level ascend to the northeastward at the rate of a foot or more to the mile: the result is, that the streams which flow towards the north have had their slopes in large part destroyed, while those which flow towards the south have steeper descents than before the change took place.

South of the Hudson, along the Atlantic and Gulf coast, there are a number of considerable rivers, the Delaware, Susquehanna, Potomac, James, Roanoke, Savannah, Mobile, as well as many other lesser but still considerable streams, none of which present individual peculiarities deserving notice in our general survey of North American rivers. All those mentioned head in the Appalachian system of mountains, and two of them, the Susquehanna and the James, divide not only the Blue Ridge portion of that mountain system, but cut through all but the more western folds of the Alleghany chain. Two other streams, the Delaware and the Potomac, entirely divide the ancient Blue Ridge axis.

It is quite characteristic of these seaboard rivers which pour into the Atlantic and the Gulf, that they do not pass directly into the open sea, but debouch in bays which widen gradually towards the ocean. This seems to be due to the fact that the region through which they flow was recently at a greater height than at present, and during the elevation the rivers cut out channels in the then shore land which was farther out to sea than the present coast: the subsequent sinking of the shore permitted the sea to extend up the lower part of the valley for a considerable distance. These bays were once a good deal longer than they are at present, for the mud brought down by the rivers has filled the upper part of them.

The rivers which discharge into the Pacific are few in number: the most important are the Colorado, which empties into the Bay of Lower California; the Columbia, which discharges through Oregon; and the Yukon, which empties into Behring Sea. All these rivers gather their waters within the Cordilleras: owing to the relatively small rainfall which characterizes the interior region of that mountain district, they have a great length for the amount of water which they bear to the sea.

The Colorado is on many accounts the most remarkable of the three greater Pacific coast streams. Its waters are mostly derived from melting snows of the Rocky Mountains; for the greater part of its length the stream receives few tributaries. It is probable that no other river in the world except the Nile flows so far without being joined by streams from the neighboring country. Like the Nile, the Colorado flows through a desert, though the desert which borders the Colorado, unlike that which borders the lower Nile, is very elevated: it lies at a height of about five thousand feet above the sea. Through this table-land the stream has cut a deep gorge, or cañon, the most wonderful narrow valley in the world. The Columbia, in the middle portions of its length, flows also through a very arid country, but the regions about its head-waters and near its mouth are more fertile. In the middle portion of its course the Columbia passes through a vast field of volcanic rock, one of the largest areas overlaid by lavas which the world affords. The Yukon is a noble stream, on many accounts the finest river of the Pacific coast of North America, for it drains a country which has a greater rainfall than the other great streams; but the region is entirely unfit for agriculture, on account of the coldness of the summer season, and thus it has no great importance to man.

As a whole, the rivers of the Pacific coast and the lands which border them are a less conspicuous feature of the country than those near the Atlantic shore or in the heart of the mountains. The reason for this seems to be that this western district has been for the greater part of the ages since it became firm land, as it is now, except near the sea-shore, a field in which little rain falls. Consequently few river valleys have been formed, and these not of great size.

We now come to the great central system of the continent, that of the Mississippi Valley. This vast stream has its tributaries situated partly in the eastern portion of the Cordilleras, partly in the western portion of the Appalachians, and in part they flow from the low watershed which separates the Mississippi Valley from that portion of the continent which drains towards the high north. Only the head-waters of the Mississippi on the east and west flow in mountainous gorges or cañons. Throughout by far the greater portions of their course the principal affluents traverse a wide region underlaid by horizontal rocks which have a generally plane surface. Almost everywhere the branches of these great tributaries, as well as the larger stream, are more or less navigable from the border of the mountains downward to the sea. Except the river system of the Amazon, that of the Mississippi has a greater stretch of shores naturally accessible to vessels of considerable draught than any other in the world. Unlike the Amazon, whose waters lie altogether within the tropics and afford no great range of climatal conditions, those of the Mississippi course through regions which have great variety of temperature and rainfall. The upper Missouri traverses a very arid country, the upper Mississippi a region of cold climate, while the lower portion of the main stream flows through lands where oranges will grow in the open air.

As a whole, the continent of North America is peculiarly well watered by rivers, and the streams are so placed as to be of great value for the uses of commerce. South America rivals it in the extent of its uninterrupted navigable waters. The rivers of this southern continent are, however, mostly in the tropics, and have a climate unfavorable for the uses of people of European origin. Africa has more great streams than North America, but the greatest of them are in the tropics, and they are all much obstructed by rapids in the lower part of their paths. The rivers of Asia afford in the aggregate more navigable water than those of North America, but several of the most important fall into the Arctic Ocean, and have only a limited value for human use.

THE FORESTS OF NORTH AMERICA.

To primitive savages dense forests do not afford advantageous places of abode. They contain less game than more open countries. Only a few of their species yield nutritious fruits or seeds, and the close-set trees are hard to clear away when it is desired to use the ground for agriculture. Even the pioneers of our own race find dense woods a serious obstacle. When the trees are cut off, the roots are in the way of the plough, and, however fertile the soil, it is often half a lifetime before the farmer has good fields. The prairies are much better for the needs of the first settlers of a country than the dense woodlands.

The natural use of woods is mainly to store the rain-water in the mass of decayed matter which rests about their roots, which water, yielded slowly to the streams, diminishes the force of the winter torrents and maintains the flow through the summer season. To man they become most important when population is dense, and there is a great demand for timber for house-building and other purposes. In the prairie countries the narrow strips of forest along the streams serve for the needs of house-building and for firewood, and the farmer finds it greatly to his advantage to have land so open that he can set his plough in the virgin soil and run it straight away for miles without hindrance.

The forests of North America at the time when the country was settled by Europeans were probably more continuous than the first men found in any other of the great lands except Europe. On the eastern part of the continent, extending from Central Texas north to near the junction of the Ohio with the Mississippi, thence eastward along the southern border of that river, and northward to the Laurentian Mountains north of Lake Erie, was the western margin of the great Appalachian forest which covered all the country east of the above-described lines, except a few small areas in Kentucky, North Carolina, and perhaps some other states where the Indians had destroyed the woods by fire. This region is remarkable for the very great number of broad-leaved trees which it contains, and for the noble dimensions to which many of these species grow. The oaks, maples, tulip trees, magnolias, walnuts, and a number of other genera attain here a measure of development unknown to other countries. In fact, this field holds the noblest forests of such trees which are known in the world. In Europe, at a time not long before the glacial period, many trees akin to the species which are now characteristic of North America flourished. Thus we find the leaves of the sassafrases, tulip trees, and other kinds now characteristic of North America, in the miocene tertiary beds of Switzerland and Germany, although the forms have long since disappeared from the European forests.

By no means the whole of this great Appalachian woodland is composed of broad-leaved trees, although the species of this group occupy the larger part of its surface. The western border of the field, the portion of it in Ohio, Central and Western Kentucky, Western Tennessee, and thence south to beyond the Mississippi, contains a few narrow-leaved forms, such as our pines, firs, hemlocks, and cedars; but in the mountainous parts of the Appalachian forests, and the level land between the Blue Ridge range and the sea, narrow-leaved share the ground with the broad-leaved forms. There are areas of a thousand square miles in extent in this region which are mainly held by pines or firs; but generally the two groups link their boughs together in a common forest. This mixture of vegetation of diverse kinds is most common in the mountainous country.

On the plains broad and narrow leaved trees generally possess different fields.

In no other part of the temperate zone are the timber trees so varied or so useful to man as they are here. It is only in the tropics that a greater range of useful woods is found. The result is that for two centuries timber has been one of the most important articles of export from this part of the continent, the European market having been to a great extent supplied from this field.

As we go northward in the Appalachian forest and approach the St. Lawrence River, the number of the narrow-leaved trees, as well as the variety of species, gradually diminishes. North of that river firs begin to predominate; but before we attain the summit of the low Laurentian Mountains, the Arctic cold begins to stunt the growth of all the arboreal vegetation. North and northwest of this region, though forest trees continue to occupy the surface, their trunks are short and of small size, so that they have little value for construction timber. Around by the north the Appalachian wood is connected by scant forests with extensive rocky fields and prairie-like intervals of open land to the woodland district of the Pacific coast.

The woods of the Pacific coast, at least those that are of such density that they deserve the name of forests, begin in California as a narrow fringe along the coastline where the rainfall is sufficient to maintain them, and extend thence northwardly in a widening belt until, in the southern part of British America, the forest district occupies the most of the region between the crest of the Rocky Mountains and the sea. Thence to the northward the trees begin to shrink under the influence of the cold, until in Alaska they have a stunted character. The field occupied by well-grown trees extends, however, for near a thousand miles farther north on the western shore of the continent than it does upon the eastern. This difference is due to the fact that the Pacific shore is warmed by a great ocean stream, while the Atlantic coast to the north of the St. Lawrence is the seat of a cold current coming from the Arctic regions. These streams of the sea affect the climate of the neighboring land.

It is characteristic of the Pacific-coast forest that it is mainly composed of narrow-leaved trees which bear cones in the manner of our firs and pines. Among these the sequoia is one of the greatest trees of the world, being only exceeded in height by some of the eucalyptus trees of Australia. In average girth they probably surpass any other giants of the forest. This magnificent species is now nearly extinct, the woods in which it occurs occupying in all only a few square miles of area. Another species, the redwood, a kind of fir, forms enormous forests, doubtless the noblest woods of coniferous trees now existing on the surface of the earth.

Between the eastern margin of the Pacific forest and the western border of the Appalachian timbered country, occupying in general the western half of the Mississippi Valley, and much of the Cordilleran district where the waters drain to the Pacific Ocean, we find a vast territory where the forests are very scant or entirely wanting. Here and there in the Rocky Mountains, in places where from the position of the elevations in relation to the winds there is more rainfall, we have considerable areas of wood, and almost everywhere along

PALMETTO, FLORIDA.

the streams there is a narrow belt of thin forests in the naturally irrigated lands. It seems likely that when this continent was first occupied by man a large part of this unwooded area was forest-clad. It was a common habit with our aborigines to set fire to the undergrowth in order that after the conflagration the fresh growth of vegetation might afford good pasturage for the deer and buffalo. In this way the young forest trees were killed so that when the larger plants of the species perished from old age, there were none to succeed them.

Unfortunately the habit of burning the woods is common with civilized men as well as with savages, and much of this destruction by fire has taken place since the country was settled by the whites. A more extended and deliberate destruction of the woods, particularly those of the Appalachian forests, has necessarily been brought about in order to secure tilled fields. Probably about three hundred thousand square miles of what was dense woodland three hundred years ago is now tilled land.

Certain American forest trees, and other woodland plants not noted in the preceding description, deserve especial mention. In the tropical portion of the continent several species of palms are tolerably abundant, particularly near the shore. Some of these species are native, but others have been brought to this country from South America and the Old World. Only one important group of palms, the palmettos, naturally dwell within the United States. These palmettos, of which the larger varieties attain the height of thirty feet, are abundant in Florida, and occur along the Atlantic coast as far north as the southeastern corner of North Carolina. This variety of palm is often called the cabbage tree, for the reason that the large unopen bud at the top of the stem somewhat resembles that vegetable and is often cooked for food.

The live-oak, so called because it is never without green leaves, ranges from Cape Hatteras southward through the southern portion of the Gulf states to Central Texas. This tree rarely grows in the dense forests, but prefers a somewhat open country, where, when well grown, it forms noble domes of foliage. The wood is of remarkable strength and endurance, affording a very valuable ship-timber, much of which is exported to Europe.

In the Southern states of the Federal Union and thence southward to Central America, all the swamps contain a species of cone-bearing, narrow-leaved tree known as the taxodium, or bald cypress. This, also, is a very noble tree, not infrequently having a trunk as much as twelve feet in diameter, and without a branch for about a hundred feet in height. This plant is peculiar, in that from the roots which lie below the water of the swamp there arise spur-like projections often to the height of five or six feet above the soil. Each of these projections, which are termed knees, has, when full-grown, a bulb-shaped excrescence on its summit, which is covered with soft bark and is hollow within. They are so large, that they are often used for well-buckets or beehives. These curious structures appear to serve to give the sap of the roots a chance to come in contact with the air; for whenever, as by the construction of a mill-dam, or the downsinking of the land during an earthquake, the caps of the knees are brought below the level of the water during the summer season, the tree dies.

Another American tree, the sassafras, though not of large growth, is worthy of notice, for the reason that it played an important part in the commerce of the country for some time after its settlement by the whites. The bark of this tree, especially that of the roots, has a very aromatic flavor. This caused the plant to be much prized on account of its supposed medicinal virtues. For a long time great quantities of it were shipped to European markets. The Diospyros, the persimmon or date-plum, a species of the ebony family, a group characteristic of the tropics, is abundantly developed in the Southern states, and scantily so as far north as Rhode Island and Iowa. It bears quantities of fruit about the size and shape of plums. This fruit is extremely bitter and astringent until affected by the frosts of autumn, when it becomes sweet and palatable. It was much eaten by the savages and wild animals, and is not disdained by civilized man. In the Southern states considerable quantities of fermented liquor are made from it. This is sometimes distilled for brandy.

The paw-paw, or custard-apple, a single member of a tropical family found within the limits of the United States, extends from New York and Southeastern Nebraska to near the Gulf of Mexico. It is a low, bushy tree from twenty to thirty feet in height, bearing a large, many-seeded fruit from three to six inches in length and one or two inches in diameter, which is much eaten, and is sometimes distilled for spirits.

The trees and shrubs of the holly family, a group of plants which retain their glossy foliage in winter and bear bright scarlet berries, are also well developed in the southern portion of the great Appalachian forest. The largest of these species, commonly known as the American holly, attains on the southwestern border of that eastern timber-belt a height of from forty to sixty feet, and has a smooth-bark trunk a foot or more in diameter. Its wood is of a dense texture and a white color, — qualities which make it greatly prized in certain constructions. One of the species of American holly, which bears the Indian name of yaupon, was much used by the savages of the Carolina district in making what the early explorers called their "black drink": a decoction of its leaves still serves as a tea with the whites of that country.

The species of the ginseng family, a group of perennial rooted plants, one species of which sometimes grows in the form of a low tree, abounds throughout the Appalachian forest. It is interesting for the reason that its roots are very extensively collected and exported to China, where they are used for medicinal purposes, as they are also in a small way in this country. It is one of the most singular features in the commerce of this country that the inhabitants of the most remote settlements in the Appalachian district gain most of their ready money from the sale of a natural product which is principally consumed in the far-away Celestial Empire.

Other groups of trees, less peculiar, but still of conspicuous features, are developed in North America. Among these we may name the tulip tree and the magnolias. The tulip tree, known by many different local names, is perhaps the noblest of the broad-leaved American trees. It sometimes attains the height of near two hundred feet, with a trunk diameter of six or eight feet. It has beautiful broad leaves, and flowers, as the name indicates, shaped like those of the tulip. The magnolias are represented by many species: they also have very broad glossy leaves which in some species remain all winter upon the plant. They have beautiful flowers of large size and a whitish color. The magnolias are mainly limited to the Southern states, but one of the species ranges as far north as Massachusetts. In the mountain valleys of the southern Appalachian Mountains is another interesting tree, the stuartia, closely akin to the camelias of Eastern Asia.

As a whole, the American forests are much like those of Europe, except that they contain many more kinds of trees than do those of the Old World. This great variety gives our forests east of the Mississippi a richness and diversified foliage unknown to any other region beyond the tropics.

PRAIRIES.

One of the most characteristic features of North America is the wide extent of the very level lands lying between the Appalachian and Laurentian Mountains on the east, and the Cordilleras on the west, occupying by far the larger part of the Mississippi Valley, and extending northward towards the Arctic Sea. Nearly all this area west of the Mississippi, and south of British America, as well as the larger part of Indiana, Illinois, and a portion of Ohio and Kentucky, was originally, and mostly yet remains, without forest trees, except along the streams. There were also some treeless tracts of considerable area in the country farther to the east and south. These areas of open country were termed by the early French settlers of the Mississippi Valley *prairies*, the word designating in the French language what we term meadow-land.

These prairies were the seat of a dense growth of plants, largely grasses, which had no permanent stems, but with tops which dried away in the winter season.

When set on fire by the Indians, the flames would often run through this dried grass for scores of miles, destroying any young trees which might have sprung up, and thus limiting the forest to the damp margins of the streams. Besides the grasses, these prairies generally abounded in beautiful flowers. Many species belonging to the family of the *Compositæ*, the kindred of the sunflowers and daisies, attained a most luxuriant growth in this open country.

The prairies have played an important part in the history of North America. Owing to their wide extent and hard surface they shed the rain quickly to the streams and cause those water-ways to be alternately flooded and nearly dry. In the days when they were occupied by the Indians they afforded rich pasturage to innumerable herds of buffalo, elk, and deer,— creatures which in their abundance induced the savages to retain, or adopt, the wandering habits of the hunter rather than to seek subsistence in the more elevated occupation of the husbandman. When the whites came to the prairie country, they found the soil surpassingly fertile and very easily won to the plough. For the first hundred and fifty years after the English settlements were founded in North America the farmers had to struggle with the dense forest, each acre of which required about fifty days of labor before it could be made fit for ploughing. When in the beginning of this century our people came to this open ground, they found fields of rich and virgin soil lying wide open before them. A large part of the growth which the population and wealth of this country has made during the present century, has been due to the readiness with which these soils of the prairies can be brought to yield a crop. The prairies are particularly suited for grain crops, and their vast harvests of this staple food have long been the source of a great export trade with Europe.

Although the soil of the prairies is at first extremely fertile, often yielding as much as forty bushels of wheat to the acre when first brought under the plough, they unfortunately do not retain their fertility for any great time. In the course of thirty years the average yield of wheat is reduced to about half the original quantity. This part of the country suffers under certain disadvantages of climate. East of the Mississippi the rainfall is tolerably abundant and constant from year to year. A little west of that stream the prairies come to feel the arid conditions of the Cordilleran district, and for more than half their area from Central Texas and Central Kansas westward, droughts make tillage hazardous. In fact, more than half of the Western plains cannot be trusted to produce good crops without irrigation.

CLIMATE.

The climate of any country is determined by the proportion of heat, moisture, wind, sunshine, and clouds which occur there, on the proportion of these at different seasons, and even at different times in the days of the year. It is easy to see that there is no definite thing which can be termed the climate of an extended region, as all these elements which go to give character to the weather constitute its climate. Between the top and bottom of any hill a thousand feet high there is usually a distinct difference in all these features, which shows itself in the variation in the plants. The north side of such a hill will have one climate, and the south side, at the same level, another; even on the sunshiny and shady sides of a house or a large tree we may find differences in condition which are in fact of a climatal nature. Thus it is not possible to regard the climate of a country as a matter common to all of its parts, or even to a very small portion of its surface. Still there are certain general features of the climate of North America which deserve attention, and will now be described.

This continent is a very much more united land than either Europe or Asia; it has few great peninsulas, and its inland seas are not large as compared with those of the Old World; as we have already seen, it is not divided in an east and west direction by any high mountains. The Laurentian ranges, the only considerable elevations which run in an east and west direction, ceased to grow upwards in a very ancient time, and have been gradually worn down to their very roots by the action of rain and ice. There are thus no such great barriers between the Arctic cold and tropic heat as are formed by the Pyrenees, Alps, Caucasus, or Himalayas of the Old World. Hence it comes about that the summers of this continent are generally very warm even as far north as the Arctic Circle, while the winter cold extends far to the south. This extreme contrast between the principal seasons is in the main due to the shape of the surface of the continent.

We have remarked the fact that North America has a very highly elevated mass of mountains and table-lands on its western side, and a considerable system of elevations on the eastern border, with a very wide continental valley between these highlands. These elevations to a great extent fence out the interior parts of the continent from the seaboard region and deprive it of a portion of the moisture as well as of the cool air which the Atlantic and Pacific oceans would otherwise send to it. Thus, though this continent lies between the two greater oceans, it is in its interior region relatively little affected by their influence. The Gulf of Mexico has more effect on the climate of this central trough of the continent than either the Atlantic or Pacific. Being a very warm sea, and having the valley of the Mississippi wide open on its north, and the prevailing winds being such as to carry the warm and moist airs from it into the interior of the continent, it affords an abundant rainfall to a wide field of land which would otherwise be exceedingly dry. The effect of this gulf is felt upon all the central and eastern part of the Mississippi Valley, and it is probably not without influence on the climate of regions to the north of the Great Lakes.

Owing to the exclusion of the moist air of the neighboring oceans, together with the heat and dryness of the summers, the mountains of North America have few fields of perpetual snow except in the region about Alaska. This is the only part of the continent in cold regions which has a warm ocean stream flowing against its shores. The Japan current, sometimes known as the Kuro Siwo, sends a large volume of moderately warm water against these Alaskan shores. The effect is to cause a great snowfall in the highlands, and this not melting away in the cloudy summer time, forms great ice-streams which flow down the mountain valleys into the sea. This is the only part of the mainland of North America which has large glaciers; but smaller fields of ice which withstand the summer heats are found at several points in the Cordilleras south of Alaska, some of considerable size in the portion of that mountain district which lies within the limits of Canada, and a few of lesser extent in the northern part of that field within the boundaries of the United States.

In Switzerland, and most other countries where glaciers abound, they are fed from fields of perpetual snow which cover the upper parts of the mountains and slowly creep down, becoming more compact as they move onward, until they finally take shape as streams of ice to be melted in the warm air of the lower valleys. But in the case of the small glaciers of the United States, where there are no extended fields of enduring snow, the glaciers are principally fed by the snow which in the winter season drifts into the valleys and accumulates there to a great depth. Where such snow lies for a long time in this heaped condition, it passes into the state of whitish ice. It is characteristic of the western portion of the Cordilleras that a great deal of snow falls in winter, but it melts away except in the drift-heaps of the narrow and very elevated valleys, during the heats of summer.

Although the continental portion of North America has on the whole less glacial ice than either of the other northern lands, the island or peninsula of Greenland, which is an appendage of this continent, is the greatest known district of glaciers, being possibly exceeded in the depth and width of its ice-fields only by the almost unknown lands about the South Pole. In Greenland the whole of the surface except the southern extremity and a strip of land along the east and west shores is continuously covered with an ice-sheet which is so deep that it hides the whole surface. Along the shores of the land this glacier is broken by fissures, as in similar sheets in other countries, but in the interior, a few miles back from this point, it exhibits a gentle continuous slope extending up to the height of several thousand feet above the shore, and then gently declining towards the sea on the other side of the peninsula. Around the margin of vast glacial fields the ice, descending through the valleys, passes into the sea. Being somewhat lighter than the water into which it enters, and also being much rifted by crevices, the ends of these glaciers break off and float away to the southward. These icebergs, as the floating fragments from the glacial field are called, are often two or three thousand feet thick and contain several cubic miles of ice.

The deep currents of the sea, moving southward to replace in the equatorial regions the water which flows northward from that region in the Gulf Stream, drag these icebergs for a great distance southward. They often journey for a thousand miles or more towards the equator before the heat of the water and the air melts them away. These great fleets of icebergs often come directly in the path of ships passing from the ports of America to England and Germany, and are the source of much danger to these vessels. Each of these great floating ice-islands carries with it a store of the cold of the Arctic regions. It cools the water of the sea all about it, and the air as well. The result is that the winds which blow from over this ocean to the neighboring lands are colder than they otherwise would be.

Another stream of cold water from the ice-laden regions of Baffin's Bay and Hudson's Strait moves down the shore, passing by Labrador, Newfoundland, and Nova Scotia, as far south as Cape Cod; and this cold water much affects the climate of this portion of the shore-lands of North America. Wherever the winds blow over it to the coast, they bring a remarkable coolness even in the hottest part of the summer. A similar result is brought about by the current which sets southward along the Pacific coast from the cold regions of the sea about Alaska. This stream extends down as far as Southern California, becoming warmer as it goes. The winds which blow over it to the land are always much cooler than they would be if there was no such continued inflowing of these Arctic waters.

Thus we perceive that this continent has the greater part of its shores bathed by chilled waters from the Arctic regions. Around by the Arctic Sea and south to Massachusetts Bay the waters of the sea are far colder than they would be but for such currents, and the shores are characterized by the fact that the sea-winds have a low temperature. The warm currents of the ocean strike the coasts only in the regions about the Gulf of Mexico and the Caribbean Sea, and also in the region about Alaska. In the last-named district the current, having traversed a great distance under northern skies, is only moderately warm, yet it gives to the shore-land region of Alaska a climate a good deal milder than that of Labrador, which is situated much farther to the south. The result of this distribution of the warm currents, together with the absence of mountain barriers to the polar winds, is that the winter in the northern half of the continent is very cold.

In the southern portion of the continent the winter season is milder, but down to the line of Mexico and Northern Florida strong winds from the north may at times bring a bitter cold air. Southern Florida and the narrow lands of Mexico and the peninsula district near South America, lying between warm seas and with a climate controlled by their warmth, are the only portions of the mainland where winter frosts do not frequently occur on the lowlands. If there were a range of mountains, such as the Pyrenees or the Alps, extending from east to west across the northern border of the United States, the region to the south of the barrier would have a much more equable climate than it actually has.

The most important determining feature in the climate of North America is the Gulf of Mexico. This great sea, receiving the heated waters of the Gulf Stream, has a high temperature, and because of its heat sends a great deal of vapor into the air which blows over it. It is the rain from the clouds of the Gulf which seems to fertilize the greater part of the habitable portion of the continent,—the valley of the Mississippi and the Atlantic lowlands. In former geological ages this sea, at first a great strait extending to the ocean of high latitudes, exercised much more influence on North American climate than it does at present: it has been gradually narrowing in the northward until it is but a fraction of what it once was.

Indian Summer. — At the close of the long, hot, and rather tempestuous summer season which characterizes nearly the whole of North America east of the Rocky Mountains, there commonly comes a time of drought extending from about the first of September until the winter rains set in in November or December. Extensive forest and prairie fires occur at this season, which often fill the air over a large part of the continent with a hazy smoke. As there is not much wind to blow it away at this season, this smoke-laden condition of the air often continues for weeks. The lack of wind and the envelope of smoke are apt to make the temperature high, and so this period of cloudless but darkened skies has received the name of Indian summer. Frequently portions of the air become so filled with the fumes from the burning woods as to hide the sun. Drifting slowly across the country, these masses of smoke sometimes, and in a very sudden manner, bring a temporary darkness as of midnight over the sky of midday. There are a number of such dark days chronicled in different parts of the eastern United States. In certain cases the incidents have been appalling to the people.

VIOLENT STORMS.

The fitness of any country for the uses of man is much affected by the storms to which it is liable. These accidents of the atmosphere may greatly affect the interests of its human occupants in either of two ways: by the force of the winds they may endanger ships near the shore, or they may destroy buildings and crops in the interior districts. In either of these cases the visitations may be very destructive to life.

Owing to certain physical peculiarities, North America is very liable throughout much of its area to violent convulsions of the atmosphere. The absence of great mountain ranges in the Mississippi Valley and on the eastern and northern parts of the continent, the existence of wide treeless plains over a great portion of the central region, and the wide difference in temperature in the water of the neighboring seas, lead to the occurrence of violent movements of the air. The storms of North America are divisible into three classes, — ordinary thunder-storms, tornadoes, and hurricanes: although all these classes of disturbances occur in other lands, they are more conspicuous and frequently presented in North America than elsewhere.

Thunder-storms in North America more commonly occur in the Mississippi Valley and on the Atlantic seaboard district. They are frequently of great violence, and are remarkable for the very numerous electric discharges which accompany them. Usually they are not complicated with the other classes of storms, but originate in the hot days of the year when there is no general disturbance of the atmosphere. Not infrequently, however, they attend the more serious accidents of the air which belong in the groups of tornadoes and hurricanes. Although violent, these thunder-storms appear to be not more destructive in North America than in Europe.

The group of atmospheric convulsions known as tornadoes are remarkable and almost peculiar features of the North American climate. These storms consist in violent upward-going whirlings of the atmosphere caused by the effort of the warm air next the ground to break through the colder part of that envelope which lies a few thousand feet above the surface of the earth. So great is the violence of this movement that heavy bodies, even those which weigh as much as a railway car, may be lifted from the earth. Bodies of cattle or of men may be carried to the height of hundreds of feet before they are cast again upon the surface. The strongest trees are frequently uprooted, and all but the most massive buildings, when they lie in the central path of the storm, are apt to be destroyed. Where they pass a pond or small lake, the up-rushing air in the whirl of the tornado will sometimes remove all the water from the basin.

Fortunately the destructive path of these storms is very narrow, rarely exceeding two thousand feet, and they often are only four or five hundred feet in width. In most cases the portion of their course in which the winds are strong enough to do much damage does not exceed twenty or thirty miles in length. These storms generally occur where other classes of atmospheric disturbances moving across the country push a quantity of cold air above a layer of warm which lies against the ground; this warm air being lighter than that which is above it, moves upward with a spinning motion much as the water whirls as it flows through the hole in the bottom of a wash-basin.

Tornadoes are most frequent and destructive in the parts of the Ohio Valley which lie north of that river, and in the territory adjacent to the upper Mississippi. They occasionally occur in Kentucky, Tennessee, in the northern portion of the Gulf States, and on the Atlantic shore-land district as far north as Massachusetts.

SCENERY OF NORTH AMERICA.

The aspect which any country presents to the eyes of men has much effect upon their minds. It is a well-known fact that mountaineers become more attached to the places in which they have dwelt than do the people of the plains. Even the sturdy Swiss, in the days when they were hired as mercenary soldiers to other countries in Europe, often died from homesickness when they were forced to dwell in lowland countries. The same was true of the mountaineers of the southern Appalachians during the late Civil War. It seems, indeed, to be a truth of importance that all countries of picturesque aspect have an educative value upon men who are bred in them, and even upon those who by journeys are able to behold their beauty.

As a whole, the continent of North America is very much less picturesque than the continent of Europe, whence our ancestors came, and this for the reason that a much smaller portion of its surface as compared with its area is occupied by high mountains. Moreover, the greatest mountainous region, that of the Cordilleras, the only one in which the elevations attain to anything like the heights they have in the Alps or Pyrenees, is very sterile, with few streams and lakes, and with hillsides which lack the associated forests and meadows which lend so much charm to the Alpine districts.

The wide fields of perpetual snow, with their dependent glaciers, are the most beautiful and ennobling features which mountains possess. These are lacking in North America, save in the coast ranges of the Cordilleras north of Oregon, and in the frozen deserts of Greenland. At only a few points in the Cordilleras which lie within the United States do small snow-fields remain through the arid summer.

While in Europe not more, perhaps, than one-third of the surface is away from the sight of high hills or mountains, more than two-thirds of North America presents to its dwellers the aspect of a slightly varied plain, in which the streams have cut but shallow valleys. Even within the Rocky Mountains, the peaks of which rise at the higher points to elevations about as great as the Alps afford, the general surface of the country is so elevated that the eye rarely perceives, except near the Pacific coast, a mountain slope which from base to summit has an altitude of more than four thousand feet; while in the Alps the observer, standing at the height of a thousand feet above the sea, may often behold the snowy crests rising to the height of twelve or thirteen thousand feet above his point of view.

The coast-line of North America is also less picturesque than that of Europe; and this for the reason that the higher mountains along its shores do not come so near the sea; except in parts of the Pacific coast north of San Francisco and in Greenland and Mexico, there are hardly any elevations which deserve the name of mountains which are visible from the ocean shore. Moreover, there are no volcanoes in North America so placed as to give the charming effects arising from their sterile but beautiful cones placed upon a luxuriant and cultivated shore, such as is afforded by the Bay of Naples and the coast-line near Mt. Etna.

For all these differences which exist between that most beautiful part of the world, the European continent, where our race was cradled, and the sterner fields of North America, we must not suppose that our own land is lacking in beauty, or, indeed, in majesty. Each of the continents has peculiarities of form, climate, or living inhabitants, which serve to make the impressions it affords the eye, though in themselves beautiful, somewhat different from those yielded by other countries. If the student has a true love of nature, and will train his eye and mind in the knowledge and understanding of the earth which is just about him, he will everywhere gain that sense of the majesty and beauty of his dwelling-place which is the best fruit of all the naturalist's labor. Although the dweller in the plain-land is deprived of the perpetual charm which every morning brings with the sight of the mountains, he may win for himself a nobler impression, one vastly more enlarging in every way, than any which the ignorant mountaineer can possibly receive, by gaining an adequate knowledge of the history which has led to the construction of the ground about him.

First among the natural attractions which the scenery of North America affords we may reckon the forests, which, as we have before noted, have a splendor unknown in other parts of the temperate zone. Each species of tree has its characteristic elements of beauty of form, foliage, or flowers. Whoever has learned to appreciate the grace and dignity of these trees has gained a liberal education in the beauties of nature. Where the forests are lacking, as in the prairie country, the lesser plants exist in great variety and afford blossoms of rare beauty. There are few sights in the world more charming than these flowery plains in the blossoming season.

The rivers of North America, owing to their great size, lend an element of dignity to many of its landscapes which is too little appreciated by our people. The lakes of this continent are very much more numerous than those of any other land, and they give a singular charm to the scenery of the districts, in all more than one-half of the continent, in which they occur. Even the deserts of the Cordilleran district, which extend from Central Mexico to near the northern limit of the United States, possess many most attractive features. They are diversified by mountains, and in their southern parts bear here and there a wonderful growth of the peculiar American plants belonging to the group of the cactus.

If the reader will but clear his mind of the prejudices as to what constitutes beauty in nature which have come to us from European literature and the pictures of the scenery in that country, and will seek a sympathetic understanding of the land which is about him, he will not lack opportunity for securing that sense of the loveliness of the world which is one of the best gifts of a true education.

WATERFALLS.

North America has numerous and interesting waterfalls which merit attention not only on account of their beauty and their value in the economic arts as sources of power, but also because they throw much light upon the geological history of the country. Waterfalls or rapids are formed wherever a river in its course encounters an obstruction which it cannot readily wear away by the cutting action of the stream. All flowing water tends to cut away the rocks over which it passes. In time, any river will wear down all the obstructions of its bed, so that it will flow with a gentle, continuous, though diminishing, current from its source to the sea.

When a mountain range is formed, the streams immediately set to work to bear it away, removing the rocks bit by bit to the sea. This work they also do, though more slowly, with the lower-lying rocks of the continental plains. Where the region has recently been elevated — recently in a geologic sense, though it may have been millions of years — above the sea, the streams usually occupy deep gorges and river-beds, and have a rapid fall. Gradually the main rivers and the tributary streams cut down their beds, and, swinging to and fro, carry away the highlands on either side: all the while the underground water is dissolving out the substance of the rocks which are not touched by the streams; thus in time, if the country does not continue to rise, the

NIAGARA FALLS.

surface is brought down to near the level of the sea. Waterfalls are formed wherever a portion of the rock over which the stream flows is peculiarly resisting to this down-cutting action. The circumstances which may bring about the formation of such falls are numerous and interesting. The most common cause of these sudden interruptions in the uniform flow of the stream is well represented in the Falls of Niagara. There the great river which drains the upper lakes, Erie, Huron, Michigan, and Superior, flows over bedded limestones and shales which dip up the stream. The hard, compact layers of the Niagara limestone are but little worn by the clear water which courses over them. They give way only as the soft shales below them are cut out by the whirling waters at the base of the fall; the limestone blocks left without support then tumble in ruins into the gorge. In this way the face of the fall is continually working up stream at a rate so rapid that it has been estimated that only about seven thousand years have elapsed since the cataract was at the mouth of the gorge near Queenstown.

Although this is the commonest type of great falls, other interesting cataracts and rapids are formed in other ways. Thus at Louisville, Ky., the Ohio River passes over a great coral reef formed in the corniferous epoch of the Devonian age. This reef, some miles in width, and fifty feet or more in thickness, by the entangled mass of coral branches and the great amount of lime which the broken-up corals and shells have contributed to the rock, makes a hard mass which the water cannot cut away as rapidly as it does the softer materials, and so it forms a series of rapids which in low-water stages of the stream are impassable for boats. A canal enables voyagers to avoid the difficulties of the main stream.

Many waterfalls are formed where a stream passes over dykes or veins which cause a local hardness of the rocks; but these have generally the shape of rapids or cataracts, the water falling from step to step over the obstruction. Again, in mountainous countries, the torrents gathered near the summits of the peaks often pass from these high levels into the valleys cut by the rivers in a very steep descent. These rivers, because their volume is great and their streams very permanent as well as muddy, often excavate deep valleys with steep walls, while the small, clear water-rills of the uplands, which are generally dry for a part of the year, cannot cut their channels downward in such a rapid manner. The sudden descent of rivers in rapids and steeper waterfalls is often of great economic advantage. At such points the water can be led from the top of the fall to water-wheels at its base, and be made to give power to mills. The great number of these falls in North America affords not the least of its commercial advantages.

CAÑONS.

A conspicuous feature in the surface of North America is found in the deep gorges carved by the rivers in the rocks of certain parts of the country. Those profoundly excavated defiles are found in all the continents, but they are more abundant in North America than in any other. They are particularly characteristic of the southern portion of the Rocky Mountain district, but occur in nearly every part of that vast elevated country. The Spanish applied to these deep ravines the name of cañon,— a term which has been adopted into our own language. In such valleys we do not find the surface of the country sloping gently to the river-banks, as is the case in most valleys, but the water-way has perpendicular walls.

The gorge of the Colorado is the most wonderful of these cañons, and far exceeds in its proportions any similar defiles in the world. It traverses the great table-land of the Colorado plateau, where the rocks, though lifted to a great height above the sea, have been but little affected by mountain-building dislocations. The summit of this elevated country lies at the height of from five to seven thousand feet above the sea, and has hardly any distinct slope towards the precipices which border the stream. Through this field of elevated yet prevailingly horizontal rocks the river has carved a narrow gorge having a length of several hundred miles, and at places a depth of five thousand feet. So steep are the cliffs which border the river that it is only here and there possible to clamber down the escarpment to the border of the stream. The history of this marvellous gorge seems to be as follows : the Colorado River is an ancient stream which came into existence in an early age, and has been since that time continually wearing down its bed. The river heads on the lofty peaks of the main ridge of the Rocky Mountains above. Owing to the height of the country a good deal of moisture which passes from the Pacific Ocean over the Colorado plateau is thrown down as rain or snow, and through the channel of the river passes away across the nearly rainless region of that table-land. As it flows down its steep descent, this river constantly carves away the rocks, cutting its channel nearer and nearer to the sea-level. If the Colorado plateau had been a rainy country while this carving went on, the smaller tributary streams of the main channel would have worn down the neighboring district as fast as the bed of the principal river was deepened. We thus would have had a broad valley of the ordinary form occupying the place of this table-land and gorge. But the rainfall of this country has evidently been small in amount for many geological periods: there has thus been nothing to wear away the rocks in this part of the path of the stream, except where the river waters from the mountain region in the east has assailed them. We see by this example that cañons, in certain cases at least, perhaps in all, are due to the course of a considerable river through a region where the underlying rocks have been lifted to a considerable height above the sea, and where the local rainfall has long been slight in amount.

There are, besides the Colorado Cañon, many similar great river gorges in the same section of the Cordilleras: those of the upper Arkansas, the Platte, and the Yellowstone deserve mention. They all present like evidence going to show that they are due to the action of rivers which cut strongly on rocks which are not much worn by the elements except where the principal stream assails them. Other cañons occur in the eastern parts of the United States, but none which approach in magnitude or beauty the vast gorges of the Cordilleras.

CAVERNS.

Owing to the existence of very thick strata of pure limestone in many parts of North America, this continent abounds in extensive caverns: they are probably more plentiful within its area than in any other part of the world. They most frequently occur in the southern part of the Ohio Valley and in the portion of Virginia which lies between the Blue Ridge and the peaks of the Alleghany Mountains; but they exist in many parts of the country where massive limestones occur, and where the glacier of the last ice period did not cover the surface. Where this ice existed, it generally wore away the strata in which the caverns existed, and there has not been since then time enough for them to be remade. The greatest number of these caves are found in the central portion of Kentucky, where the beds of the limestones belonging to the sub-carboniferous period underlie a district several thousand square miles in area. The layers of this limestone are very thick single strata, often being twenty feet or more in depth without a partition, and the succession of these beds forms a deposit several hundred feet in thickness: they all lie horizontally as they were laid down on the old sea-floors when they were formed.

These cavern limestones owe their formation in a certain way to the growth on the ocean-bottom, at a great distance from the land, of very numerous animals which formed their skeletons or solid supports of lime which they gathered from the marine plants on which they fed. In large part these creatures were crinoids or "stone lilies," which are like star-fishes supported on tall stems of limestone. These stems were often two or three feet in height, and as the branched arms were also of lime, each of these animals in dying contributed a good handful of stony matter to the bottom of the sea. Growing in this way age after age, the beds, composed almost altogether of the hard parts of crinoids, corals, mollusks, etc., became in time very thick and massive. They contain hardly any sand or clay; often no more than two or three per cent of the mass is of other materials than decayed animal frames. In time these limestone beds were lifted above the sea; there the land-water, which lends itself to the destruction of rocks as effectively as the conditions of the sea-water aid their formation, began to attack these deposits and dissolve them away, returning the lime in the state of solution to the sea, to nourish living things again.

The rain-water excavates the caverns in the following manner: As the rocks are formed, they become jointed or divided into rude blocks by slight fissures extending in various directions through the beds. The most of these cracks run vertically through the strata; some of them are open enough to give passages through which the water may trickle from the surface to the depths of the rocks. The pure water as it falls from the clouds has only a slight power of dissolving limestone; but in passing through the soil it becomes charged with carbonic acid gas,—a chemical compound of one atom of carbon and two of oxygen (CO_2), which arises from the decay of vegetable and animal bodies in the earth. The water thereby becomes able to take a great deal of lime into solution, as sugar is dissolved in water. Passing through the rents of the strata, the rain-water dissolves the limestone, and thus enlarges the passage, until it no longer creeps along as it does at first, but finds room to move swiftly. It then cuts the rock by rubbing the fragments of hard stone against it, as well as by breaking it away. Where the water falls vertically down through the rifts, it makes tall, perpendicular parts of the cavern which are called "domes"; where it creeps along through the strata to the open rivers, it forms tortuous horizontal galleries.

On the surface of the earth of this and other similar cavernous districts the traveller notices the absence of the ordinary small valleys and their accompanying streams. In place of this familiar outline, the surface of the earth is covered by a multitude of shallow pits, from ten to twenty feet deep, and from a hundred feet to half a mile in width. At the bottom of each of these there is a hole which leads through a hard layer to one of the vertical shafts or domes of the caverns. These sink-holes gather all the rain-water and send it down into the chambers of the caves; in passing through these underground passages it enlarges their spaces, and finally escapes to the rivers and thence to the sea, bearing with it the limestone which it has dissolved from the rocks with which it comes in contact. As the surface of the country wears down, as it does at the rate of a few inches in each thousand years, the upper arches of the caves are constantly broken through. They fall in here and there, disclosing in places the underground cavern-making streams. Where a great length of the cavern arch is left, it is commonly called a natural tunnel; in Southwestern Virginia such a tunnel is used for the passage of a railway. Where there is only a small part of the arch left, it is termed a natural bridge. That of Rockbridge County, Va., is a good example of the remnant of a cavern roof, the greater part of which has fallen in.

Although the swift-running streams of the under-earth carve out large chambers, converting the once solid limestone into a mass resembling worm-eaten wood, the waters which trickle slowly through the narrow crevices of the rock and drop by drop find their way through the sides and roofs of the caverns deposit limestone in the spaces of the caverns. This is done in the following manner. Each drop of water as it passes through the rock takes up all the lime that it can hold. When it enters the open space of the cave, the water evaporates in the dry air, and leaves the lime in an icicle-shaped pendant called a stalactite. If there is more water than can evaporate on the pendent stalactite, a part of it falls to the floor and deposits its lime on an upward-growing mass called stalagmite. It often happens that the growth of these masses of lime is in time so great that the cavern becomes entirely closed by them. Thus, while swift-running water excavates the caverns, that which creeps in drop by drop serves to refill their spaces.

These caverns are occupied by many curious animals, which are generally related to those of the neighboring open air, but differ from them in certain interesting ways. They usually are without sight; sometimes their eyes seem still perfect, but have lost the power of seeing; again, as in the case of the blind fishes, the organ of vision has entirely disappeared, so that we cannot readily discover the place where the parts originally were. Other forms, like the cave crickets, have very long feelers, which aid them in guiding their way in the darkness. Near the mouths of the caves the bats find their winter quarters. When the frosty nights of the autumn begin, they fly into the caves, penetrating, it may be, a quarter of a mile from the mouth, and in the darkness hang themselves by their feet to the stalactites on the ceiling of the chambers; their bodies then become cool and lose all sensibility : they hang there as if dead until the warm days of spring come : then, though the atmosphere of the caves has not changed in temperature, — for it remains the same all the year, — the life suddenly comes back to their bodies, they shake themselves free, and fly forth again to the open air. Many of these bats die during their winter sleep, and their bodies falling to the floor afford food to the cavern rats, and to many insects : where they fall and are eaten, the clay covering of the cavern floor becomes very rich in nitrate of potash or saltpetre. During the war of 1812 several great caverns, particularly the Mammoth Cave, afforded large quantities of this material for the manufacture of gunpowder.

Where the conditions are most favorable for the formation of caverns, the whole under-earth becomes riddled by them. Thus within the limits of the cavern district of Kentucky the length of the galleries in the caves which could be traversed by man, if there were any way of getting to their chambers, is doubtless much greater than that of the roads upon the surface of the country. It often happens that in excavating a cellar or sinking a well the people find their way into a vast set of underground chambers. Owing to the fact that the sink-hole openings are generally very small, and that the underground streams discharge through small openings on the banks of the rivers, it is always difficult to enter these caves. The greater part of those which have been discovered have entrances made by the falling in of the roof of some gallery which has not become filled with stalactitic material. Thus this vast subterranean world is curiously hidden from the inquiring eye.

DEAD SEAS.

Among the inland waters of North America must be reckoned the singular basins where the rivers are poured into a depression which they never fill, the water going away, not as is usual with lakes through a river to the sea, but through evaporation into the air. Such lakes only occur where there is a certain amount of rainfall in certain times of the year, followed by other seasons of excessive drought, when the air is greedy of moisture. Lakes of this nature are saline, and generally so excessively salt that because of it no living things can dwell in their waters. They occur only in the most arid parts of the world, in regions where no crops can be cultivated except by means of irrigation. They are common in Central and Western Asia, where, indeed, they are larger and more numerous than in any other country. They also are found in Southern Africa, in Australia, and parts of Northern Africa; indeed, they exist in all the continents except Europe. They indicate dry but not the dryest climates; where the rainfall is very small, no lakes whatever will be formed.

In North America these salt lakes or dead seas are limited to the central portion of the Cordilleran system, from the northern part of Mexico to the line between the United States and Canada. Of these, the most important are the Lago di Cayman in Mexico and Utah Lake — the latter being the northernmost of these dead seas. Between these two great basins there are hundreds of smaller salt-water lakelets and pools, some of considerable size, but mostly pools having only a few square miles of area. Altogether they do not include anything like the area of the Caspian Sea or the Sea of Aral.

The saltness of these lakes without outlets is easily accounted for. The rivers which flow into them carry in their waters certain small amounts of various substances which serve to give the salt taste to the ocean waters. As the water dries away into the air, it leaves these saline matters in the basin. In course of time the quantity of these materials becomes greater than the water of the lake can contain, and they begin to fall upon the bottom of the basin. If this process is long continued, the bed of the dead sea becomes deeply covered with the salts. The accumulations may indeed attain a depth of many hundred feet. The artificial process by which this salt is made closely follows the natural method which we find in these lakes formed in arid countries. The sea-water, which owes its saline character to the salts which the rivers bring to it, is evaporated by the salt-makers in pools shut off from the sea, or is boiled away in pans, and so the salt is caused to fall upon the bottom as it does upon the floor of the dead sea.

We may here note the fact that all the dead seas of the Rocky Mountain district which have been carefully studied by geologists are known to have been once living lakes pouring forth by outlets to the sea. They all show beaches at higher altitudes than their present shores, and the highest of these beaches is at the level where their waters discharged by a river to the sea. It is thus plain that they were recently fresh-water lakes, which were fed by a rainfall much greater than now comes to the country wherein they lie. During this rainier time, which probably coincided with the glacial period when ice-sheets covered a large part of the continent, the fresh-water lakes of the Cordilleras were of much greater area, perhaps twenty times as extensive as those salt-water basins now existing in the country. The dead seas are in fact only the trifling remnants of the ancient lake areas of this part of the continent.

CONTINENTAL SHELF.

Around the coast-line of each of the continents there is beneath the level of the sea next the shore a mass of debris, sand, clay, and pebbles, worn from the land by the waves or delivered to the ocean by the rivers, which is called the continental shelf. The width of this shelf depends upon the amount of matter which has been rent from the land and delivered to the sea since the land district against which it lies was lifted to its existing level. If the land has been long in its present position, and the waves and streams have worn away much of the earth and rocks and laid the waste down under water, the shelf may extend a hundred miles or more from the shore; if the portion of the continent next the shore has recently been lifted from the sea, the part of the shelf which remains submerged may be relatively small. It commonly happens that this continental shelf in course of ages is upraised above the level of the ocean waters, and forms dry land. Thus in the southern part of the United States, the lowland region of Western Virginia, the Carolinas, Georgia, Alabama, Mississippi, Louisiana, and Texas is a part of a recently elevated shelf of this nature. In time, these regions of plain become wrinkled into mountains or elevated into table-lands: the greater part of the existing continents have been formed in this manner, first as plains beneath the sea, and then lifted into the air to be folded into ridges and to furnish waste to the ocean floor.

This continental shelf is best developed along the Atlantic coast from Labrador to the southern part of the Gulf of Mexico. If the continent should be raised to the amount of four hundred feet, or the sea be lowered by that measure, this shelf would appear as a wide plain-land district, extending from the shore for a great distance towards the deep sea. At Newfoundland it is nearly three hundred miles wide, and is here known as "The Banks." Along the Atlantic face of the United States it is on the average about one hundred miles wide. It narrows near the southern end of Florida, but widens again along the shores of the Gulf of Mexico, where it is as marked as it is along the Atlantic coast. At its outer edge the bottom slopes steeply to the depths of the sea. It is this shelf which affords the feeding-ground of the schools of fishes which abound on the Atlantic coast. In the future geological ages it will probably be elevated above the sea and form a part of the continent.

Although some of the rocky matter which composes this shelf has been brought into the sea by the action of the rivers, the larger part probably has come there by the work of the waves and tides which beat against the shore and bear the waste of the rocks out to sea. During the last glacial period, the ice moving slowly over the land bore off from it a great mass of detritus, which it deposited on the sea-bottom near the shore ; this debris has been distributed by the waves and marine currents, adding much to the mass of this shelf, and widening it from the mouth of the Hudson River northward. In the region about the Gulf of Mexico, wherever coral reefs abound, they furnish a great deal of limy matter, which, unless swept away by strong currents to the deep sea, is added to the mass of this shelf.

If we examine the country near the shore-line of the eastern part of North America, we find that there are at various levels, up to some hundred feet above the present shore, old sea-beaches, each of which marks the presence of the sea at a higher level against the land than it now occupies. Working in former ages at these different heights, the sea has cut away a great part of the margin, and has conveyed the material, so far as it was not dissolved in the water, out upon the continental shelf. Wherever we find this shelf, we may be sure that the land has been greatly worn away to furnish materials for its formation.

CORAL REEFS.

Throughout its geologic history North America has frequently been a field where coral reefs have been extensively developed. Such reefs form where a strong current of pure water from the open seas, which has been warmed under a tropical sun, is poured in against the land. In the earlier ages these reefs were formed much beyond the tropics. In the lower Silurian they were made in the shallow water between Cincinnati and Nashville; in the upper Silurian in central New York; in the Devonian about Louisville, Ky., and again in New York. In modern times they are only occasionally found beyond the tropics, and nowhere else do they attain such a development in comparatively high latitudes as on or near the eastern coast of North America.

All the modern coral reefs of North America have been formed under the favoring influence of the Gulf Stream. This great tide of warm water is heated in the tropical districts between Africa and South America, and flows from that part of the sea against the eastern shore of the last-named continent. Diverted from its western course by the opposing land, the larger part of this stream turns towards the North Atlantic. A portion of it drifts into the Caribbean through the spaces between the islands of the Lesser Antilles; another part of it, unable to find passage through those narrow water-ways, passes around to the north and east of the West Indies. The part of the current which enters the Caribbean sweeps to the westward across that sea, and thence to the northward into the Gulf of Mexico, from which it emerges in the mighty river of the sea known as the Gulf Stream. The portion of the warm waters which flows to the north of the West Indies passes by the Bahamas, and finally mingles its currents with those of the Gulf Stream in its slow-moving mass of warm water which flows toward the polar region.

Wherever these warm waters in any considerable amount strike against the shore, or upon shallow places of the sea having a depth of only about a hundred feet below the surface, they favor the growth of those species of polyps which, from the swiftness of their development and the form of the colonies or communities in which they grow, build up great masses of limestone termed coral reefs. Where the tropical waters flow against South America, they make a great series of these reefs. Again, where they touch the islands between which they pass in entering the Caribbean, they produce yet another series of these structures. But the most remarkable of all these vast monuments constructed by the frail polyps are those which are found in the reefs of Florida and the Bahamas, which lie on the east and west of the channel through which the stream from the Gulf of Mexico pours into the North Atlantic. To this stream we owe the growth on the southern margin of Florida of several successive reefs, built one after another from the north southwardly, which have formed the southern part of that peninsula. To the Gulf Stream, properly so called, and to the current which flows north and east of the West Indies, may be attributed the remarkable growth of reefs which constitute the Bahamas. To the life-giving influence of these two streams in their farther northward course is due the growth of the coral reefs of Bermuda, which lies in the open sea about five hundred miles to the east of Cape Hatteras, being much the farthest towards the pole of any known coral island formed during the present day.

These coral islands and reefs have had an important influence on the geography of the shores, and probably much effect on the growth of the lands and seas of the North Atlantic region. They have constructed a good deal of the low-lying land about the Gulf of Mexico, and by controlling the flow of water where the ocean streams pass into the North Atlantic, they have perhaps affected the temperatures in and about the northern portion of that sea.

CHAPTER IV.

THE ABORIGINAL PEOPLES OF NORTH AMERICA.

Origin of American Indians. Their habits. The Mound-builders. Cause of the failure of the Indians to attain a civilized state due to open nature of the country. Capacity and character of the Indians. Effect of these native people on the whites.

It is not certain when or whence the first human beings came to the continent of North America. It seems clear, however, that man did not originate on this continent, but came to it from the Old World. It is much the most likely that the first settlers were from Asia, and that they found their way from the region north of China along the archipelago of the Alaskan islands, and thence down the western coast into the body of the continent. It is possible, however, that the Esquimaux tribes may have found their way to North America across the waters of the Northern Atlantic; but as that part of the sea is wide and very stormy, and as neither the Esquimaux nor the red Indians had boats fit for long voyages, it is, on the whole, most reasonable to suppose that they all came by way of the Aleutian Archipelago, the islands of which lead like stepping stones across the sea, or else by way of Behring Strait, which narrows until the shores of Asia and America are only about fifty miles apart.

The time when the first human beings came to this continent is also lost in darkness. Neither Indians nor

Esquimaux have any traditions as to the place of their origin, and being a people without alphabets, there is no chance for written history among them. Some students are of the opinion that the ancestors of our native savages were on the eastern part of the continent as far back as the glacial period. Although several inconclusive facts point to the conclusion that there may have been people on this land in that remote age, the only certain evidences which we find of human occcupation are of very much later date. So far as trustworthy observations are found, there is no evidence of the presence of human beings on the eastern side of this continent more than two or three thousand years ago. We must esteem it probable that in the time when Egypt was occupied by peoples who had attained to a very considerable advance in civilization which enabled them to build great monuments and engrave their history upon them, the greater part of the American land was untrodden by man.

On the Pacific coast, in the region now occupied by the state of California, there is what appears to be good evidence showing the presence of man in a very much earlier time than is indicated by any satisfactory evidence from the region east of the Rocky Mountains. In that portion of the country, in a time which appears to be at least as ancient as the glacial period, there were many very great outbreaks of volcanic nature. Vast streams of lava flowed down the valleys, filling the places occupied by the rivers sometimes to the very brim. When these lavas had cooled, the rivers began to flow again, but found it easier to cut new streamlets on either side of the compact lava than to remove the stone from their old pathways. The result is that in many places the original site of the streams is left with a river on either side, forming a "divide" or watershed between the two streams. Now it happens that the beds of these old rivers when covered by the lava held, as those of the present do, considerable quantities of gold in the form of grains and nuggets which had been caught between the bowlders or other irregularities of the bottom.

When gold mining was begun in California it was soon discovered that these old high-lying river-beds could profitably be worked for the precious metal they contained. Galleries were run from the hillsides into the level of the channels, and the gravel was carried out and washed so as to separate the precious material from the earthy matter. In doing this peculiar mining a number of stones shaped to serve the simple purposes of hatchets and hammers, or tools for pounding corn, have been discovered, and also one well-preserved specimen of a human skull. These remains show clearly that man has been upon the Pacific slope of the continent for a period far outrunning the term of written history, for a time which doubtless extends much farther back than the remains so commonly found in Egypt, and this for the reason that it has required probably not less than from twenty thousand to thirty thousand years for the streams to cut down on either side of their old bed to such a depth below their original position. The fact that men existed in so early a day in the region about the Pacific coast, while we have no good evidence of their presence on the eastern portion of North America for anything like as long a time, makes it seem the more probable that the settlement of the continent was from Asia, and that long ages elapsed before the settlers passed through the difficult country of the Rocky Mountains and reached the Mississippi Valley and the portions of the continent bordering on the Atlantic Ocean.

Except in the case of the Esquimaux, who are evidently a peculiar folk, the Indian natives of both North and South America exhibit a great likeness in their form and general characteristics. We find no such striking differences as occur among the various peoples of Asia, in the form and color of their body; in a general way in their manners and customs they are more nearly akin than the diverse peoples on any of the Old World group of continents. They occupied the surface of both continents from the Arctic to the Antarctic circles with a kindred life. No part of this great population had ever attained to an economic organization which deserves the name of civilization, for none of them had invented a written language or formed a highly organized political system. Certain portions of these peoples, however, those dwelling in the country from northern Arizona southward along the Cordilleras to the southern portion of Peru, had advanced beyond the savagery of the other tribes. They had almost entirely abandoned the occupations of the chase and supported themselves by agriculture. They had learned to build structures of unburnt brick and stone, and had attained a considerable skill in many other arts. They had, however, never learned to work iron, and probably did not know how to make bronze. Their weapons and tools were of stone or copper, which they apparently did not know how to smelt. Except among the Peruvians they appear to have had no beasts of burden except the dog, and no domesticated animals which could afford them food. The Peruvians alone had tamed the llama and alpaca, which afforded food and wool, and served as beasts of burden. The people of Central America, of Mexico, and of all the northern parts of the continent were without any resources such as domesticated animals other than their dogs could afford.

Deprived of the resources which the men of the Old World obtained from their domesticated animals, the agriculture was of the simplest description, and the food of the people of a very unvaried character. Ignorant of writing, no system of laws and no literature worthy of the name could exist. All knowledge was a matter of tradition, and in this state of culture no great intellectual advance is possible. Thus, though through the fabulous stories of the early Spaniards, it came to be believed that the Mexican and Peruvian peoples formed great states, we now know by more accurate inquiries that they had made but few steps in the path towards civilization beyond that attained by our ordinary red Indians.

Among the tribes outside of the portion of the Cordilleras above described the native population appears to have everywhere existed in the condition of savagery or the lowest state of barbarism. Each tribe generally consisted of a body numbering from a few hundred to a few thousand individuals, who held together somewhat in the relation of a great family. The government rested upon adhesion to a chief. This chieftain was commonly selected by the consent of the women in his clan. In few, if any, tribes was the office hereditary; but it was in most cases required that the leader should be a man of physical power and of intelligence. Often the war chief was specially and temporarily chosen for a particular campaign. Commonly each of these tribes occupied for a greater or less time a certain space of country; but as they were in a state of frequent warfare with their neighbors, as is usually the case with savages, they not infrequently drove out the neighboring tribes and possessed their land, or were themselves driven to other parts of the country.

Some of these tribes, which by one chance and another had remained for a considerable period in one district, effected a certain amount of union with their neighbors, and gained strength thereby. Thus the Iroquois, or Five Nations, who occupied the western part of New York, a position in which they were in a measure protected from incursions of other peoples, formed what was perhaps the strongest and most enlightened savage state in this country north of Mexico, and gained much strength from their union. Yet other tribes, such as the Shawnees, were nomads driven about by constant battle. They ranged from South Carolina to Pennsylvania, from near the Atlantic coast to the banks of the Mississippi. In general, we may say that the Indians east of the Mississippi were always more settled, and were more given to agriculture than those to the west of that stream. They subsisted, to a certain measure, on the products of their fields, in which they tilled Indian corn, pumpkins, and tobacco. After the first whites came to this country, many of them acquired other domesticated plants.

Although the Indians cultivated the land in a rude way, they did not plough the ground, but planted their crops in patches of soil, which they had rudely tilled with stone implements. Nor did they ever attain to the state of civilization where the land was owned by individual men, but it remained in all cases the property of the tribe. In some cases, though seldom, they built rude,

ZUNI VILLAGE.

unfloored houses of timber, which provided sufficient shelter, but they generally dwelt in log cabins, tents, or lodges made by setting poles in the ground and covering them with mats and the skins of animals. Their only considerable arts were those of pottery-making and of rude embroidery.

There are many evidences going to show that on the whole the Indians of the Mississippi Valley were rather more domesticated some centuries before the whites came to this region than when the country was first settled by Europeans. Over a large portion of that great valley we find, here and there, large earthen mounds, sometimes of gigantic dimensions, commonly in the form of conical heaps, but frequently in the shape of serpents, birds, and larger animals. These earthworks appear to have been in some way connected with their forms of worship. Many of the mounds were probably designed to commemorate the place of burial of their distinguished men. Besides these monumental works there are numerous fortifications which often inclose large areas, and are constructed with considerable skill for the purposes of defence. Although the habit of building conical mounds in their villages survived among certain of the tribes after they were visited by the Europeans, the *image* mounds — those delineating the forms of the various animals — had ceased to be built before the land was known by the people of the Old World.

It appears likely that the social condition of this people underwent a certain degradation, brought about by the eastward extension of the buffalo. After these savages had dwelt upon the land for ages, and had, in a measure, exhausted the game and been driven to the soil for their support, the buffalo appears to have extended its range from the far west towards the Mississippi River. The nomadic savages of that part of the continent had the habit of setting fire to the prairie grass in the dry season. The flames swept into the eastern forests, destroying large portions of their area, thus bringing the open or prairie land further to the east, and affording a better pasturage to the large beasts which occupied it. As the more eastern Indians, who had been but a short time accustomed to agriculture, had the chance once again to obtain food in plenty by hunting, they again became to a considerable extent nomadic, and abandoned, in a measure, the habit of trusting to the soil, and so lost a part of the slight civilization to which they had attained.

There are many reasons for believing that the Indian of North America is an abler man than we should judge from the rude manner of his life. The greater men — such as the chieftain Brant, the Shawnee Prophet, Pontiac, and many other famous Indians — have shown that oratorical ability, generalship, and other qualities which are found only in men of power, not infrequently exist along with the brutal traits of savages. It is true that our literature abounds in records of atrocities which they committed during their wars. We should bear in mind, however, that such cruelty was common among our own ancestors a few thousand years ago; and against these evil deeds we must set the many well-attested cases of kind treatment on the part of the Indians towards strangers in distress; and also the fact, that while they occasionally tortured their prisoners, they yet more commonly adopted them into their families, and gave them the privileges of the tribe; and these people thus adopted into the tribe often became, in the course of a short time, so attached to their savage comrades that they could not be induced to leave them.

It is also clear that the Indian was not deficient in inventive power. The implements of war and peace compared favorably with those used by the early peoples of the Old World whence we ourselves have come. In the last century a half-breed Indian of the Cherokee race, Sequoia, accomplished the remarkable feat of inventing, altogether by himself, a means of writing his own language. This art he taught to the young men of his tribe, and so created at once a method of recording thought such as it required thousands of years for the peoples of the Old World to attain to. If we suppose, as the facts justify us in doing, that the Indian was not kept in his low position by lack of ability, how can we account for his condition, for his failure to gain a firm foothold on civilization in the many centuries during which he occupied this country?

It seems likely that the failure of the Indian to attain much advance in his economic condition was due mainly to the fact that he dwelt in a very open land, unlike the peoples of Asia and Europe, who were nurtured in districts more or less completely shut off from the other parts of the world by decided barriers. The only extensive isolated districts of North America lie so far to the north that their lands are sterile. The mountain valleys, which are sufficiently walled about to make them safe refuges, are usually in over-dry regions, unfit for agriculture. The islands of the Antilles are in the tropical districts, where the climate is unfavorable for human advance. The greater portion of North America, about all, indeed, of its fertile land, lies in one great area, which is easily moved over in every direction by savage peoples. It appears in the Old World that all the folk who succeeded in passing from savagery to civilization, secured their advance by occupying some limited field where, by reason of mountain ranges or broad spaces of sea, they were safe from the incursion of savage neighbors, and were thus able through centuries to accomplish a great deal of progress in the development of the arts, which is impossible without the seclusion and safety which comes from such isolation. If in North America any tribe advanced somewhat in culture, and came to have a certain amount of wealth, they were in immediate danger of being plundered by their more warlike and needy neighbors. Thus the character of the surface of North America did not favor the development of civilization.

A yet more important influence is found in the absence in North America of animals which can be domesticated and turned to human use. This continent had no wild cattle or horses, no tamable variety of sheep, no pigs or goats, no elephants or camels. The only creatures capable of domestication were the llama and alpaca, which were used by the Peruvians. These are small animals unfit to draw the plough. They afford only wool, meat, and a little service as pack-animals. It is probable that this absence of domesticable beasts was the most serious hindrance to the advance of our savages beyond the condition to which they had attained when Europeans came to the country. It is likely that if Asia and Europe had been without these animals which have served man so well, our own civilization would not have gone very much further than that of the savages whom our race displaced on this continent. Something also must be allowed for the fact that our Indians never had the good fortune to learn how to extract metals from their ores. No considerable advance in the arts is possible without this art. It is a noteworthy fact that our savages never learned the art of boat-building. Their only vessels were pirogues and bark canoes; the former consisted of large logs hollowed out by the use of fire, which served to burn the wood, and stone tools which scraped away the charcoal after each application of fire. Such vessels can never have considerable size, or be in any degree safe in open water. The bark canoe, the other form of boat, is also limited to the size of a single tree, and is scarcely more seaworthy than the pirogue or dug-out. The art of ship-building requires at least the use of metal axes and other tools. It can indeed attain no considerable development until something like the saw enables the men to shape timber to their needs. Thus the American savages, through their ignorance of the use of metals, were debarred from an extended maritime life.

The fact that the low grade of our American Indians was in part due to the open nature of the country is shown by the condition of the regions in which, as in Peru, Central America, and Mexico, these Indians had gone further toward civilization. These are the parts of the continent where the occupants of the ground are tolerably well sheltered from the incursion of less advanced peoples about them. Even in Mexico, if we may trust their traditions, the somewhat cultivated people of that country were subject to very destructive incursions from tribes of wandering savages. So, too, the condition of the Peruvians, by far the most advanced towards civilization of any of our American Indians at the time when the whites came to the country, may be partly due to the fact that they had in the singular group of domesticated animals which they acquired some other resource than that afforded by the labor of their own hands. In a word, it seems likely that the social condition of our American Indians was to a great extent determined by the physical state of the district which they occupied. Our own race came to the country so provided with the arts of civilization that the lack of domesticated animals, the absence of barriers between one part of the region and the other, were of no very great consequence to us. The only risk of incursion was from the savages, and they were, through the superior arts of war of the Europeans, easily overcome. For nearly two centuries, however, our own folk felt something of the effect arising from the absence of strong geographic features in the country which might afford them some effective shelter against the savages. It was easy for a war-party of Indians to move many hundreds of miles through the tolerably open forests or the plain lands, which characterize so much of the continent, and to strike serious blows at many frontier settlements. Such forays were rarely possible in the conditions of the Old World, where the land was of old, as at present, divided by impassable forests and morasses, by mountain chains or arms of the sea.

It was fortunate for the European settlers in this country that the Indians, though brave and warlike, were subdivided into small tribes and so hostile one to the other that no effective resistance could be made by them to the scanty bands of Europeans who first came to these shores. Moreover, the arms used by the savages were of a rude and ineffective sort. The ordinary short bow and the rude stone hatchet were the chief weapons which they possessed. Although they used these valiantly, the weapons were very ineffective against firearms, and the armor in which the European soldiery encased themselves. So it was that the Spanish conquerors, though in none of their invasions had they more than a few hundred soldiers, were enabled to conquer the strongest and best organized portions of our American Indians who could bring many thousand brave but ill-armed men into the field. In no cases during the wars between the Indians and Europeans have the savages ever been able, however numerous, to make head against a thousand well-equipped and skilfully led white soldiers. In cases they have managed to defeat somewhat larger bodies of white troops, but all such successes were due to lack of skill in managing the civilized forces. If the savages had attained to a somewhat higher development, if they had even the skill in military matters of the African Zulus, they might have retained possession of the continent for centuries after its discovery by Columbus.

CHAPTER V.

NATURAL PRODUCTS AND RESOURCES OF NORTH AMERICA.

Natural conditions and resources. Value of climate, soil, and minerals to man: to the savage; to civilized man. Climate of the several great divisions of the continent. Share of the land fitted for human use. Soils of North America. Domesticated plants of the United States. Wild and domesticated animals. Mineral resources, metals, fruits, etc., of the several parts of the continent.

IN this chapter we shall consider the natural conditions and resources of the continent which affect the welfare of men. In such an inquiry we find it necessary to glance once again at the various physical features which have been set forth in the previous chapters. Of these the climate is the most important; next, the productions of the soil or those of the deeper-lying earth which are afforded by mines and quarries; and last, the relations of the country to other lands, which go to determine the ways of commerce with other parts of the world. The value of these features differs much at different stages of the development of a people.

In the earliest stage, when the folk are in the process of acquiring their natural characteristics, the climate, soil, and relations which their cradle land has to other countries are of the utmost importance. After a time, when these conditions have strongly impressed themselves on the character of the race, they may go forth to other lands, where they find very different conditions, and for centuries retain the qualities which the country of their infancy impressed upon them. Thus the Aryan people, who were raised from primitive savagery to a state of some civilization in the northern lands of Europe or Asia, most probably in the region about the Scandinavian peninsula, spread thence throughout Europe, Western and Southern Asia, mingling with other races, which they in time in good part displaced. This separation of the Aryan people was so complete that the different branches of that race lost all knowledge of their original kinship, which, indeed, has only been discovered in very modern times by a study of their languages, literatures, and customs. Although some of these branches settled in the tropics and others remained in their northern home, some became mainly seafarers, and others have dwelt in the central parts of the continents; although, in a word, they have gone to all the differences of condition which the world affords, all the branches of the race have certain common traits. They everywhere show a singular capacity for intellectual development, their religions are always ideal, their literature of a more finished order than those of other races; from them have come all the high civilizations except those of the Hebrews and the Arabs, who belong to the Semitic peoples. Greece, Rome, all modern Europe, and the present civilizations of the two Americas and Australia are of Aryan origin.

Thus when a people have certain definite characteristics impressed upon them in the cradle land, the region where their infancy was spent, they are likely to preserve these features long after they have been separated from their birthplace. Great as are the influences of these early conditions on the character of a people, they are in a measure affected by the country in which their lives are lived; gradually the nature about them determines their habits into new channels, and modifies their ways of thinking and acting. The fishermen of Newfoundland or Iceland, depending on the sea for their subsistence, are very different men from the merchants of New York or New Orleans, or the prosperous farmers of the Northwestern states; for the good reason that a man's work shapes his qualities, the nature of the earth about him, which determines his work, gives character to his thought, and is in turn reflected in all his ways of living. The effect may not at first be plain, for the habits of our forefathers dwell long with us, but in the course of a few generations men become greatly influenced by the world immediately about them. Therefore, if we would have a good idea of the effect of living in the various parts of this continent on the men who are to inhabit it in the time to come, we must consider the relations of the climate, soil, mineral resources, and general geography of these districts.

The climate of North America varies more widely than that of any other continent except Asia, and is not exceeded in range by that great continent. In respect to the climatal conditions, North America may be conveniently divided into four districts, each of which has certain portions of great importance to the welfare of men. These are the frozen north, the exceedingly arid region of the Cordilleras, the district of middle temperatures and rainfall, and the tropical country of the extreme south. All these districts differ from the countries of Europe and those of the greater part of the other continents in the fact that in North America the difference between winter and summer is greater than in those other lands. This is due to the large amount of land in the region near the north pole, which becomes covered with snow in winter and makes the winds from that direction excessively cold. A glance at the map shows how different are these conditions from those of all the other great continents except Asia. Taking the above-named districts in the order in which they are named we will proceed to consider in succession the character of their climates.

The frozen north includes all the district within and north of the Laurentian Mountains; viz. Labrador, the lands near Hudson's Bay, and the little known country to the northward of these districts. In general the region on the north polar side of the Great Lakes and the St. Lawrence, except the narrow strip of country overspread by the Canadian people, is desolated by cold. In the central part of the continent, including the valley of the Red River of the North and the Saskatchewan, and probably a small part of the country yet further to the north, the climate is so far bettered by the influence of the air blowing from the warm waters of the Pacific Ocean that the summers are long, moist, and hot enough to permit the tillage of the soil, and the production of certain kinds of grain and vegetables; always, however, with the risk that peculiar seasons may cause a failure of crops. On the west, in the highlands of the Cordilleras, north of the boundary of the United States, the elevation of the surface causes the cold to be greater, and so the fertile middle region of the British Dominion is walled in both on the east and west by countries sterilized by cold.

The frozen region of the continent includes about one-fourth of its surface, which is now and must ever be unfit for the more important uses of man; at least until some great change in the climatal conditions of the region is brought about. Within this great realm of cold the short, hot summer, with its long days and prevailing westerly winds, brings a brief period in which plants of varied kinds grow with great luxuriousness. For two or three months the vegetation flourishes almost as well as it does in tropical lands; but this respite from the cold is brief and precarious: north winds may at any time bring frosts, and at best the summer is not long enough for the development of the grains, fruits, and roots on which man and his domesticated animals depend for food. Throughout a large part of this region the earth at a depth of a few feet below the surface remains locked in frost throughout the year. The summer warmth melts the water in only the upper part of the soil, the rest remains frozen.

The greater part of this extensive north land is covered by scanty forests and wide fields of upland swamps. The woods are so low and the trees have such small and short trunks that they are worthless for timber. The only resources of value to men are to be found in the mineral stores of the rocks and the fishes of the lakes and neighboring seas. What is known of the geology does not give much promise that this land has sufficient mineral wealth to tempt miners to brave its inhospitable climate. Coal, which might help to make the land inhabitable, is probably of rare occurrence; iron and the precious metals are probably found in many places, but not well situated for working. It is thought that petroleum may be obtained in the valley of the Mackenzie River, but until the vast supplies in the rocks of more southern countries are exhausted it will have no value for exportation.

The fisheries of the seas which border the northeastern part of the continent are valuable, but they are now resorted to by sailors from the central parts of the country, who return home with their harvest and only make at most temporary settlements on the shore. It thus seems certain that this part of North America has little promise as a dwelling-place for our race. It will probably remain for hundreds of years a vast desert, a wider and more useless realm for civilized man than any other part of the earth. Even the Desert of Sahara has its oases; the very cold country of Siberia can in parts have crops of grain, and has much mineral wealth; and the central part of Australia, though now a desert, lacks only water to make it fertile; and this may be in part at least won to man's use by artificial means, by storing that which can be obtained in time of rain to be used in the season of drought : but this region desolated by cold is not to be bettered by human skill. The only use which it can have will be for a great natural park whereto, when the more southern parts of the continent are crowded with a dense population, the people may resort for the recreation which the wilderness affords. For this use it is admirably suited, its summer climate is stimulating and delightful, its scenery charming; even in winter the face of nature has a splendor from its unbroken snowfields and the surprising beauty of the recurring periods of the Aurora Borealis, which wrap the skies in a dress of fire.

Besides the desert of the high north, there is another portion of the continent which is in a certain way unfit for the best uses of man. This is the dry land of the Cordillera district. From southern Mexico to the northern part of the United States, and from the one hundredth meridian west to central California and Oregon, the land is so high and so separated from the sea-winds that the rainfall is very scanty, not averaging more than about a foot in the year, and coming to the earth mostly in the winter season, when it cannot serve the need of plants. This region, made sterile by drought, merges on the north into the frozen part of the continent, so that in a portion of the area the dryness combines with a low temperature to make the land a desert.

The arid desert district covers about one-fifth of the continent. In this region crops may in wet summers be with profit tilled on much of the surface, but the rainfall is so limited that agriculture is uncertain except where the scanty streams are led upon the ground in ditches, or where the water is stored in reservoirs for use in the summer season. Although, as in other countries of high mountains, a great part of this district is too rocky for tillage, the larger part of its surface has a deep soil which in the main was formed in times when the rainfall was more abundant than at present. As little grows upon this earth, it contains a great deal of nutriment for plants, and is, when well watered, exceedingly fertile. It is reckoned by Major Powell, director of the United States Geological Survey, that by storing the water from the winter rains in the valleys above the head-waters of the rivers, it will be possible to irrigate about 50,000 square miles of this desert land, a field considerably greater than the state of Illinois. On account of the natural fertility of the soil, it seems likely that from this barren district engineers may win to the uses of man fields having the food-giving value of all the land within the valley of the Ohio River. It is not unlikely that within a century these artificially watered districts of the great desert region of North America may support a population of twenty or thirty millions.

Although the climate of this arid district is very dry, it is very wholesome for man and his domesticated animals. The clear sunlight and upland air secure it against many diseases which overrun the lower-lying countries. It will probably develop a race of hardy mountain people, as Switzerland has done in the country of the Alps. The dry region of the Cordilleras can only give a small part of its surface to tillage, and this at much cost in labor. The crops, except at certain points, are too far from the sea-shore to enter into commerce. They will only serve for the use of the people who dwell on the ground. Scanty as are the agricultural resources of this great district, beneath the soil there is a great variety of wealth-giving minerals; no other equal portion of the earth's surface has ever yielded so large and so varied a contribution of mineral products. The precious metals, gold, silver, and platinum, are extensively mined; the base metals, even more precious to the arts, iron, copper, and zinc, and many other important substances, abound in many parts of the field; the heat-giving materials, coal, natural gas, and petroleum, exist in considerable quantities; and many earthly substances, such as natural or earth wax, soda, salt, etc., are more plentiful than in any other considerable part of the world. It seems certain that the mountainous portion of the great arid land of North America will in the next century be the greatest field of the world for mining industries. The fact that by irrigation the soil can be made to supply the people engaged in seeking this underground wealth, secures a great future to its population, for they will thus obtain cheap and varied food.

Although, as we have just seen, nearly one-half of North America is not well conditioned for man's use, it must not be supposed that this continent is as a whole a less favorable place for human development than the other great lands of the earth. The fact is that, excepting Europe, the continent is really better fitted to serve the needs of man than any other of the continental masses. Europe, owing to the fact that it has not the true continental form, but is a mere group of peninsulas and islands attached to the western coast of Asia, is exempt from exceeding cold or drought, — the two desert-making elements of climate. As a whole the Asiatic land mass is, in proportion to the area, even less fitted for the uses of civilized man than North America; for the northern part of the continent is subject to the same polar conditions which sterilize high latitudes of North America and the whole of the central parts of the continent are subject to continued drought.

Africa is so placed as to escape the effects of cold, but nearly the whole of the northern part of that continent is made desert by drought. In Australia at least three-fourths of the land so far lacks rain in the growing season that it is untillable. South America has its southern portion in Patagonia so near to the south pole that it is by the cold rendered unfit for man's uses, and in the western portion, where the Cordilleras of South America rise to great altitudes, a combination of cold and drought desolates a considerable part of the area. The valleys of the great rivers of the Orinoco, Amazon, La Plata, contain exceedingly fertile land, but the greater portion of this region is within the realms of tropical heat and affords conditions of climate which have never been found favorable for the life of our race or for that of any other people capable of making a high civilization. When we carefully look over the lands of the earth, we come to the conclusion that not more than one-half of that surface is really fit for the uses of the Aryan race; the remainder must remain unoccupied by man, or at most peopled by savage or barbarian tribes. Thus though North America has a great part of its surface in the condition of what we must call deserts, it is not in this regard in worse condition than the other continents.

North America has for our own people the great advantage that its well-watered lands are almost altogether within the region of the middle temperatures, — those states of heat and cold which permit the vigorous development of the peoples who came from northern Europe. Except a small area extending from the Rio Grande and the Colorado south to the isthmus and a small portion of Southern Florida, no part of the continent is subjected to the evils of a tropical climate; even the portions of Southern Mexico and Central America which lie within the region of the true tropics have a large part of the surface so elevated above the sea that the climate is more tolerable to our race than is generally the case with lands near the equator. Not more than about one-twentieth of the mainland of the continent is so far affected by the equatorial heat as to be decidedly unsuited for the uses of our race. If we include the West Indian islands in the lands of North America, the proportion of tropical realm would be somewhat extended; but a large part of these islands, like the tropical portions of the mainland, are elevated to such heights above the sea that they afford tolerable climates for men of our race.

From the Laurentian Mountains southward to the Gulf and westward to the one hundredth meridian we have a great field of land, of remarkably good, fertile quality, which possesses a climate which two centuries of experience has shown to be singularly well fitted for the home of people who are the descendants of Northern Europeans. West of the Cordilleras, along the Pacific coast from the northern line of Mexico to the southern portion of Alaska, is another section of continent, relatively small in area, amounting to not more than one-twentieth of the eastern fertile section, which also is admirably suited to the needs of our people. These two districts together contain about two-fifths of the continental area. In the Cordilleran district from Southern Mexico to the southern part of British Columbia we have, as before remarked, numerous areas of land capable, with engineering skill, of serving the needs of man. This region of detached fertile grounds will probably have a great value in the centuries to come; but it is not by nature alone suited to the uses of man, for it demands engineering skill to fit it for such purposes.

The eastern fertile section of North America, that extending between the one hundredth meridian and the Atlantic coast, from the Gulf of Mexico to the indistinctly determined line where the work of man is arrested by the northern cold, is divided into several tolerably distinct regions, each characterized by certain peculiarities of climate or soil or under-earth resources. The greater part of the field lies within the valley of the Mississippi or in the basins of the streams which flow northwardly towards the Arctic waters of the sea, streams which, like the Mississippi, lie also within the great central part of the continent. Much more than half of this great fertile realm is thus situated in the interior portions of the land remote from the sea and little affected by the conditions which it brings. The climate of this section ranges through a great scale of variations both as regards temperature and rainfall. In the extreme north the period exempt from frost is limited to about three months in the year, affording a scant time for the rapidly growing small grains and the roots, such as the turnip and potato, which hasten swiftly to maturity. These with grass and a few hardy fruits constitute the possible crops. The winter is so long and severe that cattle cannot be profitably reared except for domestic purposes.

From the Canadian district southward to the Gulf of Mexico the summer season continually lengthens; though the heat of the hottest term does not increase, it is protracted through a large part of the year. There is only a small portion of the Mississippi Valley within the United States that will not afford good crops of maize or Indian corn, and wheat, the great export staples of the American farmer. The central district of this valley almost to the Gulf of Mexico is fit for all the common grains except rice. From the Ohio and the Missouri southward to the Gulf the great length of the season permits cotton to be profitably planted, and this is the most important crop of that district. In no other equally extensive portion of the earth is so wide a range of soil products obtainable as in the fields of this great valley. Throughout the greater portion of its extent the animals of the barnyard, which have been the familiar attendants of man from an early period, flourish as well as in the Old World: cattle, horses, sheep, and swine prosper greatly.

Although the climate of this district is characterized by more destructive storms than in any other country extensively inhabited by our race, it seems to be on the whole remarkably well suited to descendants from the peoples of Northern Europe. Except near the Gulf coast, and in other portions of the country which are liable to agues, the people are not subject to diseases which are in any way caused by the climate. They attain as much vigor as in any other country.

The valley of the St. Lawrence, including the shores of the Great Lakes, and the lands which border the river from Lake Ontario to its mouth, have in general the same character as the country in the northern part of the Mississippi Valley. The summer is generally short and the range of crops somewhat diminished by the brief period in which plants grow. In Michigan and along the southern shores of Lakes Ontario and Erie the frosts come at a later time than in the regions north of these great water-basins. Maize flourishes as well as all the ordinary crops of the Mississippi Valley. From Lake Ontario to the sea the climate is more severe; maize does not flourish, and agriculture is belated much as it is in the parts of the continental valley lying in the basin of the Red River of the North. Although the climate of the St. Lawrence Valley is too severe for the best agriculture, it evidently suits the people of our race; nowhere in other lands on this continent or in Europe are they more vigorous than in this portion of North America.

A third area of the fertile lands of North America

lies along the Atlantic coast, between the rather unfertile soils of the Appalachian Mountains and the sea. This section extends from New Brunswick and Nova Scotia south to Northern Florida. In general, the climate of this district is more uniform in its character than that of the central valley of the continent. The winters are less cold and the summers less hot; the rainfall is also greater than in the regions of that valley; the soil is on the whole less fertile than in the Mississippi district, but it admits of a great variety of crops, except in New Brunswick, Nova Scotia, and a part of Maine; Indian corn prospers as well as all the smaller grains and roots. The great north and south extension, as in the Mississippi Valley, permits a considerable variety in the products: in the southern part of the section oranges and rice will grow; in the northern region the hardier grains and roots flourish.

In the peninsula portion of Florida we find one of the most peculiar parts of the American continent. It is a region of low lands, and more than half of its area is covered by swamps lying at a slight elevation above the sea. The soil is generally sandy except where it is formed by the decay of old coral reefs which have been elevated above the ocean level. This peninsula is wrapped about by warm waters of the Gulf of Mexico, and by the Gulf Stream, which flows in the basin between Florida and the Bahamas. It therefore has a very warm winter climate, while the summer season, owing to the tempering influence of the neighboring seas, is of moderate heat. The result is, that in the southern portion of the Florida peninsula we have a tropical land, where, as in the region about Biscayne Bay and thence southward to the extremity of Florida, the pineapple, cocoanut-palm, and various plants of the true tropics find suitable conditions.

On the Pacific coast, from San Diego north to the southern border of Alaska, there is between the sterile — because dry — mountain ranges of the higher parts of the Cordilleras and the sea an irregular narrow strip, on the average not more than two hundred miles in width, though it has a length of more than fifteen hundred miles, which, like the Atlantic coast-belt, but in a greater degree, has its climate affected by the neighboring ocean, from which it receives a considerable share of moisture. Although a large portion of this area, particularly its southern part, is too dry for the best uses of the farmer, it is characterized by a much more equable climate than any portion of like extent in the more eastern districts. It is excellently well adapted to a wide range of fruits, and produces in certain portions very large crops of grain Here, too, as in the other section, the people appear to be very vigorous, giving evidence in their condition that the climate is well suited to them.

Although the difference in climate in the various parts of the fertile region of North America is to a considerable degree caused by the variety of the seasons as regards heat and cold, the character of the climate in these areas is even more affected by the amount of rain which they receive in the time of the year when plants are growing. In the Mississippi Valley and along the Atlantic coast the quantity of this rain generally increases as we go from north southwardly. Thus in the region about the head-waters of the Mississippi the annual rainfall, together with the amount of water which may be melted from the snow which comes in the winter season, is, on the average, about thirty inches, while along the Gulf of Mexico it amounts to more than twice as much, or about sixty inches.

On the Atlantic coast we find, in the region of Maine and New Brunswick, an annual fall of water from the skies, in the form of rain or snow, amounting to about forty inches, and again in the southern portion of the coast adjacent to the Gulf of Mexico the amount of rainfall is increased, amounting to about sixty inches. The reason for this increase in the amount of the rainfall as we go southward is mainly found in the fact that in the country about the Gulf of Mexico there is an extensive region of sea subject to a very high temperature: the water evaporates rapidly, ascends to the clouds, and these are borne inward by the winds, and pour the waters upon the land. The further we go from the warm tropical seas, the less the amount of contribution which comes in this way to the earth, for the reason that the air has parted with its moisture before it attains the inland stations. The western portion of the Mississippi Valley exhibits a rapid decrease in the amount of its rainfall as we approach the eastern base of the Rocky Mountains, the reason for this being that the winds from the Mexican Gulf blow prevailingly towards the northeast, and thus the moisture is drawn away from the Rocky Mountain district. When we attain to even three or four hundred miles of the base of those mountains, the rainfall in the summer season is usually so scant that crops can hardly be cultivated with any certainty of yield, except where the soil can be watered by canals led from the slender streams.

In general, the fertile lands of North America receive more water from the skies than those of Europe. If this rain fell at a time most favorable for crops, hardly any portion of its surface would suffer from droughts; but this rainfall comes in the largest measure during the winter season, when it can be of no service to plants, and the summers are frequently periods of drought. The reason for this is simple: in the winter time the difference between the temperature of the tropical seas, where the vapors ascend upward to the clouds, and that of the land to the northward is very great. Moving northward, the clouds are quickly chilled, and so compelled to give up their vapor in the form of rain or snow. In the summer time, however, the land is very warm, and so the moisture is not taken from the clouds as in the winter season. In Europe, where the summers are less hot than in America, and where the prevailing winds blow from over the northern Atlantic, a region of seas warmed by the Gulf Stream, the yearly rain is more even in summer and winter seasons than in the territory of North America. The very warm seasons of the Mississippi Valley and the eastern coast frequently bring periods of drought over large districts. Although these droughts are sometimes destructive to crops, they are on the whole not more detrimental than the excessive rains which so often occur in the summer season of European lands. They are more serious in the district west of the Mississippi, where at best the rainfall is so small in quantity that not much of it can be spared without damage to the fields.

On the Pacific coast, owing to the fact that the sea is cooler than the waters of the Gulf of Mexico or the Atlantic Ocean next the southern part of North America, the rainfall is much less in amount than in the central and eastern portions of this continent. Again, the

western shore of the continent is cooled by a strong
current setting down from the north, and so the winds
which blow over it to the coast bring less moisture to
the land than those which come over the Gulf of Mexico. The consequence is that this shore is on the whole,
particularly in the southern part, much less well watered
than the fertile parts of the continent. While on the
Atlantic coast the rainfall increases as we go from north
southwardly, on the western coast of the United States
it decreases to the southward. Thus the peninsula of
Southern California is made a desert for lack of water.
In the middle portions of the coast near San Francisco
the rainfall is much greater. It is greater still in Oregon and Washington, and in British Columbia to the
north of the line of the United States. In the southern
portions of the state of California only a narrow strip
next the shore is sufficiently watered for tillage. In the
valley of the Columbia River the well-watered district
is much wider. All along this coast the high mountains
near the sea act as barriers to prevent the moist air
from penetrating any considerable distance into the
continent. Behind the Sierra Nevada we have the
driest portion of the continent, the interior region of
the Rocky Mountains, which, as before remarked, is unfit for tillage except where the land may be irrigated by
artificial means.

SOILS OF NORTH AMERICA.

As all the needs of man depend very much upon the
character of the soil, we shall now consider the nature of
this covering which affords subsistence to plants, and
through them to all animals, including men. As in all
other countries, the soils of North America are composed

of the worn-down rocks which have been taken from the solid state, broken into fine bits, and exposed to decay, mainly by the action of frost and water. All soils are composed of rocky matter which, under the action of rain-water, is on its way from the original bedding-place back to the sea, where the material is to be remade in the form of new strata. The broken-up, stony material of the soil is commingled with the dead and decaying fragments of plants and animals, and its fertility is in part due to the intercommingling of these two kinds of material. In large measure the fitness of the soil for the farmer's use, as well as for the growth of wild vegetation, is determined by the character of the rocks whence the grains of the soil have come. If the rocks were in their time formed of the remains of animals, as were all limestones, then the soil is fertile; if it happens that the rocks originally contained no fossil animals, they are likely to be sterile: thus while limestones by their decay always make fertile soils, sandstones generally produce soils of a sterile character.

The soils of North America are divided into three different classes. On the north, within the limits of the region occupied by the ice during the glacial epoch, the pebbles and sand and finer-grained mud composing the soil are in all cases carried for a considerable distance from the point where they originally lay in the bedrocks, the bits from different places churned together so that the resulting soils have a more uniform character than in other regions. Generally, however, these soils are very deep; and, though rarely of the highest fertility, owing to their depth they remain permanently fruitful. In the region south of the area occupied by the ice in the glacial epoch the soil of each field is generally derived from the rocks immediately beneath the surface. Where the ground has a considerable slope the debris from the rocks may have slipped down the hill or been washed by the rains to a lower level, but it is a conspicuous feature of this region that the soils have the measure of fertility determined by the organic character of the under-rocks. We can often tell the change in the character of the underlying rock, although that rock is not exposed at the surface by the sudden alteration in the evident fertility of the soil as shown by the trees or by the tilled crops. This difference in the soils due to the variations in the character of the underlying rocks is particularly conspicuous in the Southern states of this country. By observing the effect of this difference on the life of the farmers, we perceive how far the peculiar character of the soil may influence the life of man. Thus in Kentucky the central portion of the state is underlaid by limestones which contain the fossilized forms of animals whose remains afford good food for plants and which have by their decay formed a very rich soil coating. All this limestone area is extremely fertile; the people have grown wealthy from farming, and attain a high state of civilization. In the eastern part of that state the rocks are mostly composed of sand, and afford very lean soils. In this section the people have remained poor, and the progress of civilization has been very much retarded.

A yet further effect due to these peculiarities of soils may be seen in the history of the civil war between the states of the North and South. All the fertile lands of the South were occupied by farms tilled by slaves. In the regions of lean soil it was not profitable to use slaves in farming, for the reason that no crops could be reared which were valuable for export. The result was that the mountain portion of the South, the Appalachian district, from the head-waters of the Ohio and the Potomac southward to western North Carolina, Northern Georgia, and Eastern Tennessee, were occupied by people who had no interest in slavery, and who were not effective supporters of the Rebellion. They were largely Union men, giving little help to the Southern cause. It seems not unlikely that the failure of the Southern Confederacy to attain its independence may in considerable measure have depended upon this matter of soils.

A third group of soils is formed of the deposits made on the banks of rivers in times of their overflow. These alluvial terraces are built up in times when the river carries its flood waters over a considerable area occupied by forests or other plants on either side of the stream. Penetrating into the interstices of these usually thickset growths, the current of the water is arrested and a good part of its mud falls down upon the earth. With the succession of floods through many thousand years, sheets of fine-grained soil become very extensive. Thus in the lower part of the Mississippi Valley, below the junction of the Missouri, the alluvial plains occupy an area of nearly thirty thousand square miles. Because a large part of this alluvial deposit is composed of richer soils taken from the margins of the smaller streams near the head-waters of the main river, they always have a higher measure of fertility. Alluvial plains along the great rivers always afford lands entitled to rank among the richest of those which are tilled by man. Although alluvial soils are most common in the region south of the district, they are to a certain extent found within that ancient realm of the ice. They are rarer and less extensive in the ice district, for the reason that in such a country the deep layers of gravel and sand retain the water of the flood times and deliver it slowly to the streams, and thus avoid the peculiar flooding which brings about the construction of such alluvial plains as those which exist in the Mississippi Valley.

In general, it may be said that the richer soils of the United States lie in regions which are to the south of the area occupied by ice during the glacial period, or in parts of the field where the ice was thin and did not by its deposits greatly affect the character of the soil. On the other hand, the earth affords in glacial fields soils which are more enduring to the tax which tillage puts upon them. They do not wear out so rapidly, and this for the reason that the pebbles are numerous and constantly in process of decay, and by this decay continually yield new stores of plant food. Thus in Virginia and the neighboring states a good deal of the soil has so far been worn out by tillage, so much of its fertile materials have been shipped away in the ashy matter of the exported products, that they no longer yield crops which are profitable to the farmer; but in New England, though the soil was originally poorer than in those states south of the glacial area, the soil is, on the whole, about as good as when the country was first settled.

There are certain peculiar kinds of soils in North America which deserve particular mention. The greater part of the area which has been brought to the use of the farmer has been won from old forest lands. It may be said in general that all the regions east of the Mississippi, except a portion of Illinois and Indiana, were originally wooded. To win these forest-covered soils to tillage requires a great deal of labor in order to remove the forests and to get the ground clear of the roots of the trees. In doing this work the pioneers generally followed a method which they learned from the Indians. They spared themselves the labor of cutting down the trees and burning their great trunks and branches by cutting a ring of bark from the trunk near the surface of the ground, which caused the trees to die. Then cutting away the underbrush, they proceeded to plant their crops in the interspaces between the great trunks. Gradually the deadened wood decayed, so that in ten or fifteen years it practically disappeared from the ground. Even with this simple but very advantageous practice the process of winning a forest-covered surface to tillage is slow and laborious.

So, too, in the countries originally covered by ice the first settlers had a hard struggle to fit the soil for the plough. The larger part of these lands which were recently ice-ridden are covered with great bowlders, broken from their bed places in the rocks and scattered over the surface of the ground. These stones had to be removed from the path of the plough, built into walls, or, if they were too heavy for removal, buried at a depth beneath the soil. In the greater part of the region recently occupied by glaciers it requires from fifty to one hundred days' labor to remove the stones from an acre field so that the plough may do its work. Generally this bowlder-strewn region was forest-clad, so the labor of removing the wood must be added to the task which was imposed on the soil-tiller in the preparation of his land for use. It is difficult to conceive how great has been the toil of those who have preceded us in this country, who have necessarily given their lives to the subjugation of the land.

In the greater part of Illinois, Indiana, and Wisconsin and in the most of the country west of the Mississippi the conditions are as favorable for the beginning of tillage as they were unfavorable in the eastern part of the United States. When in the process of the settlement of the country the pioneers came to the central and western portion of the land, they found an exceedingly fertile region where forests were rare, being generally limited to the immediate neighborhood of the rivers. This vast expanse of country, containing almost as much fertile land as was included in the forest country of the eastern part of the United States, was not only without woods, but usually without the covering of bowlders which was such a hindrance in the region in and about New England. This prairie district did not begin to be settled until about the end of the first quarter of the present century. We see in part the peculiar advantage afforded by this open land to the farmer in the fact that while it required about two hundred years to push the settlements of the white man from the Atlantic coast westward to the Ohio and Kentucky, it took less than half a century to carry the settlements for nearly twice that distance farther to the westward. Of course something of this rapid march of the people to the westward is due to steam transportation on the water and the land, but in large part the swiftness of the movement is owing to the peculiarly open character of the country which has been settled in the last half-century.

We do not certainly know the causes which led to the formation of the prairies. In large part they are doubtless due to the fact that the rainfall diminishes as we go westward towards the Rocky Mountains, and many of our trees cannot stand the lessened moisture. In part the prairies are probably due to the fact that the Indians were in the habit of burning the grass in the open or unwooded districts, and the undergrowth of the forests as well, in order to secure better pasturage for the wild animals which they hunted. By these annual fires young saplings were killed off, and when the older trees died, the forest disappeared. In this way century by century the original forests were pushed back to the eastward and replaced by prairies. That this is the case is shown by the fact that when what is now called the "barrens" of Kentucky was first occupied by whites, the larger portion of the western section of the area was without woods because of the frequent fires set by the savages. When the Indians were driven away and these annual conflagrations ceased to ravage the country, the woods rapidly regained the field.

In the region of the Rocky Mountains there are vast fields of bare rock lying where the slopes are so steep that the soil cannot maintain itself upon them. Over yet larger fields there is a thick soil formed in an earlier time when the rainfall was greater than now, and when the conditions which make the soils were present in a way in which they no longer exist in that country. The existence of a greater rainfall in recent times is proved by the fact that all the dead seas, those lakes without an outlet to the ocean, which now frequently occur in that region, show by old shore benches around their margins that they have recently shrunk to a small part of their former size. In these parts of the continent the soils are not only sterile for lack of moisture, but they are very often made even more desolate than they would otherwise be, by the fact that certain solid substances work up from the depths of the earth and make a crust upon the surface. This crust is so alkaline that it kills many plants which otherwise might withstand the drought. There are but few vegetable species which are adapted to grow upon it, and none of these are of any use to man.

The conditions which lead to the formation of these alkali plains is worth the attention of the observer, for the reason that their history shows us a beautiful process of the soils, — one which generally greatly serves the needs of vegetation and only in exceptional cases is hurtful to plants. We will therefore turn aside for the moment to trace the history of this peculiar salt coating which is visible in the alkali districts of our western plains and in some of the valleys of the Rocky Mountains. In all fields, except perhaps in those small areas of the earth where scarce any rainfall occurs, there is a constant and tolerably rapid decay of the rocky matter contained in the grains of the soil. By this decay a certain amount of lime, potash, and soda, in the form of various chemical combinations with other materials, is brought into the state in which they may be dissolved in water. In ordinary soil in a region of sufficient rainfall a portion of this material is constantly washed away, and so the amount of these substances is kept within hurtful limits, within the limits in which they are advantageous and not damaging to plants.

When, however, a soil which has been formed in a period of more abundant rainfall comes to be very dry, as is the case in our western lands, the occasional rains soak the soil with water, but do not send such an amount of fluid through the porous material as to wash away the excess of alkaline matter. Then when summer droughts come, and the heat of the air causes the water next the atmosphere to pass away in vapor, the alkaline material which this water contained, not going away in the process of evaporation, remains as a crust on the surface. As soon as the surface becomes dry, what is called capillary attraction draws up more water from the depths towards the surface. This water brings yet more alkaline matter, and gradually the coating of the salts next the surface become thicker and thicker.

Beginning in the eastern portion of these plains with a certain amount of rainfall, say twenty inches each year, we find no alkaline coating created; going further westward, where the rainfall is less considerable, we begin to find the crust formed in situations favorable for its accumulation. Yet further west, with a diminished rainfall, the coating formed in the dry season is often so thick that it is not altogether dissolved by the rains of the wet season, and so the surface is rendered sterile beyond the sterility which is given by drought. In all fertile lands these movements of salt water towards the surface in times of drought have a beneficial effect, for it is not more than sufficient to bring the desired food to the roots of the plants. Ordinary droughts, though they may in some cases harm the crops of one season, are apt to help those of the following year when the rainfall is more abundant, and so in a general way the upward movement of these salts is beneficial. It is only where the rainfall has not sufficiently leached away enough of the saline matter that it becomes injurious to plants by forming an alkaline encrustation.

DOMESTICATED PLANTS OF THE UNITED STATES.

The value of a country to mankind depends more upon the useful plants that will grow within it than upon any other natural feature. On the amount of production of those articles which serve as food for man or his domesticated animals the agriculture of a country necessarily depends. Measured by the plants which fit the soil and climate, North America may be deemed extremely well suited to human use. All the grains, roots, and fruits which were known in the Old World before the discovery of America do well in one part or another of the country; except some of the peculiar kinds of millet grown in the central parts of Africa, all the grain crops are to a greater or less extent tilled in this country.

In addition to the small grains, wheat, rye, oats, barley, etc., which came to this country from Europe, America has furnished to the world from its own soil the large and very productive grain known as maize or Indian corn, which in North America, between Mexico and the northern part of the United States, flourishes so well that it produces nearly twice as much food per acre as any of the grains in the Old World. Although maize will grow tolerably well in many countries, the peculiarly hot and rather dry character of the American summer suits it particularly well, and it may be regarded as an essentially American crop. Besides maize the American land has yielded two valuable food plants, — the potato and the tomato. The potato has been carried from America and extensively introduced in the cooler parts of all the continents. It differs from any other of the edible roots or tubers in the fact that it flourishes through a wider range of climate than any food-producing plant of the same general nature. It grows well as far north as any of the grains flourish, and it also yields tolerably abundant crops near down to the tropics.

In general, the food-producing plants of North America very closely resemble those of Europe. In the more southern portion of the country, however, certain tropical or subtropical vegetables, such as the banana and plantain and the sweet potato, are more successful than in any part of the Old World occupied by Europeans. From the Isthmus of Panama northward to the southern portion of Mexico, and including the southern part of Florida and a portion of California coast, vegetables of a tropical character such as palms, pineapples, guavas, as well as the sugar-cane, attain their highest perfection. This region also affords crops of some of the ordinary grains, but they do not attain their best development there. The food plants of the United States proper are evenly distributed as regards their perfection of growth over the whole country. With the exception of the sweet potato, the ochra, and some of the melons which are limited in their best development to the southern half of the United States, essentially the same kinds of food-yielding vegetables can be grown through all the area of those states. North of the line of the United States the number of the plants which can be grown for food purposes rapidly diminishes. Indian corn does not flourish in any part of the Canadian district. Many of the roots are not successful there. That part of the world, however, contains a wide area suitable for the small grains.

The whole of North America, as far north as it is fit for the purpose of tillage, is well adapted to the growth of the grasses which when dried afford the principal winter food of our ordinary domesticated animals. A long, hot summer, with the generally large supply of rain with intervening periods of very dry weather, favors the growth and harvesting of these crops. The actual value of the staple crops which are cut and dried for the barnyard animals in northern regions usually exceeds that of any other single agricultural product, and as regards the production of these articles of food for beasts, North America has in general an advantage over any other district of equal size known in the world. Taking the continent as a whole, it supports more species of plants suited for the food of man than are tilled in Europe, and probably as great a number as any other continent affords.

Of the plants which though not serving for food yet aid the work of man, North America has many important varieties, some of which are indigenous; others have been introduced from foreign lands. The most important of these, which do not come in the group of food-producers and which attain peculiar success in North America, are the cotton and the tobacco plants. Of both these articles North America produces the largest amount which enters into the commerce of the world. Cotton is not a native plant, it having been introduced from either Asia or Africa. Tobacco, at least the species which enters much into use, is in its origin peculiar to the New World, and it is so much better suited to the climate of North America than to any other region it may be regarded as a characteristic feature of its vegetation. The cotton crop of North America is now all produced in the region south of the Ohio, the Missouri, and the Potomac rivers, principally in the southern Atlantic states and those which border upon the Gulf. The plant will grow over the larger part of the tilled area of the continent, but only in this southern field is the summer long enough to permit it to ripen its seeds and thus produce the fibres of cotton which are found upon them. Tobacco, on the other hand, is cultivated from the northern part of the United States to Central America. It is a peculiarity of this plant that the quality of the product varies very much in different parts of the country and even on adjacent fields; but it can be reared in any part of the land where the summer is moderately long and hot.

In the tropical regions of America another plant characteristic of the continent, the Agava, or century plant, is serviceable for making a very strong fibre serving many of the purposes of hemp. A fermented drink much used in Mexico is made from its juices. It is only in the fruits that the products of the soil of North America are exceeded by those of the Old World. Certain fruits, as for instance the orange, the banana, and the apple and peach, are more successful in the United States than in the Old World; but the grape, the nectarine, the fig, and the date, and many other smaller fruits, are, on the whole, more successfully reared in the Old World than on this continent.

ANIMALS.

The native animals of North America differ more in their character from those of Europe and Asia than do the plants of the two countries. While the general likeness between the animal life of the two regions is great, there are many singular features to note. We shall not give any extended account of the less important creatures such as the radiates, molluscs, or articulated animals, which though very interesting to naturalists are little known to the common reader. We shall pass lightly over them and give most of our attention to the higher and more familiar creatures found among our back-boned animals,— the group to which man himself belongs.

Among the lower creatures of the sea and land, the so-called invertebrates, or creatures lacking the peculiarity of a bony internal skeleton of the back-boned kind, we find several forms which are so interesting that they must receive at least a passing notice. In the kindred of the mollusca, or shell-fish, we note the fact that in the rivers of North America, particularly those south of Canada, we have a very wonderful variety of beautiful creatures commonly known as fresh-water clams, called by naturalists Unionidæ, or Naiades. In the Mississippi Valley, especially in the head-waters of its streams on the eastern side of the valley, these forms are more plentifully developed than in any other part of the world. Almost every considerable stream has its peculiar species which is not found in other waters. It would be possible for the naturalist who is well acquainted with the variety of these creatures, by taking the individuals from any of the lesser rivers, to tell on just what waters he had been placed, even if he had been conveyed to this station in ignorance as to the course of his journey. The Naiades are peculiar in many ways. In the first place, they are capable of travelling with considerable freedom by means of an extended organ commonly called the foot, which is essentially like the instrument by which the snail crawls over the surface of the land. This contrivance is of great use to them, because they are often swept down the streams in times of flood and have to crawl back to a place proper for their needs. The females have also a pouch along the side of the gills in which the eggs are stored and hatched, in place of being thrown forth into the water, as is the case with other shell-fish. By this means the young are secured against the danger of being swept away in times when the river flows very swiftly. Like their kindred in other lands, these Naiades frequently produce very beautiful pearls though not those of most value for ornament.

It is interesting to note the reason why these Unionidæ have undergone such an abundant development and have attained so great a diversity in American waters. This reason seems to be in part at least as follows: the rivers south of the Ohio, at a good height above the sea, have been for many geological periods in about their present state. The land has not been lowered beneath the sea; glaciers have not overridden its surface, and thus the creatures have been able to go on from geological period to geological period, gradually changing and developing their peculiarities. There is, perhaps, no other region in the world where an equally extensive system of rivers has for so long a geological time been preserved from submergence beneath the sea and the destruction which glaciers would bring, — the accidents of long-continued drought which might dry up their waters, or other mischances which might interrupt the growth and development of these forms. We thus see how the variety and beauty in the group of animals and plants may be determined by the geological history of the region they occupy. Unlike most other forms of living beings, these slow-moving creatures cannot migrate to meet the needs of changing climate, and so are dependent on the conditions of the part of the world in which they dwell.

Among the snails, the remote kindred of the water molluscs, we find certain peculiarities characteristic of this country. In the Old World there are several species of very large shell-bearing snails which, to certain peoples, prove an attractive article of food. None of these large forms are native in North America, and so even among our aborigines, pressed by hunger as they often were, these creatures were rarely used for food. Yet another interesting feature in our mollusca consists in the great development of oysters in the salt and brackish waters of the eastern coast of the United States. Although oysters are tolerably abundant along many other shores, this group attains a greater luxuriance on the eastern coast of North America than in any other region. The forms grow to a larger size, and apparently find the conditions better suited to them than those of any other part of the world.

Among the kinsmen of our ordinary crab and lobster the American coast affords a peculiar crustacean, known as Limulus, or king crab. This creature is peculiar to the waters of the Pacific Ocean and to the coast of North America as far north as Nova Scotia. The creature is interesting, not only on account of its very peculiar form, but from certain singular features in its personal and race history. It has the curious habit of shedding at once in an annual molting the skin over all the external parts of its body, leaving its envelope split open along the broad front margin in such perfect state that the collector often supposes he has the real animal in his possession, when, in fact, it is only the abandoned shell which has grown too small for the creature in the course of growth. Equally interesting is the fact that this singular animal is the last survival of a series of similar forms extending from the Devonian time to the present day. Its kindred were once distributed far and wide in the ocean waters, but are now no longer found in the Atlantic except on the eastern coast of America.

The fishes of North America contain numerous interesting forms. The waters of the Mississippi and some of the streams which head near its tributaries abound in gar-pikes, commonly called alligator gars from the fact that the surface of their bodies is protected by a strong coating of bone-like plates, forming an effective armor. This creature, like the king crab, is also a survival of a pattern of creatures which were once common the world over, but are now limited to American waters. In the Mississippi there are several other fishes which recall the ancient life, and they, like the Naiades before referred to, show that this system of rivers has proceeded from the distant past.

Among the peculiar animals of North America, species of rattlesnakes and some other reptiles deserve mention. The rattlesnake is a most peculiar serpent in that it has upon its tail shapely bits of hard dried skin, which when shaken by the rapid movement which takes place in the hinder part of the serpent's body when it is excited, produce a shrill humming sound quite like that made by the cicada, or locust, when it is calling its mate. Although there are a number of other poisonous snakes in North America, these species of crotalus are by far the most to be feared, for the reason that they are the most plentiful and widely distributed. They range from the tropics northward to near the northern limits of the United States, but are most venomous and abundant in the southern half of the continent. One other noteworthy serpent alone can here be referred to. This is the Elaps, or coral snake of the Carolina district, a beautiful creature closely akin to exceedingly deadly forms which occur in South America. A singular feature of the Elaps is that, although it has poison glands and fangs like other deadly serpents, it is not known ever to use them, and is reckoned as innocuous.

In many parts of the region bordering on the Gulf of Mexico, and thence southward to the Isthmus, alligators abound, and in places they attain a great size. In the tropical portion of the continent there are numerous crocodiles, a larger and fiercer kinsman of the alligator; but this species only extends beyond the tropics in the extreme southeastern corner of Florida, where there is a little colony of them containing in all perhaps a few hundred individuals.

The birds of North America are, in general, very much like those of Europe; indeed, the common names of the sparrows, wrens, robins, etc., which were first invented for European birds, were reasonably applied to many American species which, though not just the same as their European kindred, resemble them closely. There are, however, some peculiar birds in North America which have no close relations in the Old World; the humming-birds, the turkey, the mocking-bird, etc., give a singular character to the winged life of this country.

Among the suck-giving forms there are a number of creatures peculiar to this continent. Of these the most conspicuous is the bison, commonly misnamed the buffalo, which at the time when the country was first discovered by the whites existed in exceeding abundance on the open plains of the Mississippi Valley, and occasionally penetrated in small bands through the woods as far as the shores of the Carolinas and Virginia. It is probable that nowhere else in the world, at least in modern geographical times, was there any so large a beast existing in such vast droves as these bisons. They have now been so far destroyed in the advance of civilization, that in place of the millions which existed at the beginning of this century, there are probably not five hundred now living within the limits of the United States. A few thousand probably survive in the forests north of the line between the United States and Canada.

The grizzly bear, the largest and most ferocious beast of his kind, greater than any known in Europe in historic times, still abounds in the mountain districts of the Cordilleras from the Mexican line northward to the high north. In the United States, and southward to South America, especially in the woodland districts, opossums are found. These creatures belong to the group of suck-giving animals, but differ from those familiarly known to us, in the fact that they have pouches on the abdomen in which the young are nurtured for some months after their birth. There are three species of these opossums known in North America; the group is very much more abundant in South America, where it is represented by about thirty-five varieties. No kindred of these forms now live on any other of the continents except South America and Australia. When white men first visited Australia, all the suck-giving animals had this peculiarity of structure. Among the lesser mammalian animals of this country there are some very beautiful forms which are familiar to some of the readers of this book. These are the various kinds of ground squirrels, all of which are akin to true squirrels which inhabit the trees. These ground squirrels of the western plains, commonly known as prairie dogs, are very interesting little creatures, particularly attractive from the fact that they dwell together in colonies. The ground squirrels of the eastern part of the United States are less conspicuous because they are solitary animals.

All the other noteworthy animals of this continent are more or less perfectly represented in Europe and Asia by related kinds, so that when the European settlers came to this country they were able to name most of the conspicuous animals by their evident likeness to European kinds.

Although the animals of North America are in a general way like those of the Old World, there are many kinds existing in Europe and Asia, and even more in Africa, which find no representatives in North America. Of these we will note a few of the more important. Southern Asia abounds in monkeys, some of them of large size. North America has but few species of these interesting animals, and none of them range north of Mexico. The hyænas, jackals, tigers, leopards, among the beasts of prey of the Old World, are wanting in the New. Their place is imperfectly occupied by our American panther and our several species of wild-cat. The horse, though originally developed on the American continent in early Tertiary times, had disappeared from both North and South America before the coming of man. The true camel and the dromedary, which along with the horse have played so large a part in the history of man in the Old World, appear never to have existed in America. In their stead we have in South America the smaller and less valuable vicuna or alpaca. Wild bulls and wild goats were lacking in the Americas, the Rocky Mountain sheep, an apparently untamable animal, being their only representative in the New World.

Of the various species of bulls known to exist in the Old World, although forms of great size, there existed but one in this country down perhaps to the time when man first came to it, and that had long ago passed away before the country was settled by Europeans. Rhinoceroses and hippopotamuses, together with a host of strange beasts peculiar to Africa, have had no foothold on this continent. As a whole, the larger back-boned animals of North America were very far inferior in variety and grade of development to those of the Old World group of lands. In this respect the animal life of the New World is in singular contrast to its plant life. This is more clearly seen when we remember that while the American continents have given a great many valuable vegetables to the use of the world, including the maize, potato, tomato, and the so-called Peruvian bark from the chincona tree, which affords quinine, it has not furnished a single valuable animal to the use of civilized man, unless we count the turkey such an important contribution. If we make a list of all the domesticated animals which serve mankind in an important way, including in the list the familiar barnyard fowls, we have a total of about twenty; including the bee, the cochineal, and the silkworm, etc., there are about twenty-five tolerably well domesticated species of animals which have largely served the interests of man. Of these, twelve are suck-giving animals which have afforded, through their strength, their wool, their meat, or in the case of the dog by their companionship to man, help in the advance of civilization. But one out of this list, the turkey, as before stated, is derived from America, and this creature is perhaps least of all in value.

MINERAL RESOURCES OF NORTH AMERICA.

In their savage state-men depend almost altogether for the goods which the world gives them upon the native animals of the land and waters, and the wild plants which yield nuts, fruits, or fibrous bark. From the bodies of the animals they obtain food, and from their skins raiment; even their bones serve them for rude tools, points for their spears, etc. A slight advance in the arts brings men to the stage where they work certain kinds of stone into the shape of weapons or domestic utensils. Yet further on in the development of their industries they burn certain kinds of clay in the shape of pots for cooking and storing food. Slowly they learn to plant certain seeds and to reap the harvest. It is only, however, when men rise above the state of savagery and set their feet firmly on the paths which lead to civilization that they look to the under-earth for any contributions to their life. In time, however, they are led to the use of metals.

Copper, which occasionally occurs in its native state as a metal buried in the rocks, appears in most cases to have been the first metallic substance to attract the attention of men. At first they dug it from its bed-places with rude tools. Gradually, however, they learned to use fire with rude blowing instruments, made from the hides of animals something in the fashion of the blacksmith's bellows, which enabled them to produce the metal not only from the fragments containing it in the native state, but also from the ores, or combinations of the metal with other substances. This art of smelting copper by the use of fire aided by a blast appears to have originated in the Old World, and to have had no place among the natives of this country. As soon as men found the use of fire in winning metals from the earth, they were put in the way of helping themselves to resources which were denied to them in their more primitive state. They soon began to mingle the molten copper with tin, and thus made bronze, which is very much harder and better suited for tools, ornaments, and weapons. They naturally came in a short time to smelt iron ores, and thus to find their way to the use of a cheaper and harder metal than they had before known. With advancing civilization this use of the underground resources in the form of metals and other mineral products has gone forward very rapidly, until now there are hundreds of substances won from the underground and converted to the needs of man.

We easily see that while to the American Indian and other savages of simple needs, the character of the under-earth was of no consequence, as he looked to the surface alone for his supplies, the nature of the rocks beneath the country occupied by civilized men is a matter of the utmost importance to them. While the soil is now, and must ever be, the principal source whence men obtain the objects of necessity and the simpler luxuries in the way of food and raiment, the under-earth affords to cultured men a share of their needs only less important than that which is secured from the soil.

The importance of the mineral supplies which may be won beneath the earth's surface is increased by the fact that these valuable products are not found everywhere, but only in favored places. All parts of the world which are by climate fit for the uses of man have soils which will produce food in a certain abundance, but probably not more than one-tenth of such regions have below their surface mineral resources of sufficient value to repay the costs of winning them by mining. The result is that in such favored regions it is generally profitable to the people to devote a great part of their attention to the industries which will secure these products of the deeper earth. Even if the soil of such districts be barren, it may be advantageous for men to dwell there and win their living by mining work. Therefore, in taking an account of the conditions of North America which may affect the welfare of civilized men, we must attentively consider the distribution of its mineral resources.

Although North America has been known to Europeans for more than four hundred years, and the greater part of its surface has only been visited by white men during the present century, we have a tolerably good knowledge of its mineral wealth. We are, it is true, ignorant of what in the way of valuable minerals may lie beneath the surface of a large part of British America, Alaska, and Greenland, but these lands are so inhospitable that until the mineral wealth of all parts of the world have been exhausted, it is not likely that much attention will be given to them. In Mexico and in the Cordilleras northward to a distance of some hundred miles beyond the Canadian boundary the country has been very assiduously searched for mineral stores, and the nature of that wealth is tolerably well known. The same may be said of the mountainous district of the Appalachians from Newfoundland to Alabama. As a whole, we know more concerning the mineral resources of North America than of any other continent except Europe.

For convenience we may divide the mineral resources of any country into several classes of materials. As the simplest, we have the stones, which may serve for building purposes or for architectural ornaments of various kinds. Next, we have the deposits of metals, such as gold, silver, iron, copper, tin, zinc, etc. Thirdly, the resources which yield heat or light, such as coal, petroleum, or natural gas. Fourthly, substances which may afford mineral manures, or materials which may be used in the refreshment of the soils exhausted by the tax which tillage puts upon them. Fifthly, we have the plastic clays, which serve in the arts of the potter, in making vessels for domestic uses, or making brick and many other less important articles. Last of all, we have a large group of important substances which contribute to our ordinary arts, such as precious stones, the earths which serve in making paint, etc.

The distribution of these several classes of substances is much affected by the history of the rocks in which they occur. Thus the metals, except iron, are generally found in rocks which have once been deeply buried, exposed to the heat which exists in the depths of the earth, and subsequently elevated into high land, where the beds which once covered them have been stripped away by the action of torrents and glaciers. Building stone, clay, and fuel materials are generally found in their best conditions, for use where the rocks have not been very much changed and where they have been preserved from the crumpling and other breakings brought about in mountain-building.

It is interesting to note that the greater part of the underground resources which are of value to man to a great extent owe their presence in veins, or beds, to the action of animals or plants which have lived in former geological ages. This effect of ancient life is best seen in our coal-deposits. Falling seeds, leaves, trunks, branches, and roots of trees which in other days were accumulated in wet places, formed extensive bogs. When woody matter falls upon tolerably dry ground it entirely decays, and the carbon, of which it is almost altogether composed, passes by decay back to the air. Two atoms of oxygen unite with each atom of carbon, and the result is that the carbon ceases to be a visible substance, and becomes converted into a gas, disappearing in the air, in the course of time to be reappropriated by the leaves and again built into woody matter. The water of a swamp prevents this complete decay and causes the carbon to remain for a while in the form of peat or muck. When now this peaty matter is depressed beneath the level of the sea and sealed in by accumulations of sand, clay, or limestone, the carbon gradually takes on the form of coal, and in this condition may be preserved for geological ages. It is thus easily seen that when we burn coal and make avail of its light and heat, we are served by the plant life of ancient days. In gathering the carbon from the atmosphere the plants do their work by virtue of the energy imparted to them through the sun's rays. They can only do this work when the sun is shining upon them. Thus the vegetation which forms the coal-beds is really imprisoned solar energy in the rocks. It is not too much to say that every coal fire yields us the energy of the sunshine of past geological ages, and that we could not have this store but for the action of the plants.

The same is the case both with petroleum and rock gas, — natural gas, as it is commonly called. These substances which are now of great value to man, are mainly, if not altogether, derived from the decayed animals and plants buried on old sea-floors. Imprisoned in the rocks, these fossil remains undergo a gradual decomposition, and as a result of this chemical change we have the fluid petroleum and the chemical compound known as natural gas. Where the rocks lie in their original level position, the beds of clay, which form layers in all thick series of bed-rocks, confine the gases and oil, as substances may be held in a bottle by means of a cork. If now we bore through these layers of clay between the porous sandstone in which the oil and gas have been accumulated, these substances rush forth with great force and may be gathered for use.

It is easy to see that where the rocks have been crumpled, folded, and broken, as they necessarily are in mountain-built countries, the gas and oil have a chance to escape, and thus it naturally comes about that the fields containing these substances lie in parts of the continent in which disturbances of the strata have not taken place. In a somewhat similar way coal-beds are best preserved in regions where the strata have not been tossed about in mountain-building; for where such breakings have occurred, the beds containing coal, which are always of a rather frail nature, break up easily under the action of frosts and streams and are apt to be washed away, or if they remain, are only found in small patches not well placed for the miner's use. Thus it comes about that our fuel deposits formed by the intervention of organic life are best preserved in regions of little disturbed rocks.

In a less definite way the most of our other important minerals owe something of their accumulation in profitable deposits to the action of living beings in former geological times. The history of this relation of our metals and other wealth-giving substances to animals and plants is somewhat complicated, but of such a nature that we should take pains to understand it. This history is in brief as follows : the rain-water when it falls upon the lands contains no mineral substances, but is ready to dissolve a great variety of materials; when it falls upon the surface of the earth, it commonly passes through a bed of decayed vegetation, the familiar mass of rotten leaves and twigs and trunks which we find beneath our feet in any old forest. As before noticed, this decaying woody matter is, by combining with the oxygen of the air, constantly passing back into the atmosphere in the form of carbonic acid gas, or carbon dioxide, as it is sometimes called. The rain-water has a singular power of absorbing this gas, a capacity which is made use of in making soda-water, which is simply water charged with gas. It therefore absorbs a great deal of this carbon dioxide on its way downward through the soil. When so charged with this gas it acquires a vastly greater power of dissolving materials than it had before. Thus, where pure rain-water will absorb but one part of lime, it can take up fifty parts when it has all the carbonic acid gas it can hold.

So, too, with all the other substances, including most of the metals, water, which can hardly dissolve them at all in the pure state, can take them in solution in perceptible quantities when armed with this peculiar gas. On its way downward through the earth and through the rocks, which it penetrates, it dissolves from them a great deal of mineral matter of very varied kinds. These it bears to the sea. When the sea-water is evaporated, all these substances are left behind in the ocean, constantly increasing the dissolved matter which the water contains. The result is that sea-water has in solution greater or less portions of all the substances, including the metals, which water can remove by the process of solution from the rocks. The very salt taste of the sea is due to the fact that certain of these substances, common salt and some other saline materials, are so large in quantity that they affect the palate.

If the rivers continue to bring these mineral substances into the sea, leaving them there when the waters come back to the lands, through the air, the sea would in time become so charged with these materials that it would be, like the waters of the Dead Sea of Syria, or Salt Lake in Utah, unfit for the existence of marine animals or plants. The fact is, however, that these living beings of the sea are constantly removing these dissolved substances from the water, building them into their bodies, and in time giving them back to the solid earth in the form of deposits accumulated on the sea-floor. It is probable that this withdrawal of mineral matter from the water goes on about as fast as it is introduced into the ocean from the land. But all forms of animals and plants do not take different substances from the water in the same proportion. Some kinds of sea-weed appropriate particular materials. Certain animals, as, for instance, the creatures allied to crabs and lobsters, take out phosphate of lime; other shell-bearing creatures remove carbonate of lime from the waters. The result is that where a deposit on the sea-bottom is composed, as is often the case, of the remains of animals and plants of peculiar kinds, which have grown upon the ocean floor for a very long time, the deposits accumulated by the death and decay of the creatures contain a peculiarly large quantity of one or another of the forms of mineral substances; and so it happens that in strata we may have beds, or many successive layers, which are rich in particular mineral materials. If now these beds become deeply buried, the waters they contain become heated, and in time drain away by the pressure of steam and other gases, which impel them upward to the surface. The mineral substances of the rocks may be still further concentrated into veins, it may be of copper, silver, phosphate of lime, etc.

The way in which these veins are formed is very simple. As long as the waters that penetrate them are hot and under great pressure they are constantly dissolving the mineral substances. If, when they have taken up a great charge of the materials, the way is open to the passage of the substances to the surface through a crevice, such as may be formed by a break in the rocks, they move up through the opening. As they rise towards the air their heat is constantly diminishing because they come into cooler rocks; the pressure is also lowered, and so the mineral matter is to a certain extent deposited in a cavity, through which the water is passing, and so forms a vein accumulation which the miner can afterwards explore for the substances he seeks. We thus see how it is that veins are most likely to be formed in mountain-built rocks, for there the strata are most liable to the breakage which makes the cavities in which the veins are formed; and we also see how organic life serves as an agent in the process by which mineral matter is concentrated into a shape to be of use to man.

As regards the under-earth resources, the territory of North America is somewhat naturally divided into three great fields, corresponding in position to the site of the three most considerable systems of mountain elevation. On the eastern shore we have the Appalachian mountain belt; on the western face of the continent, the Cordilleran district; and north of the St. Lawrence, the third important field, that occupied by the old worn-down Laurentian Mountains. In addition to these three principal divisions, there are a number of subordinate areas, also grouped about and within the lesser mountain districts,—the Adirondacks of northern New York, the Ozarks of Missouri and Arkansas, the Black Hills, a geographic dependency of the Cordilleras, and some other smaller areas hereafter to be mentioned, which are not distinctly connected with any mountain systems.

Beginning our survey with the best-known field, that which has longest served the interests of man and has contributed the most to the economic prosperity of the country, the Appalachian district, we find ourselves surrounded by a region of varied mineral wealth. As before described, the Appalachian Mountains may be taken as extending from northern Newfoundland to northern Alabama, and from the central parts of the Ohio Valley to the Atlantic sea-shore as far south as Richmond, Va., and thence in the interior districts southward to central South Carolina and Georgia. This mineral field occupies somewhere near the twentieth part of that portion of the area of the continent which by its climate is made fit for the uses of civilized men.

The most important feature in the Appalachian mineral district is found in the very large proportion of carbonaceous substances which occur within its area. No other mountain system of the world contains within its disturbed district or in the table-lands adjacent to its mountain-built rocks, so large an amount of these precious materials which yield light and heat and the power which drives steam-engines, for the uses of man. These carbonaceous materials are, as before noted, divided into three groups. First and most important are the deposits of coal. In general, the coal-beds of the Appalachian district lie either to the east or west of the principal axes of that system, and this for the reason that the central dominant part of the chain is composed of rocks which were formed and uplifted in a mountainous shape before the Carboniferous age, or that stage in the earth's history when the most abundant deposits of this nature were produced. There are thus two areas of coal-fields in this part of the continent, the western field of largest area containing more than nine-tenths of all the coal in the eastern part of North America, and the eastern, or seaboard, basins, which hold a smaller amount of this material.

The western field occupies an almost continuous area extending from northern Pennsylvania southward to central Alabama. Outlying parts of the field forming considerable areas contain good coal, — those of western Kentucky, Illinois, and Indiana; but the principal mass of the valuable coal-areas of the Appalachians lies in the district immediately adjacent to, and partly included within, the Alleghany Mountains. Here and there, by the mountain folding and the irregular wearing away of the rocks which has resulted from their folded condition, many small detached masses of coal have been formed, separated by slight intervals from the main field; but as a whole the coals lying to the west of the Blue Ridge, or principal axis of the Appalachians, lie in a great connected area. To the east of the Appalachians the coal-fields have been, to a great extent, worn away by the action of the sea-waves, which, with the changes of level of the continent have acted with great force all along the Atlantic border. In place of the continuous belt of coal-bearing rocks, which lies on the western side of the Appalachians, we have on the east half a dozen detached basins, some of which were formed, not during the Carboniferous age, but in the ages immediately following upon it.

Beginning with the northern portion of the Appalachian basin, we observe the existence of some deposits of coal in Newfoundland. So far none of these coal-bearing strata of this remote island have been worked, and it does not seem likely that they will prove of much value. Next south, in Nova Scotia and Cape Breton, there are some small areas which contain good coal. It is expensive to work these deposits, for the reason that the beds have been much disturbed by mountain-building, and their tilted positions make it difficult for miners to win the material. The most important of these mines are situated in Cape Breton, where the coal is followed in dipping strata beneath the sea-level, and in places below the floor of the ocean.

From Nova Scotia southward to Massachusetts and Rhode Island, the whole of the deposits containing coal have either been stripped away by the action of the sea and that of glacial ice or lie buried beneath the level of the ocean. In the region about Narragansett Bay, partly within Rhode Island and partly in Massachusetts, we have the next more southern field of coal-bearing rocks. In this interesting basin the coal, unlike that of Nova Scotia, which is of an ordinary soft or bituminous character, is a very hard anthracite, so much changed, indeed, from its original nature that it cannot be burned in an open fire or in a profitable way in making steam; therefore, although the amount of coal in this basin is large, it has not proved of much service in the arts. In this field the beds containing the coal are exceedingly crumpled and twisted by mountain-building action. The region has evidently been at one time the seat of tolerably high mountains, though at present, by the long-continued action of river glaciers and of the sea at higher levels than it now occupies, the surface has been planed down to a nearly level form.

From Rhode Island southward to southern Virginia there are no traces of coal occurring in economic quantities. In the region about Richmond, Va., there is a small basin containing an abundance of coals which were formed during the age commonly known as the Trias, which followed almost immediately after the great coal-making time. This Richmond basin, like that of Rhode Island, has been very much disturbed by mountain-building forces, and was probably at one time the seat of lofty elevations; but it too has been planed down by the sea until its nearly level surface is only a few feet above the present level of the ocean. These coals of the Virginian district, unlike those of Rhode Island, are extremely inflammable and yield a large amount of gas even before they are burned: the quantity of this gas, which when mixed with atmospheric air readily explodes, causes the mines to be of a very fiery character, liable to great explosions of what the miners term fire-damp. On this account, and also because the beds lie in very inconvenient positions owing to the mountain-building to which they have been subjected, this basin is of no great economic value. Yet further south and further inland in North Carolina there are two or three small fields of similar coal which have been somewhat mined at various times, but have proved essentially valueless because of the irregularity of the strata and the quantity of gas which exudes from the deposits.

The coal-fields on the western side of the Blue Ridge, extending from the northern part of Pennsylvania to central Alabama, are on the whole not only more continuous than those of the Atlantic shore, but contain more beds of useful fuel. Including the fields of southern Michigan and those of Indiana, Illinois, and Kentucky, which were once united with the main field, but have been separated from it by the wearing action of rivers and frost, this western coal-field is the largest, richest, and on the whole the most extensive of any deposit known or likely to be discovered in the world, unless it should be the great coal-field of China, the character of which is not yet well known. These several parts of the Appalachian coal-fields contain a total area of near 100,000 square miles of workable beds. This area is at least several times as extensive as that occupied by the coal-fields of Great Britain. Both by their position and their extent, the coal-bearing rocks of the Appalachian district are better suited to the needs of man than those of any other country. They are so placed as to be near to the most fertile lands of the continent and to the sea-shore. In the Mississippi Valley the great streams of that river system provide the miner with cheap ways by which he may take the fuel to market.

The greater portion of the coal in the Appalachian district is of the soft variety. That is, the coal burns with a smoky flame, for the reason that it yields a great deal of matter which when heated passes into the state of gas. In central Pennsylvania there are a number of small fields originally connected with the west Appalachian coal-area, but now divided from that area and from each other by the mountain folds in which anthracite or hard coals are found. Anthracite is that form of coal in which the material burns with little or no flame, for the reason that it yields no gas. Although these little basins have in all not more than five hundred square miles, the coal usually occurs in very thick beds, and on account of its superior heating powers is of great value. The Rhode Island coals are also anthracite, but as before remarked are too hard for use, having been changed, since they were buried, so far from their original character that they are only of value for particular uses, such as smelting ores. There are no other known localities of anthracite occurring in quantities sufficient to have value in the Appalachian district.

The stores of petroleum and natural gas contained in the Appalachian district are altogether limited to the region west of the Alleghany division of that system.

They occupy the field of table-lands which lie on the eastern flank of the Mississippi Valley in the neighboring portions of the basin of the Great Lakes. They are indeed beyond the true boundaries of the district, which has been dislocated by the Appalachian mountain-building movements, but the most of this oil and gas field is within the region which has been somewhat elevated by the same forces which have crumpled the beds further to the east. It is probable that the same oil and gas found in these horizontal rocks originally occurred in the mountain-built rocks of Pennsylvania and the neighboring districts, but the breaking of the rocks which was brought about by the mountain-building gave the gas an opportunity to escape, and it forced along with it the oil, leaving the strata without either material.

The oil and gas of the region west of the Mississippi is now found in patches scattered over the region from near the Mississippi to the foot of the mountains on the west. The fact that these substances are found only in particular localities is readily explained when we understand the conditions of their formation and preservation. To form oil and gas, which are generally associated together, it was necessary for a quantity of the remains of animals and plants to accumulate in strata. By their gradual decay these remains produced those valuable substances, but it was required for their preservation in the strata that there should be porous rocks such as coarse sandstones, in the crevices of which, the spaces between the grains, oil and gas could be stored. It was also necessary that in the bed above where the decomposition took place there should be dense layers of a clayey sort serving to confine the gas and prevent it escaping to the surface. It was furthermore important that no breaks should exist in these overlying dense layers, lest the gas should go out, driving the oil along with it, and escape to the air.

It is easily seen that these conditions necessary for the formation and storage of petroleum are not likely to occur everywhere over a large district; and so we have only here and there conditions which permit us to obtain oil or gas by boring through the overlying strata to the bed in which it is stored. When thus obtained, we find the gas is always under great pressure. At times this amounts to as much as one thousand pounds to the inch, or from five to ten times the pressure of steam in an ordinary engine boiler. The gas rushes forth with great energy; where oil was formed with it this oil is driven out with great violence and may be gathered for the market. In other cases there is no oil found, or the quantity is so small that it is not profitable, though the gas may be abundant: the supply is often conveyed in pipes to distant points and used for a great variety of purposes.

The petroleum, or rock oil, from these wells of the Ohio Valley now affords the principal supply of kerosene used in the world: the only other region with anything like so great a product is that on the shores of the Caspian Sea, about the town of Baiku, where the conditions of its natural storage appear to be essentially like those of the American district. Along with the rock oil contained in the fluid as it comes out of the ground is found a great variety of valuable substances. When in its natural state this oil is a black fluid. By various processes there is separated from it paraffine, which is used for making wax-like candles; very inflammable oils known as naphthas, which though not fit for lamps may be used for making gas and in various other arts; a great variety of dyes known as aniline colors; certain peculiar oils, which serve for lubricating machinery; and a great range of other less important products. Although the Caspian field promises in the end to afford a supply of petroleum possibly as great as that obtained in the Ohio Valley, no other region in the world is known to afford such quantities of rock gas as are obtained in the last-named district.

Among the ores of the metals found in the Appalachian district we must give the first place to those of iron. Ores of this nature — that is, various combinations of iron with oxygen — abound throughout the Appalachian region. Beginning on the north, we find these ores abundant in Newfoundland, where, on account of the inaccessibility of the island, they have not been much studied. They are also plentiful in Nova Scotia and Cape Breton. New England has no noteworthy iron ores except in the region bordering on New York state, where there are some considerable deposits. In New York and Pennsylvania iron ores occur in greater plenty, but it is in Virginia, western North Carolina, eastern Tennessee, northern Georgia and Alabama, and eastern Kentucky that we find the great iron district of the Appalachian mountain system.

In all this southern region the iron ores are principally found in beds, which were originally composed of limestone, afterward converted into iron ore in a curious and interesting way. Where the bed of limestone has overlying it a thick mass of sandstone, perhaps hundreds of feet in depth, and where the rain-water is free to creep down through the soils to these rocks, the water first takes up in the soil, in the manner before described, a certain amount of carbonic acid gas. The presence of this gas in the water enables the fluid to dissolve the iron oxide with which it comes in contact. There is generally a good deal of iron in sandstone rocks, so when it comes to the layer of lime the water has a good deal of that metal in solution. It then abandons the iron, taking lime in its place; and so the oxide of the metal is left where the limestone lay before. Gradually in this manner all the lime goes away, and in its place we have left a carbonate of iron. From this ore, more or less changed by the action of the water, nearly all the iron of the Southern states is made.

A peculiar advantage possessed by these irons of the southern Appalachian district consists in the fact that good coal lies immediately near the beds, and so the material for smelting the ore is easily obtained. So, too, limestone, which it is necessary to use along with the iron ore and the fuel to make the melted matter flow easily, abounds in this district. The result of these advantages is that in the states above named the manufacture of iron is coming to be a very extensive industry.

The Appalachian district, though it contains a certain amount of other metals, is so far surpassed in these resources by other parts of the continent, that they have relatively little value. A considerable amount of gold was in former days produced in Virginia and the Carolinas and Georgia; but it has proved impossible to work these mines with free labor with the same profit which was obtained when slaves could be used. In Nova Scotia a few gold mines are profitably worked, but the precious metals of the Appalachian district are on the whole of small importance. Some copper ores have been mined in Newfoundland, in Vermont, New Jersey, North Carolina, and East Tennessee, but the product has not been very great. Ores of manganese, which are used in making certain kinds of steel and for producing oxygen needed in bleaching processes, are produced in Virginia. Iron pyrite, a combination of iron and sulphur, occurs in considerable abundance in Massachusetts, New Hampshire, and Virginia. It is considerably mined, and the ore is used in making sulphuric acid. Zinc ores abound in New Jersey, southwestern Virginia, and eastern Tennessee, but at present they are not much mined.

The building stones and clays of the Appalachian region are valuable. On the coast of New England the granites are very much quarried. Vermont, Georgia, and eastern Tennessee afford a great deal of marble, which although not fit for statuary purposes, is excellent for building. The sandstones of New Jersey and the Connecticut Valley, which come from the rocks of Triassic age, are extensively, though locally, used for building purposes. From Maine to Georgia, in the central portions of the Appalachian district, slates fit for roofing and other purposes, are extensively quarried. Clays from the central portion of the Appalachian district south of New York are largely dug for pottery purposes. The little changed rocks on the western flank of the Appalachians yield at many places excellent water cements. On the Atlantic coast near Charleston, S.C., and in western Florida, in a field somewhat remote from the Appalachian Mountains, there are extensive deposits of lime phosphate derived from the remains of ancient animals which used these substances in forming their skeletons. These phosphates are dug in large quantities and utilized, when mixed with other materials, as artificial manures for cotton and other crops. Less valuable deposits of a similar kind are found at a number of points in North Carolina, and recent discoveries of the same substance have been made in western Florida. These latter, though as yet but partly explored, promise to be of great value.

The mineral resources of the Laurentian district are not well known. All that part of it from which the waters flow towards Hudson Bay is hardly yet explored by travellers. It is only the portion which drains into the St. Lawrence which has begun to be examined. This region is remarkable for the large quantities of iron, copper, and phosphate of lime which it contains. The greater part of the deposits of iron and copper yet discovered lies on the southern shore of Lake Superior, in what is called the upper or northern peninsula of the state of Michigan. In this region the copper is found in the metallic state, a form in which it seldom occurs in any quantity in other countries. So large is the supply obtained from the mines in this district that it contributes to commerce more of that metal than any other equal area in the world. In this region also there are very extensive deposits of iron, of which the most valuable occur in the form of magnetite, a dense black ore which has the property of attracting the magnet. This region is now the seat of what is perhaps the largest production of iron ore obtained in any equally extensive area in the world. The ore is very rich, containing from sixty to seventy per cent. of iron, and on this account can be profitably transported to great distances. The larger part of it is taken to the furnaces of Pennsylvania and Ohio and Illinois, where it is used in making steel.

Phosphate deposits, which are principally used for

making artificial manures, abundantly occur north of the shore of Lake Ontario. The products of these mines are shipped to Europe. There are also in the region north of Lake Erie and Lake Superior some silver deposits, but this region has not produced much of this precious metal. The rocks of all this district were formed long before the coal-bearing rocks began to be deposited, and therefore they contain none of this valuable material. Immediately north of Lake Erie there is a small district which has yielded some petroleum, but only in unimportant quantities. As a whole the Laurentian district appears to contain much less mineral wealth than that which is found in the region to the southward.

The Adirondack district, immediately around the foot of the mountains of that name, affords a good deal of iron of magnetic character, but these stores have proved of less importance since the discovery of the great iron ore deposits in northern Michigan. This region once yielded some lead, but the mines have become exhausted.

The central portion of the Mississippi Valley, though almost destitute of mountains, has some interesting mineral fields. Thus on the line between Illinois and Iowa there is a district which formerly contributed a great deal of lead to the commerce of the world, though it no longer is advantageous to work the mines. In southeastern Missouri and southeastern Kansas there is an interesting field where extensive deposits of lead and zinc occur, which have long been profitably worked. Yet further south, in the region about the Ozark Mountains of Arkansas, there are extensive deposits of the valuable ores of manganese.

In the Cordilleran district, from the foot of the Rocky Mountains west to the Pacific, the whole of the continent is mountain built, and thus offers a favorable seat for the formation and disclosure of mineral deposits; except as regards fuel materials this region probably contains a larger store of mineral wealth than any other equally extensive area in the world. The variety in the substances afforded from this district is also greater than in any other land. Beginning with the fuel resources, we note that in this field there are few coals of the same geological age as those on the eastern part of the continent. In general, the eastern coals were formed in the so-called Carboniferous period, while the Cordilleran coals were laid down in later stages of the earth's history. The deposits of rock oil and gas are also rare, and though as yet little known, apparently have no great promise. None of the coal-fields are of as great area as those of the Appalachian region, but they are fortunately scattered through the country, occurring in Colorado, Wyoming, California, in Oregon, and in Washington. The deposits of petroleum known to be of value are limited to the central portion of California. Although these stores of fuel are usually in quality much inferior to those which occur in the eastern part of the United States, they have, owing to their position, a great economic importance. The whole of the Cordilleran district has but a scanty supply of wood. The mines and smelting works where ores are treated demand a great deal of fuel, which but for these small basins of rather inferior coal would have to be brought altogether from the eastern part of the Mississippi Valley.

The iron ores of the Cordilleran district are abundant

and of very good quality. They have as yet been little used, for the reason that they are far from great markets and generally remote from fuel suitable for use in furnaces. The most important mineral resources of this district are found in the ores containing gold, silver, and copper. In no other region are these metals, especially the first two named, found in quantities sufficient to justify mining over so large a field. California was the first part of North America to produce any considerable quantities of gold. From 1848 until the present date over one thousand millions of dollars' worth of that metal have been produced within the limits of this state. A very large quantity of gold and a nearly equal value of silver have been obtained from the great vein in Nevada known as the Comstock lode, one of the largest known deposits of precious metals in the world. Perhaps the most extensive system of mines in the world are in operation in this deposit. The mines of the Comstock lode are remarkable not only for their extent but for the high temperature which is encountered. The miners not infrequently work in a heat of 120° F., at the depth of not more than two thousand feet below the surface. Profitable gold mines are also worked at various points in the eastern portion of the Cordilleras as far north as southern Alaska.

The gold of this Cordilleran district was at first found in deposits of gravel, formed along the path of ancient rivers. Wherever the gold occurs in veins, the process of downwearing, to which the country is subjected by breaking up the rock, releases the gold from its matrix: in the form of little pellets it starts on its journey to the sea. Being very heavy, it finds lodgement among the pebbles of the stream bed or in crannies of the rock over which the water flows. Unlike the other metals, nearly all of which save platinum combine with oxygen, forming more or less soluble combinations, and are thus readily borne away by the streams, gold, not being oxidizable, remains uncorroded in the stream beds, and does not go away to the sea until it has been pounded into very small bits by the action of stones driven over its surface by the torrents. In many parts of the Rocky Mountains, particularly in Colorado and California, the ordinary rivers, or those which flow from beneath ancient glaciers, accumulated vast amounts of this gravel containing gold. In many cases the rivers have in recent times abandoned their old stream beds and left these gravels lying high above their present channels. Sometimes the deposits of sand, clay, and gravel, containing the precious metal, are one or two hundred feet thick, the richest portion of the gold-bearing material lying at the bottom of the deposit near the bed-rock.

Where the auriferous gravel is thin and the gold relatively large in quantity, the miner wins the precious metal from the mixture by simple means. The easiest way is to take up the gravel and wash the gold from it in a large round-bottomed pan, by stirring the gravel with water, which causes the heavy gold to settle on the bottom; gradually removing the pebbles, the miner finally obtains a hand full of fine sand, composed in the main of magnetic iron, but containing the most of the gold which was originally held in the rejected gravel. The more effective way is to wash the gold in a trough with little partitions across its bottom, and an inclined bed; the gold-bearing material is put in at the upper end, and a stream of water is allowed to flow through the trough, the whole mass being moved on rockers in the fashion of an old-time cradle. In this way the gold is caught just above the bars of wood. The process is aided by pouring a little quicksilver from time to time into the trough; the quicksilver combines with the gold and helps to hold it in position as the sand and gravel pass by. A still more effective system of winning gold from detritus is to have, instead of the cradle, a long sluice-way of planks, three or four feet wide, and perhaps a thousand feet long, with very many little partitions of wood, which rise a few inches above the bottom. A stream of water is made to course through this channel, and the gold-bearing gravel is dumped into it.

Where the gravel is very thick, it often happens that the gold does not amount to more than a few cents to the cubic yard of the mass, and none of the simpler systems are applicable. The miner then seeks to bring a stream of water from a distance in such a manner that at his works it may have a head of two hundred feet or more, so arranged that he may lead the water down to the workings by means of pipes. He then allows this water to flow from a nozzle like that which sends a stream from a fire engine, only the stream commonly has a diameter of from four to six inches or more, and flies out with several times the force which it does from our fire apparatus. Directing this stream against the steep bank of gravel, he washes the whole mass of debris into the sluice-way. The stream is often strong enough to move bowlders a foot or two in diameter and to take them swiftly through the sluice. This was at one time a common method of mining the gold deposits. It has been found, however, that the large amount of debris thus carried into the streams has not been taken away to the sea, but encumbers the paths of the rivers, causing their bottoms to rise to such an extent that they flow out over the tillable lands, covering them with masses of sterile sand and gravel. In consequence of this it has been found necessary to stop, by law, mining by this hydraulic method.

The silver deposits of the Cordilleran district of North America are widely distributed over the southern and western portions of the mountainous belt, from southern Mexico to the northern part of the United States. Unlike the gold, which usually occurs in pure form, silver is almost invariably found in the form of oxides and much of it in combination with the ores of other metals. The largest production of silver has been from the Comstock lode, where it is found associated with gold, and in the district of Eureka, Nev., and that of Leadville, Col. Next after the silver country of South America, in the Andes in and about Peru, these North American localities have produced more of this metal than any other mines in the world.

The copper deposits of the Rocky Mountains are in the main limited to the districts of Nevada and Montana; while about Lake Superior the greater part of the copper is found in the metallic form, in these Cordilleran districts, though the supply is large, it occurs in association with other substances, and not in the metallic form. Consequently it is generally more costly to produce the metal than in the mines of northern Michigan.

The Cordilleran district also affords a large number of other valuable metals and non-metallic earth products. Iron, manganese, and lead abound. A little of the iron is worked in Colorado, and the lead is extensively produced from the silver mines, where it occurs in the ores from which the silver is extracted. Tin occurs, but probably not in sufficient quantities to be profitably worked.

This region abounds in various classes of substances, such as salt and soda, which have been produced by the long-continued evaporation of lake waters. Their plenty in this part of the world is due to the interesting fact that in very recent geological times the amount of rainfall has greatly diminished. There were numerous large lakes which of old discharged by rivers to the sea, but which are now represented by shrunken salt-water basins such as the Salt Lake of Utah, or have entirely disappeared, leaving deserts where their waters once stood.

The building materials of the Cordilleran district are, owing to the complicated geology of the country, extremely varied. They include not only the ordinary crystalline and sedimentary rocks, but many kinds of stone formed by volcanic action.

Little is known concerning the mineral resources of the Cordilleras north of the line between Canada and the United States.

The region is difficult to explore for its metals, for the reason that it is much more brush and forest clad than the parts of the district to the southward. This covering of vegetation hides the rocks from the prospector's eye. On the other hand, from the Canadian line southward to southern Mexico, the surface is generally destitute of woods and often without a covering of soil, so that the character of the rocks and their mineral contents are relatively well revealed. In large part, the rapid extension of mining in this great field is due to the ease with which the mineral wealth is discovered.

CHAPTER VI.

EFFECT OF THE FORM OF NORTH AMERICA ON THE HISTORY OF THE COLONISTS FROM EUROPE AND THEIR DESCENDANTS.

Position of first European settlements. Difficulty of penetrating into the interior. Successive steps of the westward movement of the people. Commercial growth. History of Spanish conquests. Influence of geographic conditions on slavery; on the issue of the Civil War. Influence of the Mississippi River.

WE have already seen how the form of North America greatly affected the way in which it came to be settled from the Old World, and also the influence of its surface on certain features in the early history of these colonies. We shall now go further and trace the way in which the shape of the surface has influenced and is now affecting the development of the country.

The first European settlements of North America were placed along the shore of the Atlantic and the Gulf of Mexico. The very earliest European peoples to come to this continent were probably the ancestors of the present Norwegians or Danes. These Scandinavians found their way to Iceland, occupying the southeastern portion of that country in 870. From that outpost they rapidly pushed on to Greenland, settling the southern and western portion of that country, thence creeping down along the shore until they came to some point, the place of which is not yet known, in the region south of the Gulf of St. Lawrence, where in the tenth century they made temporary settlements. This early colony was maintained but a brief time. Thus the first European colonists occupied only the northeastern outskirts of the continent. The French, the English, the Dutch, and the Spaniards contended with each other for the possession of the continent with the result that in the beginning of this century the Spaniards held the whole of the Gulf of Mexico and claimed the greater part of the Pacific coast; the English, the section of what is now the United States, east of the Rocky Mountains and north of the Gulf states, though their real possessions were practically limited to the region north of the states of Mississippi and Alabama and east of the Mississippi River. Already at the beginning of the century, two nations, which had originally held large areas of North America, had yielded their territory to the English; namely, the French and the Hollanders. To the United States fell that portion of the territory occupied by the British, south of the Great Lakes, and a considerable part of that south of the St. Lawrence River.

The extension of the English colonies was limited not only by the resistance of the aborigines, but by the fact that they had no good way into the interior of the continent. The French had used the channel of the St. Lawrence; the Spanish and French for a little while, the channel of the Mississippi, and so won their way to the great fertile districts of the Mississippi Valley. The English were separated from that field by the ridges of the Alleghanies, a rough country occupied by very dense forests. If Canada had, at the time of the Revolution, joined the United States, the way into the interior of the continent, through the chain of the Great

Lakes, would have been open to the whole of the English people, but, owing to the fact that the Canadian country remained in the possession of the British, the people of the United States could not use it. There was a natural way up the valley of the Mohawk from the Hudson, but about the head of that river was the stronghold of the most warlike of the American savages. Until they were subjugated, and the people of the American Union obtained control of ports on Lake Erie, the Great Lakes were useless to them. This end was not attained until the beginning of the present century. The first good pathway through the Appalachians was from the Virginia settlements, by way of the Shenandoah Valley, thence across the head-waters of the Tennessee, a tributary of the Ohio, and then over Cumberland Mountain to a low gap, which gave access to the plain lands and open woods of the Ohio Valley. Hence it came about that the first people of English blood to found settlements on the waters of the Mississippi were the Virginians, who took with them their African servants, and founded slavery west of the mountains. Also by way of the upper Tennessee River the state of Tennessee was settled.

For a long time after Kentucky became occupied by the Virginians the Indians and their allies, the British, still held the country north of the Ohio. In the latter part of the eighteenth century the mother country had pretty thoroughly dispossessed the French from all the territory now occupied by the states of Illinois, Indiana and Ohio, and Michigan. It was more than thirty years after Kentucky passed into the control of the English people before the region north of the Ohio and south of the Great Lakes was possessed by our people. Gradually good wagon roads were made through the northern part of the Appalachian district, a country much more difficult to traverse than that of Virginia because the undergrowth of the forest was thicker and the surface was scattered over with bowlders, and intersected with swamps, as is the case in all glaciated countries. The great advantage of routes to the west by the way of the upper Tennessee was that the forests were less tangled and the surface of the ground much more even than in the glacial country to the northward.

Although the numerous wagon-ways which were built between the years 1815 and 1840 from the old settlements of the Atlantic coast to the Mississippi Valley enabled a large number of emigrants from the older states to gain access to this country, it was not until railways were pushed through these mountains that the rapid occupation of this wide and fertile land began. It was a great advantage for the railways, as well as for the earlier wagon roads, that as soon as they had passed the relatively narrow region of mountains they entered upon broad plains which were generally but partly forest clad, so that the cost of constructing these roads was not great. From 1815 to 1840 the settlements in the Mississippi Valley were mainly limited to the forest country which occupies the eastern portion of that valley. It was necessary for every farmer to hew down the forest from all the fields which he won to tillage, and after this serious task was accomplished it was generally from ten to fifteen years before the stumps disappeared from the ground to such an extent that tillage was easy.

After 1840 the immigrants broke through into the

prairie district, and rapidly drove out the Indians from those great plains. In this region the task of winning farms did not demand more than the tenth part of the labor required in the forest-clad portions of the country. The construction of railways proceeded with amazing celerity. The great rivers of the Mississippi Valley afforded ready access to a large portion of the surface, and so the white population swept over the plains with great rapidity, winning, in fifty years, a larger area of the continent to the uses of civilization than had been won in the two centuries of previous growth.

If the whole of this country had been clad with forests, as is much of the eastern portion of the Ohio Valley to this day, the movement of the population could not have been anything like as rapid. It is probable that if the country had been densely wooded, the frontier could not, at the present time, have advanced much beyond the line of the Mississippi. We thus see how important to man are the simpler physical features of the land. The Appalachians restrained the colonial population to the Atlantic coast. The rich forest-lands of the Ohio Valley gave a new field for a portion of this people, but it required more than fifty years to push the farming country up to the edge of the prairies of Indiana and Illinois, while it has taken scarce a third of the century to extend the culture from the margin of the front district to the base of the Rocky Mountains.

We thus see how profoundly the general shape of the continent affected the early history of the Europeans within its area. The great fertile basin of the Mississippi was not accessible to the English or Dutch settlements, nor was it easy to be entered by the French or the Spaniards. The swift current of the Mississippi, and the vast marshes which border it for a great part of its length, made it difficult to settle the valley from the Gulf of Mexico. The way through the St. Lawrence Valley is frost-bound for half the year and is interrupted by the rapids of the St. Lawrence and the Falls of Niagara, as well as by the highlands between the great lakes and the Mississippi waters. So the French and Spanish were kept from more than a nominal control of the heart of the continent until the British settlements gained strength to break over the barriers of the Appalachians and possess this imperial domain.

The most important commercial growth of the United States dates from the extension of settlements to the Mississippi Valley. At first the descending waters of that stream, and afterwards the Erie Canal and its connected artificial water-ways, and yet later the railways, have conveyed the crops of this fertile land to the sea-shore, whence they have gone to the markets of Europe. The greater part of the ability and energy of this country since about 1790 to the present day has been devoted to the subjugation of this central valley of the continent.

For a long time after the Mississippi Valley had become the seat of extensive settlements derived from the Atlantic coast, the Cordilleran region remained almost unknown. The branches of the Mississippi River which extend towards it are, with the exception of the Missouri, unnavigable, and this stream at the head of its convenient navigation lies several hundred miles to the east of the mountain wall. Moreover, the plain country which extends eastward from the foot of the Rocky Mountains, is, for a considerable distance from their base, so dry as to be mostly unfit for farming purposes. Added to this is the fact that the Rocky Mountain district, and the plains which border it, were ranged over by large tribes of warlike Indians, who found their support in hunting the buffalo, and were thereby kept in a nomadic and very savage state. It was not until the Mexican War led to the acquisition of California by the United States, that these mountains began to be carefully explored. The discovery of gold in the region about San Francisco in the year 1848 speedily gave a certain commercial importance to this region and made it necessary to connect it by other means than the sea with the remainder of the United States. At first this connection was by means of wagon road of a rude sort; but the rapid extension of the transcontinental commerce led to the construction of several railways across the Cordilleras. The first railway connection between the Mississippi Valley and the Pacific coast was completed in 1870. Since then three other railways have been constructed across the continent and a great many branch roads carried through to different parts of the Cordilleras. The result has been that the last half of the present century has been characterized by the subjugation of this region to the uses of our race.

We may thus divide the westward progress of the English-speaking peoples in North America into three periods; the first extending from the time of settlement in the early years of the seventeenth century to near the end of the eighteenth, a period of 150 years, in which this people were confined almost altogether to the narrow strip of fertile lands to the eastward of the Appalachians. Next, a period from about 1790 to the middle of the nineteenth century, in which they obtained, substantially, control of the Mississippi Valley. Third, the last forty years of the present century, in which they have overcome the difficulties which beset the occupation of the Cordilleran district. The movements of the population in Canada have been in a certain way parallel to those in the United States. That portion of the English-speaking people have recently won their way beyond the difficult grounds at the head of Lake Superior, and entered on the possession of the wide strip of fertile lands which lie in the valley of the Red River of the North, the Saskatchewan and other neighboring streams. They have also, by means of a railway, broken through the barriers of the Rocky Mountains, and obtained connection with their considerable settlements on the Pacific coast. These three stages in the development of the English-speaking countries, the Atlantic coast stage, that of the valley of the Mississippi, that of the Cordilleras and the Pacific coast, are thus seen to correspond to the great physical divisions of the continent.

It is worth while to notice in some detail the history of Mexico, as affording a contrast between two European races, the English and the Spaniards. Mexico was occupied as a Spanish colony more than a hundred years before the English-speaking people obtained a foothold in the northern part of the continent. From Mexico access to the Cordilleras, the Mississippi Valley, and the Pacific coast of California is relatively easy, but with these advantages the Spaniards in the beginning of this century, when Mexico had its largest area, had won only a small area in Texas, and a portion of the coast of California beyond the original limits of their colonies. In two centuries and a half, during which the English-speaking people have subjugated the greater part of the continent, the Spanish settlements have made but trifling gains in population, and have added but little to their domain.

The difference in the success of these two peoples is probably due in part to original differences in the population, and in part to differences in the character of the countries which they have occupied. The Spaniards who settled in Mexico did not displace the Indian population, but combined with the aborigines, making a mixed race of relatively feeble capacity. The British everywhere displaced the native people, and have remained essentially unmixed with the aboriginal population. In Mexico the greater part of the country so far lacks rain that tillage produces little more than the food required for local consumption. The foreign exports have consisted mainly of the precious metals. The English-speaking people acquired possession of that part of the continent which is well suited to the production of great staples of agriculture, and thus were enabled rapidly to accumulate wealth.

The swift growth in population of the English part of North America has largely been due to the great body of immigrants which have come to that region from northern Europe, particularly those of English, Scotch, Irish, German, and Scandinavian origin. These people are attracted to the United States, not only by the rapid development of its industries consequent on the access which was gained to the Mississippi Valley, but also because the climate of the Northern states of the Union is so much like that of the countries from which they came. The rapid growth in population in the Mississippi Valley, as well as on the Atlantic sea-board, has made it possible for these English-speaking people to push the Spaniards and the French from the northern shore of the Gulf of Mexico, and from the Pacific coast, to Texas and a portion of the Cordilleras. By the circumstances of their development, by their native character, and by the physical conditions the English-speaking people have gained a firm hold on the continent of North America; they have possession of all the parts of it which are well suited to the development of the race. Those portions which are occupied by Mexico and the Central American states, and also the West India Islands are, because of the climate and the nature of the soil or because of the quality of the population, undesirable territories for the descendants of northern Europeans.

The soil and climate of the United States, and in a less pronounced way of the portions of the Canadian domain, which lie in the valley of the St. Lawrence, and in the Winnipeg district, are well suited for varied and profitable agriculture. Nearly all the crops which are tilled in the Old World do well on one portion or another of this surface, and in addition to these resources of the Old World America has in maize a peculiar resource. This plant is nowhere else so successful over a wide area as within the limits of the United States. Since the settlement of the country it has been the principal grain crop of the continent. A large portion of the more southern district of the continent is well suited to the growth of cotton. The soil is fertile, the summer is long and moderately dry, both of which conditions favor the growth of this plant, with the result that more than one-half the world's supply of this staple is produced in North America. Tobacco is also well suited to the climate and soil of North America, and is more largely produced in this than in any other continent.

Although the agricultural conditions of North America are and have been favorable to the growth of a farming population, and thereby to the best interests of its civilization, the peculiar fitness of the country for the culture of cotton and tobacco has been in certain ways disadvantageous to it. The institution of negro slavery was very profitable to the planters who grew these crops; the consequence was, that this institution was maintained and extended in the southern portions of the United States long after it had completely disappeared from all other lands in the control of the English race. The consequences of these conditions have been very great. In the first place, the profitableness of slavery led to the importation of a great number of Africans, who have increased rapidly in numbers, and now amount to somewhere near one-tenth of the total population. The political difficulties connected with slavery led to the greatest civil war in modern times.

In the limits of the slave-holding district, and in the history of the Civil War, to which the institution gave rise, we see certain very interesting effects of the conditions which climate and soil bring about. Slavery was profitable only in the regions where cotton and tobacco could be profitably cultivated. Both of these crops demand large amounts of labor of a cheap sort; labor which can be entirely at the farmer's command. They can be grown to the best advantage on considerable plantations. They require a long summer which shall be rather dry. The result was that it was only in the Southern states of the Union that slavery was maintained, although it at first existed in all the American colonies. It disappeared from the region north of the tobacco and cotton fields; it found no place north of the Ohio or Missouri Rivers, and was hardly profitable in Maryland, Kentucky, or Missouri, where cotton cannot be advantageously grown. Moreover, the highland district of the Appalachians, which occupies about one-tenth of the portion of the South which is fitted for agriculture, and projects far towards the Gulf of Mexico, was, by the roughness of its surface and the peculiarities of its climate, essentially unfit for plantations where the crops should be tilled by negro labor. This district never was to any extent occupied by slave-holders, and thus it divided the South by a wide region characterized by free labor alone.

When the Civil War came, the South found itself at a great disadvantage on account of this peculiar topographic feature of the country. All the seceding states, except Tennessee and Arkansas, have extensive sea-fronts; and as the South was not a maritime country, partly because of the generally shallow nature of its ports, it failed to obtain any strength on the sea. It was, therefore, cut off from free commerce with the Old World, and thus deprived of its natural sources of supply of materials for war, as well as of its chance of finding a market for its agricultural products.

Moreover, the principal river of the continent, the Mississippi, cut the Confederate states in twain. As soon as the Federal fleets and armies obtained control of this river, the Southern people were at a hopeless disadvantage in this contest. The Northern states, with their system of small farms and free labor, afforded a very much larger share of able-bodied soldiers in proportion to the population than could be obtained in the Southern states, where a large part of the soil-tillers were slaves. In this way we see that while the physical conditions of the country favored the development of slavery and thus brought about the Civil War, they likewise gave a great advantage to the Northern states in their effort to subdue the rebellion which arose from the presence of that social system.

CHAPTER VII.

THE COMMERCIAL CONDITION OF NORTH AMERICA.

Conditions of commerce. Continuous increase of exchange between countries. Railroad transportation of the continent: coast line; harbors; rivers. Lakes and seas. Sources of power: iron; fuel. Underground water. Earthquakes. Natural conditions affecting the settlement by Europeans. Relations to Indians. Exports: furs; timber; fisheries. Importation of slaves. Isthmus of Darien.

In the early days, all civilized peoples depended but little on supplies drawn from other countries. Each considerable community produced from its own labor nearly all it consumed. In this early state only luxuries, ornaments, or rare articles of food came from abroad. Gradually, however, it has been found most advantageous for each country to produce those articles which nature has fitted its soil or rocks to yield. In the present state of the more enlightened countries none of them could maintain their populations in comfort, except for the contributions of other lands. Each year this interchange of products of the soil, of the mine, or of other intelligent labor, rapidly increases, and it is evident that in the future the fitness of any country for civilized man will depend not only on what the country can produce, but on the ways by which the products may find access to the markets of the world, and by which the people may in turn receive the articles for which they exchange their own products.

In the broad fields of a continent the question of

internal transportation is almost as important as that which concerns the intercourse with other countries. In an area such as North America the larger part of the needs of any region may be supplied from the lands diversely situated in other portions of the continental area. Thus the crops of the farmer in Minnesota may serve to feed the cotton-planters of the Gulf states, and the wool of Texas may supply the mills of New England. The coals of Pennsylvania go to the recesses of the Rocky Mountains, and the preserved salmon from Puget Sound are sold in every state in the Union. The great variety in the soil and climate and under-earth products of North America has led to the institution of a vast internal and external commerce, the extension of which is greatly favored by the physical features of the continent.

One of the geographic advantages of North America for its internal as well as its external commerce, is the vast extent of its coast-line and the sufficient nature of the harbors along the coast. From Labrador to the mouth of the Chesapeake, these shelters for ships, where they may receive and discharge cargoes as well as escape from the dangers of the sea, are very numerous and advantageously situated. From Chesapeake Bay, southward, along the shore to the Isthmus of Darien, the harbors though less good are by dredging and jetties made to serve for the needs of ships of moderate size. On the Pacific coast from the Isthmus of Darien to southern California the harbors are not good. It happens that they are less necessary along that part of the continent, for the reason that the interior country of this isthmus district is relatively narrow; there is not much sent away by the sea or taken in from ships. From the southern part of the United States on the Pacific coast northward to Behring Straits the harbors are on the whole excellent. On the coast of California they are not numerous, but sufficient for the needs of trade. That at San Francisco is one of the finest in the world. From southern Oregon northward the coast is better provided with such shelters than any other part of the world except Scandinavia.

The extended coast-line of North America makes it easy for a large part of the states to communicate with each other by the way of the sea. Twenty-two states of the American Union face on the sea-shore, and none of the colonies or separate governments of the continent lack this contact with the ocean. The internal water-ways are also very favorable for commerce. The chain of Great Lakes, and the St. Lawrence through which they discharge, make a northern water-way into the centre of the continent. Although by water-falls and rapids, Lake Superior was separated from the other lakes, and all these lakes from the sea, they are now connected by canals passable by large ships. It is likely that in time Lake Superior will be similarly connected by means of canals with the other lakes which stretch far to the northwards.

Of the many rivers in North America the Mississippi affords the most extended system of channels for commerce. This stream and its tributaries furnish water-ways to a large part of the states which occupy the great valley of the continent. Its navigable waters extend to seventeen states, from many of which it is possible to go by large vessels directly to the sea. Including the districts which face upon the Great Lakes, all the states and the territories of the Union, except seven which lie within the Rocky Mountains, have good natural waterways to the ocean. So, too, all the habitable portions of British America, except the Cordilleran district in the western portion of Canada, are more or less well placed for communication by water either with the St. Lawrence or Hudson's Bay. Mexico and the Central American states being in the peninsular district of the continent have no great rivers, but the interior country is mostly not far from the coast.

The greater part of the continent of North America is composed of tolerably level land over which railways can easily be constructed, and the mountain districts, even the elevated portions of the Cordilleras, are from the divided nature of the ranges more easily traversed by such ways than the greater elevations of the Old World. Thus the surface of this land is extremely well adapted to the interchange of products of labor between the different portions of the country.

The great inclosed seas of North America, the Gulf of Mexico and the Caribbean, afford a wide field for commerce; except in the period of heavy storms, known as the hurricane months, extending from the middle of August to the first of December, these waters are remarkably well suited for navigation. They have a greater area of fertile soils along their shores than we find in any other mediterranean seas in the world. They afford a ready intercommunication between the great central valley of North America and the northern portion of South America. On the north and east they are bordered by the wonderful chain of isles known as the Antilles, which next after the Malayan Archipelago, is the largest and most fertile group of islands in the world.

The position of North America with reference to the commerce of the world is extremely favorable. On the east lie the western shores of the Old World, in such a position that there is a swift and easy water communication with several states of Europe, and by way of the Mediterranean with a portion of Asia. On the west there is open sea to the eastern coasts of Asia, the islands of the Malayan Archipelago, Australia, and New Zealand. None of the other continents, save perhaps Europe, are on the whole so advantageously placed with reference to commerce. In the days before steam navigation the stormy nature of the North Atlantic made the passage to Europe at once slow and dangerous. These difficulties have been overcome by steam vessels, and thus it now requires only a week for a journey from the ports of the United States to those of Europe where of old it required about six times as long.

The only part of North America which is not advantageously situated for connection with the rest of the world is the northern portion of the continent. Although these lands of high latitude are much intersected by straits and bays which afford excellent harbors, the long-continued winter keeps them generally in an ice-locked condition. The great inland sea of Hudson's Bay is only accessible to ships for about four months in the year, and its western shores are so far destitute of good harbors, and slope so gently out to a great distance in the form of mud-flats, that it would be difficult to make it useful for purposes of navigation.

For two hundred years a great deal of effort was given to finding a passage by the sea from Davis Strait to Behring Strait. Although it was finally proved possible with great labor to take a ship through this way, at least in favorable seasons, the channels are so blocked with ice that it can never be a useful commercial route. Moreover, the principal necessity which led the English people to search so long for a route by way of the Arctic Ocean to the ports of the Pacific has passed away. Of old, when the Spanish had control of a large part of the tropical seas, it was very desirable for British ships to avoid these waters in the journey to the far East. The passage around the Cape of Good Hope also required a great deal of time. In modern days the dangers which ships used to encounter from the Spanish fleets or from pirates have disappeared. Moreover, the ship canal through the Isthmus of Suez has removed the necessity of sailing to near the south pole in order to go to the ports of western America or China.

If the northern portion of North America were a fertile country, the inconvenience arising from the lack of access to the harbors brought about by the long winter would be very serious, but the greater portion of the district which can produce any articles of importance to commerce is easily accessible to the Great Lakes, or to the railways which may connect them with Canada and the United States.

The conditions of the soil, climate, and under-earth resources in North America make it plain that this continent is to have very important relations with the rest of the world, arising from an abundant production of food articles, and of certain important metals, as well as materials to be used as fuel. It is already the principal food-exporting continent, furnishing more grain and edible animals to European markets than are obtained from any other land. Among the metals which may be made the articles of commerce, iron, copper, and lead have the foremost place. It is a great advantage for the continent of North America that its abundant supply of coals will enable it to win these metals from their ores at less cost than in any other region, except perhaps in China and certain small parts of Europe.

The coal of North America and the sources of supply of petroleum are more plentiful than those of any other continent, except perhaps Asia. South America, so far as is known, is relatively destitute of these materials, and the stores are likely to be drawn from the northern continent. It is a peculiar advantage of these stores of fuel that they lie mainly in portions of North America which are near the sea, and to a large extent they are upon the great navigable rivers, the Mississippi and its tributaries.

Among the resources of North America which have already exercised a great effect on its commercial development, and are likely to have a still greater influence in the time to come, we may set the abundance of the means by which power may be won for manufacturing purposes. This power is available for arts of all sorts which demand machinery. In large part it comes from the streams of considerable fall which are used to drive mill-wheels. The northeastern portion of North America and a part of the Southern states which lie within the highland of the Appalachians is exceedingly well fitted to afford these stores of energy. In New England and other portions of the north, where sands and gravel of the glacial period are very thick, they hold a great deal of water in their interstices and so keep the rivers well supplied. There are also many lakes which act as reservoirs to feed the streams. In this way the mills are supplied with power throughout the year. In the southern Appalachians, where the rivers drain from great forests, these woods act as a sponge, and deliver the rainfall slowly. Moreover, in that part of the continent the rainfall is large and is apt to be well distributed through the year.

Thus it comes about that the eastern portion of the United States is on the whole a more favorable region for water-power than any other part of the civilized world. The wide distribution of coals in North America makes it possible to obtain cheap fuel, which is applied to machinery through the use of steam. So also very extensive fields of the continent containing natural gas afford an additional source of the energy required in the arts. These conditions make it certain that North America, at least the portion of the continent east of the Mississippi, is likely to be the seat of very extensive manufacturing industries. To these very favorable conditions we must add that this district is everywhere near the sources of abundant food supply; so that, unlike Northern Europe, which has to obtain a large part of the food for its people from other parts of the world, this region has a farming country close by its under-earth resources.

UNDERGROUND WATER.

The condition of the underground waters of a country is a matter of much economic importance to its people. Not only is the supply for domestic purposes generally drawn from this source, but the springs which discharge the water which has journeyed far underground often contain mineral and other substances which give them a healing value; or they are valuable on account of the high temperature which is given them because they have penetrated into the heated deeper earth. North America abounds in mineral springs, probably being in this respect only less rich than the European continent. The most important of these are placed, as is usual with such sources, in the mountain districts, where deep rents in the earth permit the exit of water that has penetrated far underground. In the Appalachian district there are a number of places where deep-journeyed waters emerge. They extend from the line between the United States and Canada to Alabama, the springs occurring in Canada, Vermont, New York, Pennsylvania, Virginia, Tennessee, the Carolinas, and Georgia.

In this eastern part of the United States there are no springs of a high temperature, the greatest heat being about 100° F. The waters are generally valued for their mineral and gaseous contents rather than for the qualities that are given by their heat. In Virginia alone, of all the country east of the Mississippi River, do we find springs warm enough to be of use in the treatment of disease because of their heat as well as their other qualities. In Arkansas there is a group of hot springs whose waters, though very pure as regards mineral matter, have a high temperature, and have been found valuable in the treatment of many diseases. In the Cordilleran district, on account of the recent development of volcanic action, the rocks beneath the mountains are still in many places extremely hot, and as a result we find in these regions a remarkable development of heated springs. The fact that this region is far from the great centres of population makes these springs as yet of small value; but it seems certain that in the time to come they will be of much service to man. In this region there are also great numbers of springs which, though of ordinary temperature, contain a variety of mineral substances, and are certain to prove of great use in the treatment of diseases.

Scattered widely over the non-mountainous regions of North America we find many less important sources whence there come to the surface a class of waters which have a somewhat peculiar origin. These waters arise from no great distance underground, and originate in the stratified rocks which were deposited in the sea, where the interspaces between the bits of material of which they are composed were filled with the brine of the ocean. When these rocks are buried beneath other deposits, the slow chemical changes of the remains of animals and plants which they contain cause the formation of gases, which exert a great pressure and force themselves, along with the water in which they are dissolved, through the joints and the other lines of weakness of the strata to the open air. These gas-impelled springs are generally quite saline, but they contain a great quantity of substances which the fluid has taken up from the rocks through which it has passed.

In the ancient days these salt springs were greatly resorted to by the native plant-eating animals of the country, which drank eagerly of their waters and thereby secured the share of salt which they needed. About certain of these "salt-licks," as the pioneers termed them, we commonly find in the swampy places vast numbers of the bones of the great extinct beasts of this country which passed away soon after the close of the last glacial period. Thus at Big Bone Lick, in Boone County, Ky., where several salt springs emerge in a boggy field, the ground about them is crowded with the bones of a variety of great animals which have perished from the country. In the upper layer we find the skeletons of the bisons, elk, and deer; lower down those of caribou, gigantic musk oxen, elephants, and their kindred the mastodons, as well as an extinct species of bison, probably the ancestor of the form that abounded in this country two hundred years ago. These salt-licks were useful to the frontiersman, as they were to his predecessors of an earlier time. By boiling down their waters he made salt for domestic purposes, which in the early days of the country it would otherwise have been necessary to convey from the shore of the Atlantic Ocean by wagons or pack-horses.

The ordinary springs of eastern North America, and the wells which often take their place as sources of supply for country houses, generally afford tolerably pure water. In nearly all the region where the earth is covered by glacial debris there are few springs of any importance, but water of excellent quality can be obtained by means of wells from the beds of sand and gravel. In the limestone districts which occupy a large part of the Mississippi Valley, and also much of the other parts of the continent, the wells and springs afford water which contains a rather large amount of lime and other mineral matter. The quantity of this material is rarely so great as to induce serious disease, but in certain districts it appears to lead to the formation of concretions of a stony nature within the human body, producing maladies which sometimes prove fatal. In the Cordilleran regions and the arid plains which lie on their eastern border, because of the relatively slight rainfall which prevails there, the wells and springs are often excessively charged with substances which make their waters unpalatable and even unwholesome; in fact, many of the drier parts of this district are made almost uninhabitable from this cause. In time, however, this evil will in part be remedied by means of reservoirs in the hills, which will serve to retain the pure snow-water through the summer season, which is the time of drought in that part of the continent.

Over a certain portion of the arid lands to the east of the Rocky Mountains it is possible to obtain water by means of wells bored through the superficial rocks to strata, such as porous sandstones, into which the rain has percolated, displacing the water which was built into the rocks at the time that they were laid down. When the rocks have a basin-like shape, the water will often mount up through the tube and attain the surface. A simple illustration of the principle on which these gravity artesian wells work can be secured by placing two deep saucers one within the other, filling the interspace between them with water. If now we imagine a hole drilled through the bottom of the upper saucer, we clearly perceive that the water must ascend by means of the opening. In this diagram the saucers represent layers of rock composed mostly of clay and therefore impervious to water, and the space between the saucers a layer of open-texture sandstone through which the water can creep from the hills, where it enters the layer to the lower level of the basin.

In many cases the water yielded by a boring does not come to the surface because of the basin-like arrangement of the rocks, but is forced out by the pressure of gases, as in the case of the salt springs before mentioned. Where these rocks were formed, as was the case with many of the beds in and about the Rocky Mountains, in fresh-water lakes, they naturally contain no saline material, and when they are pierced by borings and the imprisoned gases drive out the water in the manner in which it is drawn from a soda fountain, the well is fit for the use of man. Considerable areas in the region about the head-waters of the Missouri River and in Texas are now supplied with water for the farms by borings made in such strata.

As regards the measure of rain-supply in proportion to its area, North America is only exceeded by South America and Europe; and as regards the distribution of its rainfall, it has less diversity in the share which comes to the different parts of its surface than any of the great lands except the last named. It has no such extensive deserts as that in the western portion of South America, the desert of Central Australia, or that of interior Asia, where the share of rain is too small to permit much culture. The only region where the rainfall is too small in amount to permit the soil to be of some service to men either for tillage or pasturage, lies in the central portion of the Cordilleras, Northern Mexico, and the great promontory of Southern California, in all not more than one-twentieth part of the continent; and even in a large part of this very arid country there are numerous streams which flow from the hills where the melting winter snows afford them supply, so that the country is not unbroken desert, and in some places can be made fertile by irrigation.

EARTHQUAKES.

The fitness of any country for the use of civilized man is often much affected by the occurrence of severe earthquakes, which are destructive to life and property, and very discouraging to the people who dwell on the treacherous ground. We shall, therefore, consider the extent to which this continent is liable to these tremblings of the ground. The measure of this danger is not yet well determined, for the reason that a large part of this country has not been long known to Europeans, and if the shocks come at distant intervals it may well happen that, though the accidents occur in any given district, they have not yet been observed.

Beginning with the Isthmus of Darien, and the lands commonly known as Central America, we find that this southernmost part of the continent is the most earthquake ridden of all its lands. Ever since the first Spanish settlements were founded, the cities, notwithstanding the fact that they were substantially built, have frequently been ravaged by these convulsions. There are certain parts of this district that are exceedingly subject to shocks of a severe kind, while other portions have been relatively free from them. Thus the old city of Guatemala, in the central part of the peninsula district, was abandoned on account of the frequent and disastrous shocks to which it was subjected, and a new city of the same name was founded on a site about thirty miles to the eastward of the old location, where, though not safe from earthquakes, there have been less frequent and serious troubles from them.

As we go northward into Mexico, the disturbances of the earth become less menacing to life and property. On the eastern side of the widening land the shocks grow rapidly less important as we approach the Rio Grande, but on the west they continue to be frequent and of moderate strength until we pass north of San Francisco, in which city a number of considerable movements have been observed since the country was first settled by civilized man. In the whole of the eastern half of the Cordilleran district, at least as far north as the region near the line between the United States and Canada, the earth is subjected to occasional tremors, but they do not appear to have been of much violence. North of the southern boundary of Canada the Cordilleran district appears to be exempt from tremblings of a notable sort.

The Mississippi Valley in its central part appears to be liable to occasional shocks of great severity, of which as yet but one has come into the experience of the white people. In November, 1811, the region between the junction of the Ohio and the Mississippi rivers, and the northern part of Louisiana, experienced a succession of shakings of such violence that the forest trees were beaten against each other and the strongly built log houses of the pioneers were shaken into ruins. Extensive areas of the alluvial lands sunk, and into these depressions the Mississippi River poured in such volume that for a time its waters not only ceased to flow toward the sea, but actually ran up stream. The shocks, which began in 1811, continued with diminishing energy, but with great frequency, until 1813, when the region again came to rest.

A portion of the New England States and Canada has repeatedly been visited by earthquakes of considerable violence. The most serious effects of these shocks were observed in Eastern Massachusetts when, in 1685, 1727, and 1755, noteworthy shakings occurred. The shock of 1755 was one of the most violent which has been observed in the United States; it was not destructive to life only for the reason that the people mostly dwelt in timber houses, which are by far the best structures to resist such catastrophes. The earthquake of 1727 affected only a small district in Eastern New England, principally the country immediately about the mouth of the Merrimac: in this disturbance the shocks continued for about seven years, and though not severe were accompanied by very loud roaring and rumbling noises proceeding from the under earth.

The last noteworthy earthquake district on the continent of North America is that of the region about Charleston, South Carolina. This part of the country had experienced several shakings of no great severity in the course of the two centuries which had elapsed since the settlement by Europeans; but in 1882 a much more serious disturbance took place, which injured a great many buildings and killed many people. The movement of the earth was not indeed of great energy, but the masonry of that district is made with very poor mortar, and the buildings otherwise not well suited to withstand earthquakes. Hence the shaking was disastrous in its consequences. It is a noteworthy fact that in the district ravaged by the Charleston earthquakes, the buildings which were built under the supervision of the United States engineers escaped damage.

Although little is known concerning the causes of the earthquake shocks, it is likely that they are in many, if not in most cases, due to the disturbances of the earth's crust which take place in the formation of mountains; the bending, folding, and breaking movements which we see have taken place in the process of mountain-building. While the greater part of these dislocations take place in a very slow manner, they now and then occur with enough suddenness to cause a sharp jar. It is perhaps because the mountains of North America are generally of relatively ancient construction, and in most parts of the continent have probably ceased growing, that this land is as a whole tolerably exempt from disastrous movements of the earth. This exemption is not only proved by the experience of the people, which indeed does not extend for any great period into the past, but by certain geological monuments which bear witness to the fact that for long ages extensive areas of the land have been exempt from any great amount of trembling. These witnesses consist of numbers of tall, chimney-like, pinnacled rocks, such as are often found standing near the borders of streams, where they have been left in the process of erosion. These natural towers would have been overthrown by a considerable earthquake, and as we can by geological evidence often prove that they have stood in their present shape for thousands of years, they afford excellent evidence of the stability of the earth in the districts where we find them. By means of these and other tests, we may, notwithstanding the brief period of written history in this continent, conclude that the greater part of its surface is fairly secure from violent shakings, and that on the whole the continent is rather more exempt from these movements than the lands of the Old World.

THE NATURAL CONDITIONS OF NORTH AMERICA WHICH AFFECTED ITS SETTLEMENT BY EUROPEANS.

As the importance of North America to man has to a great extent depended upon the circumstances of its settlement by European colonists, we will now consider the conditions which determined the occupation of the continent by settlers from the various states of the Old

World, and the way in which the various states of Northern Europe came to have a share in this western land.

The continent of North America was first known to the people of Scandinavia about five hundred years before its discovery by Columbus; the Northmen naturally found their way to it through their previous settlement in Iceland, made in the ninth century of our era. Thence, in about a hundred years, they journeyed westward to Greenland, and as early as the year 1000 at least, one of those hardy navigators, Leif, a son of Eric the Red, who was probably the first to see Greenland, sailed to the southward along the shore of the continent to somewhere south of Nova Scotia. As the Northmen were not to any extent a commercial people, and as in those centuries they were living apart from the rest of Europe, their voyages remained unknown to the other and most civilized folk of that part of the world. When, nearly five hundred years later, Columbus discovered the New World, the people of Western Europe were interested in the results of his explorations in a way that it was impossible for the Northmen to be at the time when Eric and Leif made their journeys.

The Spaniards, French, Dutch, and English were at this time keenly interested in a trade with the southern part of Asia. In this age the only path for this commerce was through the countries in the eastern part of the Mediterranean, which were held by the Mussulmans, with whom the Christian world was in a state of chronic warfare. Moreover, the Catholic portion of Europe was at this time affected by an intense desire to diffuse Christianity among the heathen, and their people contained many ardent spirits who were ready to give their lives and fortunes to this object. Still further, in these states a patriotic spirit led to the desire to extend their domains far and wide over the earth.

The result of these conditions in the cultivated parts of Europe, was that the discovery of America by the expedition of Columbus, unlike that by the early Scandinavians, excited the liveliest enthusiasm. The Spaniards and French, the Dutch and English, hastened to plant colonies in the new-found lands. The difficulties which beset these efforts are hardly conceivable in the present state of the world. Of course nothing was known of the nature of the country which the enterprising states sought to win. Even the currents of the Atlantic Ocean, and the character of the shores which were to be approached, were yet to be made out. Therefore it was in a blundering way that the first settlements were made. We can perceive that the physical conditions of these lands, and those of the sea which had to be crossed to approach them, greatly affected the history of the European settlements in the New World, both in their founding and in their subsequent development.

The Spaniards being the discoverers of America, and in that day the most maritime people, naturally had the first chance in the struggle for the possession of the New World. Following the path taken by Columbus, they soon secured control of the Mediterranean district of America, the region bordering on the Caribbean Sea, and the Gulf of Mexico. The path to these possessions was the easiest and safest route across the Atlantic Ocean. The trade-winds, those steadfast air-currents of the regions near the tropics, make voyages in the tolerably direct route from the Straits of Gibraltar to the West Indies the safest possible sailing. The Caribbean Sea and the

Mexican Gulf are, except in the hurricane season, very secure waters for ships. The climate of all these parts of North and South America which first came under the control of Spain is essentially like that of the mother country. The natives of this region were mostly rather inoffensive Indians, who tilled the soil and were more easily subjected than the hunting tribes of the more northern lands of the continent. They were soon reduced to the state of slavery, and were of some service to the conquerors in tilling the soil and in other forms of labor.

The Spaniards, like all the other adventurers who thronged to the New World, were very intent on finding profitable mines of gold and silver. They were in this regard more fortunate in their share of the new-found continents than the settlers from the other states of Europe; for they quickly discovered very extensive deposits of silver in Mexico and Peru, and also some which yielded gold. During all the subsequent centuries until the present, the colonists of the other nations won none of the precious metals from North America, except what they captured from the Spanish ships.

Although the Spanish colonies of the West Indian islands, Mexico, and the peninsula district of Central America were all in a region of great fertility, and were provided with labor from the enslaved aborigines as well as from the negroes brought from Africa, they were only moderately successful; they have contributed nothing to the general culture of the world and relatively little to its commerce. The reasons for this relative failure of the Spanish settlements are probably as follows: In the first place, the climate of the Caribbean district of America is tropical, and thus not favorable to much vigorous labor; in the second place, these regions remained until this century entirely subservient to the mother country. They were heavily taxed to yield revenue to the Spanish crown, and had no semblance of freedom; lastly, the quality of the people was greatly damaged by a general intermarriage of the conquerors with the natives, so that few Spanish colonies ever had a pure European population: they were composed of half-breeds, or of a mixture of white, Indian, and negro blood.

About one hundred years after Spain began to plant her colonies in the southern portion of the continent, when her great strength at sea made it impossible for any of the other pioneers of Europe to dispute this part of the New World with her, England, France, and Holland began actively to seek a share in the lottery of the New World. For many years before these states undertook to plant colonies in North America, the enterprising sailors of Northern France had resorted to the coast of Newfoundland for the excellent fisheries which that region then, as now, afforded. These fishing grounds of the Banks determined that in the further sharing of the New World, the French should come into possession of the most important gateway to the central part of North America — the valley of the St. Lawrence. Following the path of the adventurous pilots, the fishermen of their country, the French pioneers settled on the neighboring shores of the mainland, and took possession of the great Laurentian valley; following up this noble stream, they found their way into the broad, central trough of the continent, the regions of the Great Lakes and the Mississippi, and for a century or more they disputed with the Spaniards the possession of the country watered by that stream. Another natural way into the interior of the continent, that by way of the mouth of the greatest river of the continent, was closed to other European states by the fact that Spain held the Gulf of Mexico, and debarred the ships of all other nations from approaching its shores.

 The Dutch, who industriously sought to find a passage across North America to the Pacific Ocean, by which they hoped to gain access to the East Indies without having to pass the Cape of Good Hope, found their way to the Hudson River, settled on the shores of that noble inlet of the sea, and thus secured the control of the natural passage by way of the Mohawk, through which it was easy to penetrate to the interior of the continent. The English were laggards in the race for the possession of the New World. They came several years after the French; nearly all the shore of the continent which the above-named countries did not claim or possess, except New England, was claimed by Spain. The Spanish, indeed, had recently butchered the unhappy Frenchman who had settled at the mouth of the St. John in Florida, and from their vantage ground in the Caribbean district, seemed able to make good their title to all the lands as far north as the Delaware River. The French had settled on what is now the coast of Maine, and regarded the greater part of New England as within their rightful domain. The first holdings of England in North America were thus limited to the portions of the Atlantic coast which the other stronger, or more fore-thoughtful, pioneers did not deem worth seizing.

 All these European colonies north of the Caribbean district, as compared with the Spanish possessions about that sea, seemed, at the time they were settled, most disadvantageously situated. In the first place, they were separated from Europe not by a calm ocean, over which the trade-winds made the passage safe and certain, but by one of the most turbulent portions of the earth's great waters. The difficulties which came from the need of crossing this stormy ocean were of a serious nature, due to the small size and poor construction of the ancient ships, as well as to the diseases which came from the crowding of many people in the confined room of their holds. Ship fever, scurvy, and famine often ravaged the crews and the passengers when the baffling winds and strong currents prolonged the voyages. It was not uncommon for a ship or fleet, seeking America by the northern way, after a month of struggling with the head-winds and currents, to be beaten back to the port whence the voyage was begun.

The ocean current, which, flowing to the westward, helped the Spanish colonists to their destination, flows in the opposite direction in the northern part of the Atlantic, and hinders ships passing from the ports of France, Holland, and Great Britain to the Atlantic coast of America north of the Antilles. Even with the swift steamships of this day, this eastward setting current may make a difference of a day in the duration of voyages to and from New York and Liverpool. In the olden time, when the clumsy ships rarely sailed, even with favoring winds, faster than six or eight miles an hour, and were almost helpless in head-winds, the movement of the waters was often sufficient to prolong the voyage so that it required two or three months of very trying experiences before the sea-farers won the American shore. The slow growth of the colonies in the American continent north of the Gulf of Mexico is doubtless in large measure to be attributed to these difficulties of the voyage across the North Atlantic. The journey became a name of terror; it was indeed as formidable as an expedition to the Arctic regions is at the present day.

There were other difficulties presented by the physical conditions of the northern part of the continent itself, which caused the settlements of the French, English, and Dutch to lag behind those of the Spanish. The greater part of the coast of North America has a trying winter climate. Except in the district now occupied by the sea-board portions of the Carolinas, Georgia, and Florida, from which colonists were long debarred by fear of the assaults of the Spanish, the shore-lands are affected by long and cold winters. The forests afforded little in the way of food, and the greater part of the fishes at this season desert the shore. All the region was occupied by dense woods, and north of New York the greater part of the ground was beset with bowlders left by the glacial period over the surface of the earth. It was thus difficult for newcomers to maintain themselves on the ground; for a time they had to be supplied with food by importations from the mother country, and these shipments were often lost by storm, or the ships which bore them were driven back to the land whence they set forth. So it came about that some settlements were broken up by starvation. The Spanish settlements escaped these trials, due to the northern climate; in the realm they occupied there is no winter cold. It was almost always easy to obtain food from the waters, the forests, or from the agricultural Indians about the Southern colonies, and communication with the mother country was relatively easy and certain.

The character of the Indians on the northern part of the Atlantic coast served also to hinder the settlement of the country. These aborigines were much less given to agriculture than the native people of Mexico and Central America. They subsisted mainly by hunting and fishing. They were warlike, and owing to their habits, not easy to subjugate; they could not be reduced to slavery. While the Spaniards made the natives serviceable as laborers, the other colonists had little profit from them; on the contrary, they soon found themselves waging desultory war with the most of the tribes. These difficulties with the natives were worst in the case of the English settlements; the colonists from Great Britain rarely entered into friendly relations with the savages. Some attempts they indeed made to Christianize and civilize them; but these undertakings were in the main fruitless, and the Indian soon came to be looked upon as a dangerous wild animal to be controlled with a gun. They were driven back before the advancing lines of settlement, embittered by ill treatment, and became a constant menace to the life of the feeble colonies.

The French of the St. Lawrence district generally pursued a more humane course with the native tribes of the country. They mingled with them on amicable terms, often intermarried with them, and reared families of half-breeds, who became semi-civilized folk, of little use to the state, but serving to unite the foreign and the native people. The plans and methods of the French settlers led in other ways to a closer relation between them and the natives. The authorities of that country, like the Spaniards, appear to have looked forward to creating great dependencies of the mother country which should be populated mainly by the Indians, under the leadership of Frenchmen. This scheme never had a place in the English plan; they, on the contrary, intended their settlements to be true colonies or offshoots from the life of the mother country. The result was that while the Spaniards and French generally adopted the Indians into their new states, the colonists from Britain rapidly swept them away, or isolated them in small communities where they could be left to their own devices. The result was that the English colonies, though they extended slowly, were always composed of a far abler population than those of France or Spain, for they were essentially like the country whence they came. In five or six generations they became strong enough to dispossess the Spaniards and French from all the parts of the continent which they cared to appropriate.

A part of the difficulty which beset the early colonists of the northern portion of this continent, was due to the fact that at the outset the land of this district produced little which could enter into the commerce of the world. After a generation the culture of tobacco in the Virginia district gave the colonies of that part of the coast a considerable export trade and enriched their landowners; but north of that part of the shore, the only important exportable articles were the native products of the earth and waters, — timbers, furs, and fish. All these articles early became valuable to the settlers, and their development quickly and permanently affected their manner of living and the nature of their societies.

The fur trade, which had no place in the Spanish settlements for the evident reason that in the warm climates wild animals are not covered with close-set hair, was the first and long remained the most important basis of commerce between the northern portion of the New World and the Old. Owing to its cold winter climate many of the animals of this country afforded excellent pelts. The black bear, beaver, wild-cats, foxes, mink, sable, buffalo, and several other animals whose skins were of value, abounded in the forests and prairies. These creatures were generally taken by the Indians, who were good hunters and had some skill in the furrier's art. As soon as they were provided by the whites with firearms and steel traps, they gathered great quantities of these furs, and bartered with the whites for the products of civilization. In this incidental way only did the colonists of this part of the land find the Indians of profit to them. For a time the gain they made from this commerce was of a great advantage to the whites; it enabled them, indeed, to meet the expenses of their pioneering life, which otherwise would have been so unprofitable that it is doubtful if the early settlers could have maintained their hold in the country. Incidentally this fur trade had another important influence on the European colonies: it led to the development of an enterprising body of frontiersmen, who pushed into the interior of the continent, exchanging their wares for the hides the Indians had to sell. These people were a means whereby friendly relations between the newcomers and the aborigines were in part maintained; moreover, these traders brought information concerning lands which would probably long have remained unknown had it not been for this profitable commerce in furs.

The effect of this trade in skins was as disadvantageous to the Indians as it was profitable to the whites. It brought them alcoholic drinks, which seem to be even more damaging to savages than to civilized people; it was the means by which a variety of European diseases, such as smallpox, which can readily be conveyed in clothing, were disseminated through the wilderness people. In general it brought the evils of civilization to a people who were not by nature fitted to avail themselves of the good side of culture. Even guns, powder, traps, and fish-hooks, although they made the pursuit of wild animals easier, turned these wild men away from agriculture to the ensavaging pursuits of the chase, and thus served to degrade them. Moreover, the possession of modern arms, which the Indians acquired by bartering furs, made them much more dangerous enemies to the whites than when they were armed with flint-tipped arrows and stone hatchets.

The whole of the eastern coast of North America originally bore luxuriant forests, and the timber of these woods was, next after the furs, the principal element in the early commerce between the New World and the Old. The more cultivated parts of Europe had long been deprived of the trees fit for ship-building and for other large constructions. As there were no railways, and but few canals by which the products of the remoter forests could be brought to the great Atlantic ports of that country, much of the supply came from America, principally from the region north of Cape Hatteras. For many years there was also an export of the bark and roots of the sassafras, a tree which affords an aromatic substance which at that time was supposed to have a medicinal virtue. The roots of a plant known as the ginseng then, as now, commanded a high price; it was once plentiful along the central parts of the Atlantic coast, but it has been nearly extirpated by the continued search which has been made for it. These plant products were of importance in the development of the colonies, for they enabled the people to secure the means necessary to pay the great costs required in the settlement of the wilderness country, where houses, roads, bridges, and the thousand other things necessary for man's use have to be procured anew, when men inherit nothing but their strength and energy from the generations which have gone before.

The sea-fisheries of the region north of New York were early turned to use, and a considerable export trade came from them. Unlike the fur trade and the timber industry, this occupation was carried on in competition with the fishermen of Europe, who resorted to our shores and returned with their cargoes at the end of each season. Still the employment was pursued with profit, and in New England as well as in the region about the St. Lawrence the people to this day follow the occupation of their ancestors who settled on this shore. It was the good fortune of the European settlers that they found the waters of the Atlantic coast rich in a number of species of fish, which were not only well suited to their own immediate use, but also fitted for preservation by drying and salting, so that they could be carried to distant lands. Among these, the cod holds the foremost place. This fish finds the stormy and rocky parts of the sea-shore particularly well suited to its needs, and so it abounds in the region off the iron bound coasts of New England and the more northern parts of the Atlantic shore; consequently the profit it has given to the people is limited to this part of the coast. The schooling fishes, particularly the mackerel and herring, have also led the seamen of New England and the St.

Lawrence district to considerable voyages, just as they tempted the people of Northern Europe to visit this part of the continent even before the first colonies were founded.

Certain species of fish, the alewives, the shad, and the salmon, which have the habit of laying their eggs in the rivers and in the lakes from which they flow, were in the primitive time accustomed to resort to the shores of the Atlantic coast in great numbers, and were of great value to the early settlers, for they provided at certain seasons quantities of easily captured food which could be readily preserved by drying, salting, or smoking for use in seasons of famine. Unlike the game of the forest, the capture of these creatures from the sea did not require the pioneers to venture into the wilderness where they might encounter their savage foes.

Another important condition of the settlements in North America was brought about by the geographic relations of this continent to Africa. We have already noticed the fact that the Indians of North America were generally of an indomesticable nature. The Spaniards, it is true, enslaved a large part of the natives of the West Indies, Mexico, and Central America, but these people, though easily subjugated, were of weak body and did not prove of much service as workmen. North of Mexico the Indian proved essentially useless for all the purposes of civilization. They would fish and hunt, they served as gatherers of furs and deer-skins, but they were incapable of steadfast hard labor. If subjected to it they soon died. The great need of the new settlements was to secure, on any terms, an abundance of cheap labor for the difficult tasks which were involved in the reduction of a stubborn wilderness to the use of civilized man.

In a small way, this need was met by sending from the Old World numbers of paupers and criminals who had been convicted of unimportant offences against the law, who were sold into a temporary slavery to pay the cost of their transportation. Even poor people who desired to emigrate to America sometimes paid for their voyage by such bondage. Although this supply of labor was for a time important, and the servitude of whites was not very revolting to the spirit of that time, it was not sufficient for the ever-growing needs of strong hands. There had for ages been a trade in slaves between the interior of Africa and the Mediterranean district. But the recently acquired knowledge of the populous districts of the Guinea coast made it easy for traders to purchase in that country, at a very cheap price, paid in goods of European manufacture, any number of negro slaves. These captives were secured by the natives in the endless wars which then as now prevailed among the African tribes, or were sold by their own petty kings much as soldiers were bartered away by the sovereigns of Europe during the last century.

This cheap captive labor from Africa exactly met the immediate needs of the European colonies in the New World. Unlike the American Indian, the negro is very able-bodied, patient in captivity, and can labor as enduringly as the white men. From their own country they could be conveyed across the calm, tropical seas, packed so closely that a ship of five hundred tons burden could bring a cargo of near a thousand men. They could, therefore, with great profit to the slave merchants, be sold at about the price of a good horse. Engaged in tobacco planting and sundry other arts, a well-chosen slave would repay his cost in two or three years of service. For a time this unhappy commerce proved of great advantage to the colonists of the New World, for it supplied them with the laborers which were needed for their pioneering work. The rapid commercial and industrial success of the settlements was in a great measure due to this extensive and forced migration of Africans to the New World. It is true that the momentary gain was dearly bought by the troubles which afterwards came in the conflict for the overthrow of slavery, but the immediate profit was great; it is indeed difficult to see how European colonies could have grown with anything like the rapidity into which they developed in the eighteenth century but for the importation of negro slaves.

It is perhaps worth while in this brief account of the influence of the geography of North America on its settlement by Europeans, to note some of the indirect effects arising from the peculiar shape of the land about the Gulf of Mexico. It was the purpose of Columbus to find a way to the East Indies and China; that illustrious explorer indeed died with the full conviction that he had found a land near to those parts of the Orient: unhappily for his anticipation it was found that the country he had discovered was not only far from Cathay, but owing to the barrier of the Isthmus of Darien, quite as remote from the Indies as are the ports of Spain. The Isthmus of Darien is so low that if the land should sink by the amount of three hundred feet there would be a good ship channel from the Atlantic waters to those of the Pacific. This slender barrier has been of incalculable influence in the history of civilized America. If it had been breached by the sea America would have been in the great highway of the world's commerce, between the fertile and populous districts of Southern and Eastern Asia and the states of Europe, and not as it is at present, the one obstacle between the Pacific and Atlantic divisions of the world. The existence of the Isthmus of Darien, and the peculiar arrangement of the islands of the Caribbean, together with the peninsula of Florida, made the seas about the southern part of North America a natural marine fortress, and enabled the Spanish long to hold this field of the ocean against the other maritime nations of Europe. It was only when the power of Spain had sunk, and that of Holland, France, and Great Britain had increased, that the firm control of the Spaniards over the region about the Caribbean Sea and the Gulf of Mexico was shaken.

This brief sketch of the effects of the physical conditions of North America on the progress of European settlements on its shores, may serve to show us how the geographic conditions of the country determine not only the internal conditions of the people who develop within its territory, but also the circumstances of its relations to other parts of the earth.

INDEX.

	PAGE
Aborigines of North America, origin of	153
Adirondack district, mineral resources of	226
Agricultural advantages of North America	193, 242
" resources of Cordilleran region	172
" " " eastern section of North America	177
Agriculture of Atlantic coast region	179
Alaska, effect of Japan current on climate	125, 128
Aleutian Archipelago, nature of	87
Altitude, effect on conditions of life	3
Alluvial soils, formation of	186
America, causes determining discovery of	263
Animals of North America	196, 203
Appalachian district	214, 215
" " building materials of	224
" " coal in	215
" " river systems	97
" mountains, comparison with Cordilleras	94, 98
" " component ranges	95, 96
" " description of	93
" " erosion	96
" " process of building	96
" " topography	97
Archæn era in North America	26
Artesian wells, principle of	257
Aryan race, characteristics	167
Atlantic coast region	179
" " formation of bays on	86
" Ocean, early difficulties of traversing	268
" " " routes over	264
Bald cypress, uses of	118
Batrachians	37

279

INDEX.

	PAGE
Bays of Atlantic coast	86, 87
Birds of North America	201
Bison, distribution of	201
Blue-grass district, origin of fertility	8
Cambrian period in North America	15, 28
Cañons	138, 139, 140
Cape Cod, influence on conditions of marine life	12, 16
Carboniferous period, climate of	44
" " in North America	34, 46
" " life of	47
" " oscillations of level of land in	40, 46
Caverns	141–145
Central district of North America, fertility of	189
Civil War, disadvantages of the South in	244
Clams, fresh water	197, 198
Climate, divisions of areas having differences in	168
" general features	123
" how affected by Polar current of Atlantic coast	128
" of Alaska, effect of Japan current on	125, 128
" " Atlantic coast region	179
" " Carboniferous period	44
" " Cordilleran region	172
" " Cretaceous period	55
" " eastern section of North America	177
" " Greenland	80
" " Mississippi Valley, range of	112
" " North America	123
" " " " conditions affecting	125
" " " " effect of Gulf of Mexico	125
" " " " " " ocean currents	123
" " " " " " rainfall	180
" " " " suitableness to man	176
" " northern region of North America	169
" " prairie region	123
" " St. Lawrence Valley	178
" " the earth as affected by ocean currents	19
" range of in North America	168
Coal, anthracite and bituminous	44
" beds, arrangement of strata in	40
" district of Pennsylvania	218

INDEX.

	PAGE
Coal, formation of	11, 209
" " " in Carboniferous period	38
" in Appalachian district	215, 219
" " Narragansett basin	217
Colonization of North America, plan of various races in	270
Commercial advantages of geographical position of North America	250
" " " Gulf of Mexico and Caribbean Sea	249
" conditions of North America	246
" development of United States	238
" inactivity of northern part of North America	250
" products of North America	251
Commerce, favored by shortened distances between points formerly remote	251
" method of growth	246
" of early colonies, disadvantages of	271
" " North America, advantage of water-fronts	248
" " " " internal	247
Comstock lode, mining in	228, 231
Continental areas, figures of	18
" formation, principle of	89
" shelf	148, 149
Continents, value for uses of man	174
Copper, early use of	205
" of Cordilleran district	231
" " Laurentian district	225
Coral reefs, effect on geographical and climatal conditions	152
" " " " Gulf Stream	86
" " influence of Gulf Stream in formation	151
" " in geological times	33, 150
" " of North America	150
" " " southeastern coast, conditions of growth	85
Cordilleran mountains	90, 91, 92
" region, agricultural resources	171, 172
" " climate	172
" " extent	171
" " mineral resources	173, 227
" " precious metals	228
" " readiness with which explored	232
" " unfitness for occupation by man	171
Cotton, production	195, 242
Cretaceous period	53, 55

	PAGE
Crinoids of Carboniferous period	35
" " Silurian period	30
Dead seas	146, 147
Devonian black shales, formation of	33
" period in North America	32
Domesticated animals, origin	204
Early settlement of interior district, difficulties	234
" " " " " effect on subsequent history	238
" " " " " progress of	235
" " " North America	264
Earthquake of Charleston, S.C.	261
" of 1811 in Mississippi Valley	260
Earthquakes, distribution	259
" evidence of former exemption from	262
" of New England	260
" probable cause	261
Eastern section of North America, agricultural resources	177
" " " " " extent	176
" " " " " fitness for occupation by man	176
Elephants of glacial period	72
England, share in settlement of America	267
Falls of Ohio River, account of	137
Figure of land-masses of the earth	18
Fisheries of early colonies	274
Fish of Carboniferous period	37
" " North America	200
Florida, character of	179
" relation of trend to axis continent	89
Footprints found in strata of Triassic period	47
Forest products of minor importance	120
Forests, importance to early settlers	113
" method of clearing for tillage purposes	188
" of North America	112, 113, 115
" picturesque value	135
" species of trees composing	114
Fossils found in salt springs	255
France, share of settlement in America	266

	PAGE
Fuel deposits, conditions affecting preservation	210
" supply of North America, commercial advantage of position	252
Fur trade of colonies, effects of	272

Geographical aspects of the earth				18
" conditions, dependence of men upon				4
" " effect on development of life				2, 20
" " " " early colonists				164
Geological changes, effect in determining present conditions				5
" development of North America				25
" records, difficulty of interpretation				25
" researches, comparison with archæological				21
" succession of life				14, 16
Geologist, methods of research				23
Ginseng, uses				120
Glacial action during ice epoch				66
" " effects on drainage				70, 109
" period, area experiencing				65
" " effects on drainage				109
" " " " migration of species				65
" " moraines of				67
" " soils formed in				70
Glaciers of Alaska				126
" " Greenland				126
Gold-bearing gravels of Cordilleran district				228
" mining				229, 230
" of Appalachian district				223
Great Lakes, conditions of drainage				106
Greenland, climate				80, 81
" geography				89
" glaciers				126
" probable insular nature of				80
" resources				81
Gulf of Mexico, effect on climate of North America				125
" " " former extent				34
Gulf Stream, agency in formation of Devonian black shales				33
" " climatal influence				19
" " conditions determining course of				19
" " course of				150
" " effect of coral reefs on				86
" " former course of				32

284   INDEX.

	PAGE
Gulf Stream, influence in formation of coral reefs	86, 151
Guatemala, abandonment of old city of	259
Harbors of North America	247
Holland, share in settlement of North America	267
Holly, uses	119
Horse, development of	58
Hot springs, value of	253, 254
Hudson's Bay, probable origin and nature of	81
Icebergs, effects	127
Indian corn, conditions of growth	12
" " production	242
" summer	129, 130
Indians, domestic arts of	158
" effect of civilization on	272
" former development	156
" " social condition	157
" ignorance of ship-building, effect on development	163
" influence of absence of domesticable animals on development	162
" " " geographical conditions on development	161, 163
" means of warfare	164
" mental capacity and traits	160
" of central North America, character of	270
" " North and South America, likeness of	156
Iron ore, formation and distribution of	222
" " of Cordilleran district	228
" " " Laurentian district	225
Isthmus of Darien, influence on history of America	277
Japan current, effect on climate of Alaska	125, 128
Jurassic period	49, 50
King crab, peculiarities of	199
Lakes, picturesque value of	135
Laurentian district, mineral resources	225
" mountains	98, 99, 100
Life, advance in during geological times	14
" degradational changes in development of	63

	PAGE
Life, effect of various conditions on	2, 3, 13, 14
" geological succession	14, 16
" in geological times, description of	14
" of Carboniferous period	47
" " Cretaceous period	53, 55
" " Jurassic period	49
" " North America, development of	28
" " Tertiary era	56
" " Triassic period	46
" process of development	16
Limestone, formation of	141
Live oak, uses of	117
Lower California, geography of	88
Mackenzie River, floods of	103
Mammalian remains found in strata of Triassic period	48
Mammals of North America	201
" " Tertiary era	56
Man, conditions necessary for development of mining life in	10
" " " " " " sea-faring life	9
" dependence on geographical conditions	4
" first appearance in North America	73
" influence of under earth on occupations of	10
" resources of, various stages in development	205
Metalliferous ores of Appalachian district	224
Methods of geological research, comparison with those of archæology,	21
Mexico, slight extension of settlements of	240
Mineral constituents of sea-water, appropriation by organisms	212
Mineral fields of North America, situation	214
" products of Cordilleran district of minor importance	232
" resources, classification of	208
" " conditions determining distribution	208
" " of Adirondack district	226
" " " Cordilleran region	173, 227
" " " Laurentian district	225
" " " Mississippi Valley	226
" " " North America	205
" " " " " extent of knowledge of	207
" " relative value	206
" springs, value	253
Minerals, varieties having economic value	10

	PAGE
Mississippi Sea	32
" Valley, account of	111
" " mineral resources	226
" " range of climate in	112
Mollusks of North America	197
Morainal accumulations, formation of islands by	84
" " of glacial period	67
Mound-builders	159
Mountain building, in Triassic period	46
" " localities of present activity	79
Mountains of North America	77, 90
Narragansett coal basin	217
Natural gas	210, 220, 221
Nautilus, pearly, of Silurian period	31
Nelson River, description of valley of	104
New England, earthquakes of	260
" " peculiar characteristics of valleys	108
Niagara Falls, account of	137
North America, aboriginal peoples of	153
" " advantage to commerce of geographical position	250
" " animals	196
" " climate	123
" " comparative fitness for fruit culture	196
" " development of life of	28
" " extent	77
" " first settlement	233
" " fitness for agriculture	193
" " forests	112
" " geological development	25
" " growth	21
" " mineral resources	205
" " minor mountain ranges	100
" " " valleys	107
" " mountains	77, 90
" " origin of aborigines	153
" " physiographic aspects	77, 81
" " population	241
" " range of climate	168
" " relative lack of picturesqueness	133
" " scenery	132

		PAGE
North America, soils		183
" " value to man		174
" " variety of sources of energy		253
" " vegetables originally from		193, 204
Northern region of North America, climate		166
" " " " resources		170
" " " " unfitness for occupation by man		171
Northmen, discovery of America by		263

Ocean currents, effect of continental grouping on 19
" " effect of distribution on climate of North America ... 128
" " effect on climate of the earth 19
Ohio River, account of falls 137
Opossum, peculiarities of 202
Organisms, principles determining the survival of 16
Oysters of North America 199

Pacific coast region, character of 180
" " " origin of continental islands 88
Palmetto, uses 117
Paw-paw, uses 119
Peat bogs 41, 42
" process by which changed to coal 43
Pennsylvania coal district 218
Persimmon, uses 119
Petroleum 210, 219, 220, 221
Physiographic features of North America; comparison with those of
    Europe 124
Plainland district, picturesque aspect 135
Polar current of Atlantic coast, effect on climate 128
Population of North America, growth of 241
Prairie lands, former destruction of timber by fire on 116
"   region, climate 123
"   "   extent 121
"   "   settlement 237
Prairies 121, 122, 189
Precious metals of Cordilleran district 228
Prehistoric man on Pacific coast 154, 155

Race characteristics, influence of natural conditions on 167

	PAGE
Railroads in North America, facility of construction	249
Rainfall, conditions determining relative amount in North America and Europe	182
" distribution	181, 258
" of North America, cause of distribution	181
Rattlesnake, characteristics of	200
Reptiles of North America	200
River systems of Appalachian district	97
Rivers of Pacific Slope	110
Rocky Mountains, former rainfall	190
" " settlement	238
" " sterility	190
St. Lawrence Archipelago	82, 83
" " Valley, absence of alluvial plain	107
" " " character	178
" " " climate	178
" " " description	105
Salt springs	255, 256
Sand beaches of Atlantic coast, cause	84
Sassafras, uses	119
Scenery, educative value	132
Seasons, effect on conditions of life	3
Sea-water, composition	212
Settlement of North America, conditions determining	262
" " " difficulties	269
" " " stages of progress	239
" prairie region, conditions determining	237
" Rocky Mountains	238
Silurian period, life	29
Silver of Cordilleran district	231
Slavery, benefits of	276
" conditions determining distribution	243
" " leading to, in early settlement of America	275
" influence of cotton and tobacco production on	243
" " soil on distribution	186
Slave trade in time of early settlement of America	276
Soil, alluvial, formation of	186
" 'character determined by underlying rock	7
" composition	7, 183
" conditions determining fertility	184

INDEX. 289

	PAGE
Soil, effect in determining conditions of life	5
" formation	6
" formed by glacial action	185
" " " " difficulty of subjugation	188
" how cleared of forests	188
" influence of former conditions on	8
" " on advance of civilization	185
" " " distribution of slavery	186
" in situ	185
" nature and origin	6
Soils of Glacial period	70
" North America	183, 184
" relative endurance of	187
Spain, share in settlement of America	264
Spanish colonies, success of	265
Springs, caused to gush by pressure of gases	257
" importance of	253
" of North America, distribution	254
" value as sources of domestic water-supply	256
Stalactite, formation of	144
Stalagmite, formation of	144
Storms, classification of	131
" of North America, conditions of occurrence	130
Taxodium, uses	118
Temperature, effect in determining distribution of life	12
Tertiary era, life of	56
Timber trade of early colonies	273
Tobacco, production	196
Tornadoes	131, 132
Triassic period, footprints of batrachians found in strata	47
" " life of	46
" " mammalian remains found in strata	48
" " mountain building in	46
Trilobites, disappearance of	35
Valley of Churchill River, character of	104
" Mackenzie River, character of	102
" Nelson River, character of	104
" St. Lawrence, absence of alluvial plain in	107

	PAGE
Valleys, classification of	102
" of New England, characteristics of	108
Vegetable life, development in Tertiary time	60
Vegetables of North America	195
" originating in North America	193, 204
Veins, formation of	213
Vertebrates, first appearance of	24
Virginian coal district	217
Waterfalls, conditions of occurrence	137
" economic value	138
" relation to geology	136
" scenic value	136
Water, dissolving capacity of	211
" influence in formation of mineral accumulations	211
" power of North America	252
" system of North America	247
Yucatan, relation of trend to axis of continent	89

www.ingramcontent.com/pod-product-compliance
Lightning Source LLC
Chambersburg PA
CBHW021954220426
43663CB00007B/809